Folk Festivals

Folk Festivals

A Handbook for
Organization and Management

by
Joe Wilson
and
Lee Udall

THE UNIVERSITY OF TENNESSEE PRESS / KNOXVILLE

Copyright © 1982 by The University of Tennessee Press / Knoxville
All rights reserved
Manufactured in the United States of America
First edition

Clothbound editions of University of Tennessee Press books are printed on paper designed for an effective life of at least 300 years, and binding materials are chosen for strength and durability.

Library of Congress Cataloging in Publication Data
Wilson Joseph T.
   Folk festivals.
   Bibliography: p.
   Includes index.
   1. Folk festivals—Management. 2. Folk festivals. 3. Festivals—Management. I. Udall, Lee. II. Title.
GT3935.W54   907'.4   81-23103
ISBN 0-87049-300-0   AACR2
ISBN 0-87049-336-1 (pbk.)

A Note on This Book

This handbook has been prepared for those who wish to present the carriers of folk traditions in festivals that are accurate and respectful in depicting folk culture. By *carriers of tradition,* we mean those artists who grew up in the tradition in which they perform or create and learned their art in family or in community as a part of daily life. Some portions of this work may be useful to those who plan other kinds of presentations, but much will be useful only to those who share our primary interest.

We direct the National Folk Festival, and much of the experience related here is drawn from it. Added to this is the experience we have had in community-based festivals: free-style fiddlers' conventions, American Indian gatherings, and smaller folk festivals. This handbook centers upon larger and more complex events, but this does not mean that we advocate festivals of this size. Rather, we hope that organizers using this material will create events appropriate to the size and aesthetic of their communities.

Folklore is deceptively complex, even for those who study it systematically. Yet people who have neither formal training nor work experience in folklore frequently produce festivals. We hope that the information we have assembled here will persuade more people to seek qualified assistance before investing substantial sums of money and energy into ventures they do not fully understand. Perhaps the sum of what we have written can serve as a warning of the most common mistake of all: the tendency of organizers to underestimate the amount of planning and preparation needed. The lack of adequate guides for planning and producing folk festivals has led organizers to make the same mistakes again and again.

Professional folklorists don't agree on either the need for or benefits of folk festivals. But new folk festivals will be started regardless of opinions in the profession, so unless improved models are described, the mistakes and misconceptions that have plagued festivals will continue.

We owe thanks to a great many people, but especially to Charles L. Perdue, Jr., for his suggestions, invaluable criticisms, careful editing, and faith that we would finally finish this book. J. Andrew Wallace, Michael Rivers, Carl Goldstein, and Michael Holmes helped by providing initial drafts concerning special subjects. James S. Griffith, Jane Bergey, and Frank Proschan provided examples contained in Part II, and Dr. Perdue supplied the bibliography. We thank Hal Bruno, Roger Abrahams, Fred Lieberman, Sandy Ives, Charles Wolfe, and Stewart Udall for their assistance in editing. And our special thanks to Nancy Dolliver for editing and organizing Part II.

A grant from the National Endowment for the Arts made this work possible, and we are grateful to the staff of the Folk Arts Program for their patient support.

Finally, most of the writing here is our own, and we take responsibility for the value judgments that are necessarily a part of this work.

— Joe Wilson
— Lee Udall

Contents

A Note on This Book v
Themes of Folk Festivals and Examples x

Part One

1. History, Concepts, Definitions 3
    Background of Folk Festivals 3
    The Function and Form of Folklore 11
    The Process and Material of Folklore 13
    Notes 23
2. Administration 25
    Administrative Structure 25
    Staffing 27
    Site, Date, Budget 30
    Legal Considerations 36
    IRS Requirements for Non-Profit Organizations 41
    Funding 43
3. Programming 54
    Establishing a Programming Concept 54
    Identifying Festival Participants 56
    Planning Workshops 74
4. Publicity 88
    Forming a Committee 88
    Prefestival Publicity 89
    First-Day Coverage 93
    Follow-Up Publicity 94
    Festival Publications 94
5. Hospitality 97
    Prefestival Communication with Participants 97
    Transportation, Housing, and Food 100

6. Production 107
   Festival Site Preparation 107
   Sound 109
   Documentation 115
   Stage Management 116
   Safety and Security 118
   Communications During the Festival 121
   Concessions 122
   Festival Breakdown 126
   Festival Recap Meeting 127

Part Two

7. Examples of Festivals 131
   Tucson, Meet Yourself by Jim Griffith 131
   Mississippi Valley Folk Festival by Jane Bergey 144
   The Open Fiddlers' Contest by Joe Wilson 156
8. A Performer's Point of View 162
9. Samples of Festival Communications 173
   For Participants 173
   For Staff 205
   For the Media 232
   For the Audience 249

Bibliography of Folklore in America by Charles L. Perdue, Jr. 261
Index 275

Illustrations

Fiddle workshop at 34th National Folk Festival	10
Informal jamming during Tucson, Meet Yourself	19
Kyle Creed playing banjo at the 39th National Folk Festival	49
Master potter Vernon Owens at 1978 North Carolina Folklife Festival	58
Mandolin Workshop at Tucson, Meet Yourself	75
Yaqui Deer and Pascola dancers at the Border Folk Festival	91
Zespol Harnasie dancers at the 38th National Folk Festival	104
Guitarist Carl Martin at the 34th National Folk Festival	113
Preparing ethnic food at Tucson, Meet Yourself	134
Basket maker, Dale Black at the Frontier Folk Festival	148
Algia Mae Hinton	249
Stanley Hicks	250
Van Holyoak	251
John Jackson	251
Haywood Blevins	252
Joe Cormier Band	253
James "Son" Thomas	254
The Olympian Brotherhood	255
Karpathian music and dances	256
Friday Workshop Schedule	257
Saturday Workshop Schedule	258
Randolph Lalio	259
Zuni youth and eagle cage	260
Zuni Pueblo of 1880s	260
Zuni silversmith	260

TABLES

First Annual Folklife Festival Anticipated Budget	35
MVFF Expenses (1977)	155

THEMES OF FOLK FESTIVALS AND EXAMPLES
(Selected from the 1978 Calendar of Festivals)

I. SACRED FESTIVALS
 1. *Seasonal:* Blessing of the Fleet, Blessing of the Fields
 2. *Music:* Sacred Harp Singing, Singing on the Mountain
 3. *Annual Rites:* Midsummer observances, Mescalero Apache Maiden's Puberty Rites Ceremonial
 4. *Miracles Recalled:* Gift of Waters, Gift of Corn, Hill Cumorah Pageant

II. HARVEST AND FOOD FESTIVALS
 1. *Vegetables:* Watermelon, Sweet Corn, Pumpkin
 2. *Animals:* Blue Crab, Whale, Catfish, Shad
 3. *Cooking:* Chili, Gumbo, Boiled Corn, Johnny Cake
 4. *Activity:* Threshing, Sugaring Down, Sheep Shearing

III. SPECIAL ACTIVITY FESTIVALS
 1. *Music:* Bluegrass, Scottish fiddling, old-time music
 2. *Local Tradition:* Mule Day, Trade Day, Dog Days Dance
 3. *Contest:* Fiddling, Piping, Hollering, Seed Spitting, Chicken Plucking
 4. *Commemorative:* Leif Ericson Day, Mud Springs Camp, Voyager Days

IV. FESTIVE SUBGROUP GATHERINGS
 1. *Ethnic:* Dances of Rumania, Czech Days, Nordic Days
 2. *Indian:* Hopi Snake dances, Rooster Pulls, Powwows
 3. *Homecoming:* Bethel Church Homecoming, Sutherland Family Reunion
 4. *Occupational:* Old Canalers Meeting

V. REGIONAL AND LOCAL FOLK ARTS FESTIVALS
 1. *Multistate:* Mississippi Valley Folk Festival
 2. *State:* Tennessee Old-Time Fiddlers' Convention
 3. *County:* Wade County Crafts Festival
 4. *Town:* Benton Buck Dancing Contest

Part One

1. History, Concepts, Definitions

Background of Folk Festivals

More than 3,000 festivals are held annually in the United States, and their continuity ranges from "first annual" events to such occasions as The Fiesta de Santa Fe, now in its 267th year. A glance at the accompanying list of Themes of Folk Festivals and Examples reveals that the term *folk festival* is used by folklorists to describe a wide range of events. To understand the differences among these events, it is necessary to consider their conceptual underpinnings and the motivations of their organizers.

At one level, a festival may be described as a public celebration of some happening, fact, or concept. Although this is not the place for a complete typology of festivals, it is revealing to examine festivals in the United States today with regard to their organizers and their primary audience. This is instructive because the motivations and aesthetics of the organizers and the composition of the audiences are as important to the overall experience as what is being celebrated.

With the exception of the first category, the classifications given below show the movement of the materials of folk culture away from the people who created them to people of the larger society. They also show how different organizers have applied their own concepts and aesthetics to problems of inclusion and exclusion. Much of the tension created by exclusion is relieved if the organizers have a clear idea of what they are celebrating, why they are celebrating it, and what presentations are appropriate to the celebration.

There is no intent here to pass qualitative judgments upon different types of events. These events exist in every part of the nation and presumably serve the purposes of their organizers and their audiences, since all types other than the first appear to be increasing in number.

INDIGENOUS FESTIVALS

These celebrations grow from particular cultures and are a part of them. Control is by individuals from a culture, and the event is directed toward the culture at large. Such events usually are monocultural.[1] Visitors may be tolerated but might also be considered a nuisance. The controlling aesthetics are determined almost exclusively from within the culture. The organizers of some indigenous religious festivals may make a conscious attempt to involve persons not of the culture, but they do not adapt the material to the aesthetic of these outsiders. Examples of indigenous festivals include Indian religious observances of the Southwest, older local fiddlers' conventions, and many Anglo- and Afro-American religious activities, such as county singings. It is interesting to note that these folk festivals are never called "folk festivals" by their organizers. This self-conscious term comes into use when organizers are less involved with the material they present.

EVOLVING INDIGENOUS FESTIVALS

These events are similar to indigenous festivals in that they grow from the culture depicted, are monocultural, are directed and controlled by persons from within the culture, and appeal primarily to an audience of persons from within the culture. They differ in that they consciously attempt to adapt cultural material to persons not of the group. This may involve adaptations of the material to an aesthetic not wholly of the group, or some commercialization of the event, or both. Examples of such festivals include some powwows, larger fiddlers' conventions, most bluegrass festivals, and many local festivals, such as "trade day" events.

An interesting new example of the evolving indigenous festival is the wagon train phenomenon of the Southeast. Wagon trains are not commercial and are directed by persons from within the culture, but some outside cultural material is adapted—for example, western regalia for some participants. Yet they also continue local arts in a

HISTORY, CONCEPTS, DEFINITIONS 5

community format: wagon making, music, dance, storytelling, lying contests, campfire foods, and other presentations of folk skills.

COMMERCIALIZED INDIGENOUS FESTIVALS

Having discovered that folk celebrations can attract broad audiences, Chambers of Commerce, tourist organizations, commercial institutions, and some individuals have become festival promoters. The effect is that the event moves partially into popular culture even while retaining support from folk culture. Examples include food festivals, many country music and bluegrass festivals, and commemorative events.

NON-COMMUNITY MONOCULTURAL FESTIVALS

Some monocultural festivals are organized by persons from outside the culture presented, have no base of support from the cultural group depicted, and make no attempt to involve persons of the culture as members of the audience. At the same time, the organizers may hold to a rigidly defined format in performer selection and presentation. The classifying factors are that the organizers are not of the culture presented and they prepare the presentation for others not of the culture. Examples include most monocultural events held on college campuses and at museums, and most of the events held at "pioneer villages" and historic sites that claim authenticity in presenting a single culture.

MULTICULTURAL FOLK ARTS FESTIVALS

These festivals, constituting a relatively recent phenomenon, present the cultural materials of many cultures. With few exceptions, audiences tend to be people who are not of the cultures presented. The organizers of such festivals tend to be academics or eclectic fans of the folk arts. Control of the event is likely to be in the hands of an institution—usually a non-profit institution. Some of these festivals feature persons reared in the cultures presented; others present only persons who perform materials drawn from cultures other than their own. Still other festivals present both. Most of these festivals primarily present folk music, crafts, or hobby crafts, but a few present other genres of folklore. Examples include the most well-known festivals—the Philadelphia Folk Festival, the Mariposa Folk Festival (Canada), the San Diego Folk Festival, The Smithsonian's Festival of American Folklife, and the National Folk Festival.

Since this handbook is directed primarily toward organizers of multicultural folk festivals, and since the experience that informs it has grown largely out of the National Folk Festival, it will be of some use here to discuss the history of the term *folk festival* and to give some background on the more important multicultural folk arts festivals.

The use of the term *folk festival* in the United States appears to be of relatively recent vintage. In 1892 it was used in advertising literature printed by Hampton Institute, Virginia, to describe the performances of musicians traveling with the Hampton Jubilee Singers. In the early 1900s it was used by the Henry Street Settlement House in New York City and by Hull House in Chicago to describe the performances of recent immigrants at settlement house events.

In 1928, Bascom Lamar Lunsford inaugurated his Mountain Dance and Folk Festival in Asheville, North Carolina. In November 1933, Sarah Gertrude Knott chartered the National Folk Festival in St. Louis and on May 14-18, 1934, held the first National Folk Festival there. These festivals differed in scope. Lunsford's was a celebration of Southern Appalachian music and dance and resembled the large fiddlers' conventions then being held in Atlanta, Georgia, Mountain City, Tennessee, and elsewhere in the South. His festival differed from the older fiddlers' conventions in that he used the self-conscious term *folk festival*. Even then, Asheville was a city that catered to tourists; the use of this term says much about Lunsford's intent, particularly his concern that a larger public know and respect mountain music and dance.

Lunsford's festival became an annual event, and it still holds to the same format. There are scores of similar Southern festivals, even though they often are called fiddlers' conventions or bluegrass and old-time music festivals.

Sarah Knott adopted Lunsford's use of the term *folk festival,* but her festival differed significantly. Among the performers at the first National Folk Festival were American Indians, French singers and musicians, cowboy singers, Mexican-American musicians, Sacred

Harp singers, singers of sea shanties, lumberjacks, costumed dancers of different ethnic origins, Appalachian musicians, and an Afro-American choir. Clearly her purpose was to present the diversity and richness of American folk culture to audiences unfamiliar with this material.

The Knott festivals were the first to feature such diversity and to present teaching workshops by performers and seminars and lectures by collectors and scholars. Among those who participated in the 1934 National Folk Festival were George Pullen Jackson, Zora Neale Hurston, J. Frank Dobie, Clarence Cameron White, Arthur L. Campa, Bascom Lamar Lunsford, and O.S. Jacobsen. In subsequent years, other folklorists and collectors were associated with Miss Knott in producing National Folk Festivals in seventeen cities. Many of these festivals were sponsored by daily newspapers, such as the *St. Louis Globe-Democrat,* the *New York Post,* the *Milwaukee Journal,* the *Philadelphia Inquirer,* and the *Washington Post.*

The prewar National Folk Festivals reached their zenith in Washington, D.C., during 1938-41 with Agnes Meyer, wife of the publisher of the *Washington Post,* as chairman of the events. The sponsoring organization—the *Washington Post* Folk Festival Committee—featured Eleanor Roosevelt as honorary chairman; twenty-eight senators were named as committee members, along with Cabinet members and scores of other Washington luminaries. Participants numbered in the hundreds and came from as many as thirty states.

Some early National Folk Festivals presented traditional folk performers and groups now widely known to collectors and folklorists. In 1939 Professor Lauren C. Post brought four excellent Cajun bands to a Dallas festival: The Hackberry Ramblers, two bands composed of Broussard family members, and the Evangeline Band. Two well-known traditional string bands from Texas were in attendance: A.L. Steely's Arlington Three and the East Texas Serenaders. W.C. Handy performed at one early festival.

These festivals presented what Knott called *survival* and *revival* performers. Both terms had been adopted from promoters of Appalachian crafts, who described weaving and other functional community crafts as *cultural survivals* and *survival arts.* These promoters started craft schools to "revive" the making of crafts for sale among mountain people who had not previously sold crafts. The terms *urban folksong revival performer* and *folk revival performer* eventually came into use to describe the performance of urban imitators of rural folk styles. These misleading terms are still used to refer to artists who have adopted or imitate a folk style rather than reviving an art which previously existed in their own families or communities.

At the early Knott festivals, revival performers were broadly defined, and in some cases neither the performer nor the style was traditional. Bird imitations by a member of the Audubon Society were performed at one festival; another festival featured a chorus of bamboo pipe players demonstrating tunes of seven nations (including "Baa Baa Black Sheep" as the English contribution). YMCA recreational dancers were presented as folk dancers, and costumes were considered important. Standards for the National Folk Festival were then different from what they are today. Unfortunately, those early standards still exist for many festivals.

The early National Folk Festivals reflected the times: a period of political unrest and economic dislocation, when the values of the society were being questioned and the championing of working people became a vogue among some intellectual and political leaders. A certain naiveté is also obvious in the works of collectors and academic folklorists of the time, many of whom were eager to associate themselves with this festival.

A later influential festival with national scope was the Newport Folk Festival. The festival was created after the imitative pop-folk group, the Kingston Trio, drew a large audience at the 1958 Newport Jazz Festival. During the late 1950s and early 1960s, the Newport Folk Festival emphasized pop-folk "stars" side-by-side with traditional performers. The Newport festivals drew large and diverse audiences and provided a forum for many excellent older Southern black and white musicians. Much of the audience had no interest in the older forms, however, and traditional musicians often were ignored by those who attended in order to see pop-folk stars.

The one festival that has overshadowed all its predecessors in recent years is the Festival of American Folklife, presented since 1967 on the National Mall in Washington by the Smithsonian Institution and the National Park Service. A three-day affair in the beginning, it grew to a week in length and, during the 1976 Bicentennial year, to twelve weeks. It has since followed a six-day format.

The directors of the Festival of American Folklife send fieldworkers to all parts of the country and to many foreign nations to seek out participants. Techniques for presenting traditional folk performers are stressed. Occupational skills, foodways, folk crafts, and narrative sessions share the emphasis on music. A few urban folksong revival performers have been presented, but the solid emphasis is upon the presentation of traditional folk performers reared in the culture whose materials are being presented. Folklorists employed by this festival have used it as a model for state folklife festivals. This festival benefits from two significant advantages: the Smithsonian's reputation and budget allocations from federal, state, and private sources, which dwarf those of other festivals.

Although festivals with a national scope do not provide realistic examples for smaller, indigenous and community-based festivals, they have created an impetus in regional presentations of folk culture. The creation of both new agencies and new programs in existing government agencies can be attributed in part to the fact that the Festival of American Folklife takes place literally on the doorstep of the U.S. Congress and demonstrates that folklife is something more than popular folksingers. Since folklore is by nature largely invisible to much of society, it seems important to provide non-academic arenas of national exposure.

National festivals also serve a function that local festivals cannot: selection for a national festival performance accords a measure of national honor to outstanding folk artists. The most meaningful honors may well be local, but folk groups — like others in our nation — have come to view appearance at large-scale events as a means of validation. Many folk artists have been honored in their own communities only after appearing at a national festival. Even though this process seems artificial to some, it is deeply pleasing to those selected for national festival appearances, and it shows an immediate and highly personal appreciation for their art. It is not uncommon to see a framed letter of invitation to participate in the Festival of American Folklife or the National Folk Festival hanging in a folk artist's home (often alongside pictures of Jesus Christ, John F. Kennedy, and Martin Luther King, Jr.).

Fiddle workshop at the 34th National Folk Festival. *Left to right:* Phil Williams, Steve Ledford, and the presenter, Alan Jabbour. Photograph © NCTA, 1979.

In addition to the types of folk festivals we have discussed, many events that are termed *folk festivals* actually focus on the presentation of *popular culture*. Common examples are dance festivals that present choreographed and costumed recreational "ethnic" dances and festivals that present commercial pop-folk and urban folksong revival performers. The organizers of these and other popular fests do not intend to mislead, and few — if any — of their patrons are misled. The term is misused because of an honest ignorance of the definitions of such words as *folk, folk dance, folksong,* and *folklore.*

The Function and Form of Folklore

Some Anglo-American folksongs have as their subject matter the evils of gambling and strong drink. Others celebrate love and respect for Mother. Council Harmon's North Carolina descendants tell stories about a boy named Jack who sometimes serves the King and himself by outwitting giants, unicorns, and robbers. Other people relate proverbs, devise complex riddles, tell scurrilous jokes about other nationalities and races, or spend years learning to play folk melodies on the fiddle.

All folklore is *functional* in the group that produces it, and such behavior is more complex than it may appear. A folksong describing the dire results of aberrant behavior or calling for the honoring of parents may have the function of reinforcing mores. Jack's exploits provide amusement, but they also serve an educational purpose by showing how wit and intelligence may be used to overcome powerful opponents. A proverb may contain the distilled experience of a people in dealing with a common difficulty. Riddles instruct in the use of logic while they amuse. Jokes that point to the real or imagined foibles of other nationalities or that denigrate other races may function to validate the culture of the person relating the joke. The joke teller's unstated position may be that people of his culture do not engage in the foolish behavior depicted in his joke.

Frequently an item of folklore may have obscure functions; it may exist only because it is customary or "right," and the actual need fulfilled might be better met in other ways.

Whether the function is as obvious as the hymn of invitation at a mountain Baptist revival meeting or as obscure as the Appalachian custom of not eating fish and drinking milk at the same meal, folklore is functional. *Function* may be conceptually separated from *form*. A particular function may manifest itself in opposite forms in different cultures. For example, in showing respect for deity, the Jew puts his hat on, the Christian takes his hat off, an Oriental may remove his shoes, and a Moslem removes his shoes and kneels in the direction of Mecca. The form of a tune may be a succession of notes with a particular rhythmic pattern, but the function of the tune may be to mourn the dead, to call to worship, to stir feelings of patriotism, to signal the beginning of a particular dance, or to lull a baby to sleep. A person from outside the culture may learn to reproduce the form without learning anything of the place of the item in the culture, what behavior is appropriate with it, or what function it serves.

Most studies of the arts in folk culture center upon forms and products rather than the behavior which creates the arts or their function in the culture. Studies of oral literature usually concentrate upon the tale or myth, not upon its carrier, and many studies of folk music deal with musical sound rather than with the musician.

While a cultural product may be studied or even replicated outside the context in which it was produced, it is in fact inseparable from context. Cultural products exist only in relation to the behavior of groups of individuals. The folk artist shapes a product according to concepts of self as an artist and within the guidelines a group has devised as appropriate behavior for an artist. The artistic product then elicits some response from its audience when it is visualized, heard, or otherwise experienced; the artist then is either reinforced, is required to change the behavior leading to the cultural product (which results in a change in the product itself), or else becomes a cultural deviant.

To see the folk arts as the behavior of groups of people, rather than as products to be understood in terms of their internal structure, broadens one's understanding of folk culture. This should be a matter of concern to each organizer because folk festival dynamics pressure organizers in the direction of ignoring the function of folklore and encourages them instead to analyze products by the potential reaction of audiences largely not of the cultures presented.

The Process and Material of Folklore

The chief identifying characteristic of folklore is that it is usually orally transmitted.[2] Folklore is ballads handed down in families, stories Grandmother learned from her grandmother, dances brought from the old country, riddles that puzzled our parents, the remedy for curing warts that Uncle Claude learned as a boy from another boy.

Culture at all levels is both conservative and creative. Today's culture is largely received from yesterday, and even in times of rapid innovation there are several times as many cultural items being transmitted from the past as being newly devised. Language, for example, is an aspect of culture subject to constant revision, but the larger part is handed through the generations. We learn to speak it as it comes to us from the people who have spoken it before us.

But while each of us may learn the larger part of language in much the same way, culture is transmitted and controlled differently by groups. In a modern industrial society such as the United States, three major levels of culture comprise the overall culture. These three levels have sometimes been visualized as a layer cake, although an ice cream sandwich might be more appropriate, as the middle layer is larger than the top or bottom layers.

The top layer is academic culture. It is largely formal, highly organized, and controlled by relatively small, elite groups. It has governmental and institutional support. It is transmitted through conservatories, graduate schools, libraries, and other institutions of education. It is Longfellow's poems, a symphony, an opera, a formal play, and other fine arts. It is written history and other elements of the humanities.

The middle layer is popular culture. It is disseminated and controlled by many individuals and by major industries, including those devoted to publishing, film, radio, television, and recording. It is transmitted through the mass media and supported by sales. It is popular magazines, the songs of Stephen Foster, soap opera, advertising art, graphic prints, and comics.

The bottom layer is folk culture. It is informal, noncommercial, and usually transmitted orally in face-to-face situations in small groups. It changes continually because it is shaped by the memories, creative abilities, and needs of human beings in particular situations. It is of the group, but the touch of the individual is on each item. A song may be traditional, but voice timbre and some of the nuance is that of an individual who may choose to vary the melody or change a word or line.

The distinction between academic culture and folk culture is easy to grasp. Academic culture is usually written in some form, identified with an individual, and has a preferred form. Folk culture is usually oral or aural, anonymous in origin, and has many forms. Many people have difficulty, however, in distinguishing between folk and popular culture. In part this is because entrepreneurs have learned that popular culture that imitates folk culture can be sold, so we find "folksong writers" and the transformation of Jesse James and Billy the Kid into characters in television serials. Of course a few items do fall on the border between folk and popular culture, but most items can be distinguished by any person who studies these traditions. Each of us has participated in all three levels of culture and is likely to continue to do so. We relate anecdotes and stories passed to us orally, share group experiences and assumptions; watch television, read magazines, visit art galleries, enjoy ballet. To understand how academic, popular, and folk traditions differ, it is useful to consider their historical backgrounds.

One of the great changes industrialization has made in daily life has been to create more leisure time and to separate work from leisure. In earlier societies, at the lowest economic levels everybody worked. Work and culture tended to fuse, so that religion, art, production, decoration, music, magic, lore, dance, healing, and other components of the culture were hardly visible as separate activities.

Prior to the industrial revolution, the only market for culture was among those who had sufficient leisure to enjoy it and the affluence to purchase it. Early academic culture was available to the privileged few, and folk culture was the culture of the masses. With the industrial revolution came industrialized art, which has now evolved into the huge complex of industries producing popular art for mass audiences. We sometimes forget that these industries stem from technological innovations beginning in the fifteenth and sixteenth centuries that made it possible to mass produce items of culture—for example, the beginnings of the popular press, mass-produced statues, reproduction prints, and the like. This production continues with motion pictures, recordings, radio, and that most pervasive of all popular culture institutions, television. Those who produce popular art normally must put profits before other considerations, and consumers richly reward popular artists and industrial executives who anticipate what mass audiences will purchase.

A small percentage of today's Americans (estimates range from 6 to 10 percent) have chosen to fill their lives with the academic art that traditionally has attracted the best educated or wealthiest portions of society. There is no consensus regarding what percentage of Americans have held to major elements of their folk culture, for it cannot be measured by sales, but it is certainly a much smaller percentage than that devoted to popular culture.

Some early producers of folk festivals hoped that they could sort out folk performers from popular performers simply by not paying performers and requiring that performed items be of the folk tradition. Alas, it is not so easy: items of folklore are performed by persons who are not part of folk groups, the folk borrow items from popular culture, and most folk wish to be paid when they perform at folk festivals. There is nothing wrong with persons of other traditions borrowing and using folklore, but a singer of folksongs is not a folksinger unless his performance has been cast in the processes by which the folk develop art. Most people do not bother with such distinctions and unquestioningly accept items of popular culture ascribed to the folk, but the directors of folk festivals need to draw careful distinctions.

What part does a folk festival have in the cultural processes? First, it should be understood that festivals cannot present very much of folklore. Culture is ideas, behaviors, attitudes, and much more that is resistant to presentation, so it is futile to expect folk festivals to show much of the beauty and depth of folk culture. Festivals present performers and products out of context, and the products best received are those developed as performing arts by the groups that evolved them.

The crucial touchstone for those who wish to engage in dignified and reasonably accurate presentations is *oral transmission and variability within a group*. One may find folklore that does not appear to be orally transmitted, but even in such cases closer examination will usually show that the item is largely shaped through oral tradition.

An example of this is Sacred Harp singing. The Sacred Harp is a hymnal, in use since 1844, whose notation uses the shape of notes in addition to their place on the staff to indicate pitch. Rural "singing school" teachers of the Southeast and Southwest teach this form of notation in two- and three-week sessions. The use of book and teacher would seem to define this as academic art. A closer analysis reveals, however, that much of the transmission process is oral and aural. A person who purchases a copy of the Sacred Harp can learn the pitch of notes from it, but the *style* of singing is not clear from the notes. In fact, no common system of notation could convey the style. Who are these "singing school" teachers? They are rural preachers, farmers, mechanics, carpenters, and others whose education usually stopped at some point in the secondary level. Their skills were learned in church, at all-day singings, and in earlier "singing schools." The Sacred Harp is a useful and essential tool, but Sacred Harp singing remains an art largely transmitted orally.

Before proceeding further, it may be useful to consider briefly some phenomena that tend to confuse first-time directors of folk festivals and to consider the types of performers commonly found at folk festivals.

SURVIVAL AND REVIVAL PERFORMING ARTS IN ETHNIC AND LOCAL CULTURES

Acculturation refers to changes produced in a culture when it is subjected to continuous first-hand contact with another culture. These changes usually result in increasing similarity between the cultures; the influence may be primarily one-way, or both cultures may be affected. The process of acculturation is normally gradual and may be viewed as either desirable or undesirable by one or both cultures involved in the process. "Americanization," aimed at turning immigrants and American Indians into reproductions of Anglo-Saxon Americans, has been a powerful, official force in the U.S., and it continues despite the recent lip service paid to cultural pluralism by government, educational institutions, and other agencies of the majority culture.

HISTORY, CONCEPTS, DEFINITIONS

When people feel their culture being supplanted, or at least begin to perceive that this is undesirable, a conscious effort may be made to preserve and revitalize the culture. Very often, preservation efforts center upon dance, song, national or ethnic customs, foods, and forms of expressive culture—those marks of the disappearing culture that survive long after even language has disappeared. Children may be taught the melodies and words of national songs even if they do not speak the language. National holidays may be observed and celebrated. The revived culture may claim to be preserving far more than it actually is.

Obviously, the expressive culture of the group has a very different function in such a revived form than it did in the original context. Songs that once had deep meaning in pledging allegiance to a nation may become a touchstone of personal or small-group identification, sung more out of nostalgia than nationalistic spirit. The clothes of earlier generations may become exotic costumes reserved for special occasions, and common inexpensive foods become the national cuisine (for example, "soul food").

Individuals and groups also experience acculturation when they move from their home area to another region of their country. They may attempt to slow the process, or at least ease it, by getting together with others in the new area who are from the same home locality and celebrating the culture of the home area. North Carolina settlers still celebrate Tar Heel Day near Seattle, and Texas Days are celebrated in Southern California. These celebrations feature regional foods and the music and dance of the home area.

Acculturation may occur when the locale of an isolated minority is under pressure from a dominant culture. Further, the group undergoing acculturation need not be a minority. Large, majority cultures may be totally acculturated when—for reasons involving status, economic power, larger armed forces, and other complex factors—the majority culture cannot compete with the minority, but dominant, culture.

Although what remains may be only a small part of the original larger culture and may center somewhat artificially upon performing arts and other expressive forms, these residual cultural aspects are important and are often good grist for folk festivals. All forms of culture have been conditioned by earlier forms, and purism is not a concern of the festival organizer. Still, the organizer has a better opportunity to show the special characteristics of a culture by holding to older, less evolved forms. This invariably requires seeking out persons reared in the culture who are less acculturated, because more often than not those who seek out the festival organizer are likely to be highly acculturated individuals.

A CONFUSION REGARDING FOLK CULTURE

A problem central to choosing participants and conducting a folk festival is a nationwide confusion regarding what folk culture is. This confusion is fed by large, well-established sales industries—publishing companies, the commercial music industry, music schools, touring agencies, Chambers of Commerce, and even the script writers for television series. Popular cult figures such as Bob Dylan and Joan Baez are considered folksingers, and forms of pseudo-folklore are created to sell breakfast cereal.

Confusion also stems from the so-called folk festivals which have long existed without conceptual and aesthetic standards for distinguishing between traditional folk performers and the various categories of non-traditional performers who sing "folksongs" and call themselves "folksingers." An authentic folk artist seldom uses such a term in describing himself. Rather, the folk performer is likely to describe himself as a Cajun musician, a Ukrainian musician, a blacksmith, a white oak basketmaker, or some other similarly specific term.

A corollary situation can be found in almost any record shop. The bin marked *folk* is likely to be filled with recordings of folk revival performers, folklike performers, and pop-folk cult figures. If the shop has any recordings of actual folk artists, they are likely to be found in sections devoted to ethnic music, old-time music, bluegrass, blues, gospel, country, or "international" music.

Thus, in common parlance, folk artists often are not called folk artists; instead, artists who are *not* folk artists are so labeled. This is a recurring problem for festival organizers because much of the public is confused about their purposes and the materials and performers they intend to present. The problem must be dealt with through the careful use of language and definition.

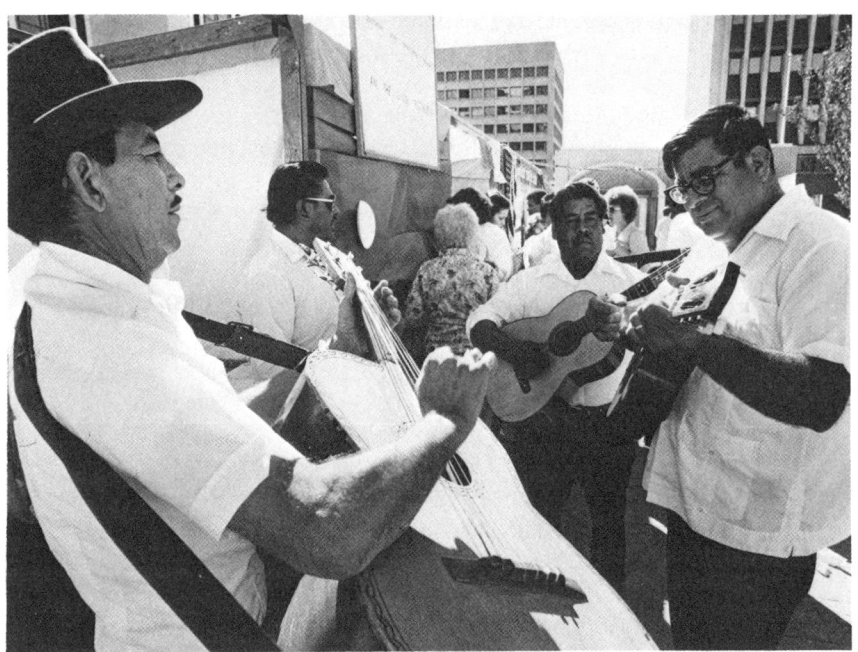

El Mariachi de Cristo Rey practicing by a food booth at Tucson, Meet Yourself. This mixed Mexican-Yaqui-Papago-Anglo group plays during Mass at a Catholic church in one of Tucson's Yaqui Indian communities. Here they are warming up before a stage appearance. This sort of informal jamming is a feature of this and other festivals. *From left:* Alfredo Nuñez, Ignacio Armenta, Pedro Flores, Richard Morales. Denny Carr photograph, 1979.

Some festival organizers feel that even the word *festival* has connotations which they do not wish to have associated with their events. To avoid the connotations of the words *folk festival,* the organizers of one highly respected folk festival chose to emphasize their interest in community-based folk arts by calling their event "Tucson, Meet Yourself."

Let's look at the major types of performers who describe themselves or are described by others as folk performers.

Performers reared in the culture from which the performed materials are drawn:

1. *Traditional folk performer.* While acculturation is pervasive and affects all, these performers are those who tend to hold closest to their culture's traditional forms and styles of performance. They are guided by the aesthetic of the group that produced the performed material and are not self-conscious in performing this material. The material may be changed or varied, but only within the aesthetic of the group which produced it. Such performers may know of other forms and styles, but it would probably not occur to them to adopt these styles. They may occasionally adapt material from outside the culture, but they still hold to the group aesthetic in performing it. Their presentation is usually within the group or community and is an accepted part of other activities rather than an event in itself — one performs at weddings, christenings, auctions, funerals, dances, and feast days rather than at concerts of the arts.

2. *Aware traditional performer.* Such performers are much like the above in that the material performed and the style of the performance is largely based upon the group aesthetic. Like traditional folk performers, they also hold to traditional forms and are unlikely to blend them with other forms not approved by the group. They differ in that the unself-conscious quality is gone; they may be aware that what they perform is "folk art," and they may regularly perform outside the group or community which produced the form. Realizing that folk art buffs prize authenticity, they may return to older forms and materials which the group has abandoned.

3. *Evolved traditional performer.* Again, the personal roots of the performer are in folk tradition, but the aesthetic and materials of the dominant culture have largely supplanted those of the group. Such performers may work full time at their art. They tend to be highly conscious of the styles in which they perform and of other forms, and they may blend forms. The material performed tends to be idiosyncratic although the flavor and style of the group which produced it may be an obvious and prized part of the performance. Some of these performers draw materials from popular cultural sources, such as radio and television, and adapt it to local tastes.

Performers who adopt elements of style and materials from cultures in which they were *not* reared:
1. *Performers who reproduce traditional folk styles.* Some performers attempt to reproduce material found in folk culture stitch-by-stitch and note-by-note, while others closely adhere to form and style but stop short of actually copying. This type of performer is found most often in folk music, and such performers usually have as their models recordings made by traditional folk artists. In the case of musicians and dancers, it is not unusual for an individual performer to present works created in several cultures, holding closely to the form or style of forms as disparate as old-time Appalachian string band music and Delta blues music. Such performers are highly selective in borrowing elements of folk culture, seldom adopting anything more than performing style. They may sing the songs of evangelical Baptists, but they are not likely to become part of a group of evangelical Baptists; their culture is usually the contemporary dominant culture.
2. *Performers who innovate upon adopted folk styles.* There is a wide range of performers in this category. They differ from those described above in that while they may use such words as *folk* and *traditional,* they are more concerned with individual creativity than with the adopted styles upon which they base their creations. They are less likely to have specific traditional folk artists as models, and their works of art are more likely to

be individualistic. As in the case of others who adopt elements of folk style, the culture of these performers is likely to be of the contemporary dominant culture.
3. *Performers who create in folklike style.* There is only a hint of folk style in such performers, and the material performed is likely to be of the artist's making. This hint of folk style may be subtle: the use of a guitar while singing, the singing of coal-mining songs, or the use of salt glaze on pottery. Nevertheless, performers in this category are the pop-folk, singer-songwriter, cult figures and craft shop operators who are most likely to be described as folksingers or folk artists by the mass media. The materials and styles of such artists are in fact a part of popular culture.

Many who are interested in folk festivals resist sorting potential performers for a festival into categories such as those presented. In their view, every person should be allowed the opportunity to perform at a folk festival, and selection should simply be an assessment of which individual performances are most pleasing. Such persons are disturbed by the fact that people are born and reared in a culture; their unstated egalitarian stance is that individuals should be able to select their culture in much the same way as they do an occupation or place of residence. That a culture is preselected for *everyone* and is a fabric of life infinitely larger than the thread of an ability to perform given items from folk culture is not viewed as a matter of such significance as to warrant decisions about what types of performers should be invited to perform. The orientation is toward individual performance, not folk culture.

At the outset, before you retain any performers, establish a policy on whether your festival will present persons who have adopted performance elements of a folk culture as well as traditional folk performers and, if so, which kind of performer will predominate. This decision should be treated with care; no other issue has so divided scholars in this field from those who have presented festivals.

While it is inappropriate to present urban folksong revival performers at a traditional festival, they may be usefully employed as presenters who guide traditional folk performers through the festivals. It is an appropriate function which has educational benefits for the revival performer while it benefits the traditional folk performers and the audience. But more than the superficial knowledge accumulated in learning songs and instrumental styles from records is needed. The presenter of traditional folk performers needs a degree of understanding of folk culture, empathy, and appreciation along with the skill to communicate with both the folk performer and mass audiences.

Presenters can help overcome the chasm which separates many traditional folk performers and sophisticated audiences. Some folk performers are not adept in communication outside their community. The attitudes and skills one needs to introduce his art in a living room or on a front porch differ from those needed on a large stage before hundreds or thousands of spectators. Large stages create in audiences an expectation of entertainment which may not mesh with the quiet art of some folk performers. The revival performer has experience which may be utilized in teaching audiences to cross cultural boundaries in their appreciation and to listen to the subtle and unfamiliar.

Like most other artistic presentations, folk festivals are social experiences. Often, audiences are attracted to performers they see as their social and intellectual peers. Audiences tend to approve of performers who, in attitude and style, reflect the audience — or the audience as it wishes to be. This phenomenon affects persons who claim an affinity for the folk arts just as it does the patrons of other arts. Thus, the revival performer can make an important contribution to the folk artist by functioning as an intelligent and erudite person who understands. To have such a person on stage introducing, interpreting, and appreciating a folk performer can indeed be most valuable.

Of course, many traditional folk performers are quite capable of handling their own communication and do not need such services. Many others are spectacular performers whose artistic skills are so obvious that description is redundant. See the discussion of presentation, pages 80-87, for more about this subject.

Notes

1. The only exceptions which appear worthy of note are "Mediterranean style"

festivals, usually held under the aegis of a Roman Catholic congregation which has parishioners of several cultures.

2. Folklore texts contain many definitions of folklore and folk art which may be useful (see Bibliography). The following carefully reasoned working definition was produced by members of the Folk Arts Panel of the National Endowment for the Arts in 1978 as an introduction to the NEA's Folk Arts Program:

> The folk and traditional arts are those that have grown through time within the many sub-groups that make up any nation—groups that identify themselves as sharing the same ethnic heritage, language, occupation, religion, or geographic area. Every Iroquois, Louisiana Cajun, and Mennonite represents a people who have developed a distinctive expressive system, a body of important works of art, and an assembly of respected practitioners of those art forms, all cherished and valuable.
>
> Folk arts include music, dance, song, poetry, tales, oratory, crafts, and rituals at their core. The particular ways these artistic forms are expressed serve to identify and symbolize the group that originated them. Each traditional tale, each pottery style, and each song is full of meaning because it has been subjected through time to a process in which the transitory, the trivial, and the inessential tend to be forgotten and discarded. What survives expresses the "soul" of the group, because it carries within the compacted wisdom of the past.
>
> For many groups in our nation—Native Americans, ethnic Americans, and others—this past exists primarily in the memories and repertoires of senior traditional artists. Accordingly, the most valuable practitioners of the folk and traditional arts are those who have been brought up within a traditional community, learning the repertoire from the older folk and absorbing the style as they live the life that the style and the repertoire represent.
>
> For this reason, individual creativity or innovation is not crucial to our program. Our program is designed to nourish the roots of that creativity. We define our responsibility as the encouragement of those community or family-based arts that have endured through several generations and that carry with them a sense of community aesthetic. Our major criteria are the authenticity of the practitioners of those arts and the excellence of their work.
>
> We do not seek to prevent artistic change and development. Instead, we attempt to help smooth the flow of culture experience, so that all people can move confidently into their own futures, secure in the knowledge of the elegance and individuality of their own cultural pasts.

2. Administration

Administrative Structure

Festival planning should begin about one year in advance of the event with the establishment of an administrative structure, selection of site and dates, and formation of a budget and timetable. The scope, setting, and philosophical concept of festivals cover a broad range—from small, free local events to national extravaganzas with a budget and logistical problems to match. Even so, there are common concerns in almost every instance.

There are five major areas of festival production—each with its own operating procedures and required skills, but all closely interrelated. These five areas of work can serve as a festival planning guide and a key to staffing needs. The material in this handbook is organized accordingly.

ADMINISTRATION AND MANAGEMENT

The festival director is usually the key person in the administrative structure of a festival. The size of the supporting staff and the degree of authority delegated is up to him or her. The director must devise a timetable and budget and must stay within them. He or she may be involved in several aspects of the festival—programming, publicity, on-site production—but the main task is coordination of all phases of the festival.

PROGRAMMING

Program decisions can be made by one, two, or ten persons; but first-time festivals are advised to establish a program committee made up of five or six energetic persons representing a diversity of interests relating to the festival. They will (*a*) establish a programming concept; (*b*) select festival participants; (*c*) assist the festival director with scheduling performers and selecting presenters; and (*d*) work closely with the publicity committee to formulate media promotion and produce posters, brochures, and a program book.

PUBLICITY

Publicity is a vital and time-consuming operation for any public event. It involves (*a*) writing and distributing press releases; (*b*) producing public service announcements for television and radio; (*c*) producing posters, brochures, paid media advertising, and a program book; (*d*) establishing a working relationship with the media and other segments of the community which may be vital to the success of your festival; and (*e*) documenting the festival when it is over.

HOSPITALITY

Hospitality involves the physical care of festival participants and staff. This includes transportation to the festival, housing and food, transportation between housing and festival sites if necessary, and generally attending to participants' needs. Hospitality begins with the first communication with participants and continues throughout the festival until the last participant is homeward bound.

PRODUCTION

Production goes hand in hand with all other work areas. It also includes a whole different area of effort: constructing and operating the festival site, arranging for stages, sound, lights, booths, or tents for the crafts area, electricity, stage crews, presentation, and a host of other considerations. In the early stages, production can be handled by one person, but as the festival approaches it becomes a labor-intensive operation requiring a large staff to get the work done on tight time schedules.

Staffing

STRUCTURE

In staffing your festival, the first step is to define a structure based on the size and nature of your particular event. It might be helpful to draw up an organizational chart, designating committee chairpersons and members, coordinators and assistants, and volunteers for each work area. You may not have the luxury of having a different person to fulfill every function on the chart, but do make sure each job is assigned to somebody and give that person enough help to get the work done. The next step is to determine specific duties for each coordinator and put it all on paper, ready to be distributed to everyone involved. This is an important step in insuring a smooth flow of communications during the festival.

ADMINISTRATIVE STAFF

Some of the work which falls into other areas as festival planning progresses usually begins before the staffing process is completed and so necessarily is done by the administrative staff. During the early stages of festival planning, negotiations and correspondence will require a considerable amount of paperwork. Although taking care of the needs of participants is a hospitality function, prefestival communication with participants involves important documents—contracts, information sheets specifying electrical sound requirements, travel arrangements—and should be handled as an administrative function. Ideally this work should be done from an administrative office or headquarters from which the festival director and staff work. You probably will have some persons working part time, possibly from their homes or other offices. In any case, insist that copies of all festival communications be kept at the central office, and transfer pertinent information in writing to each coordinator.

Publicity and public relations are treated in this handbook as a separate function, but your publicity chairperson should work out of the central office as much as possible. Files on press releases, media contacts, arrangements for publicity features, and so on should be maintained in the central festival files.

Bookkeeping also is a function of the administrative staff. It need not be done by a professional—any competent person can set up a simple, standard bookkeeping procedure. The following suggestions should be helpful:

1. If your festival committee receives grants from state or federal agencies, familiarize yourself with the fiscal reports required and keep books which will allow you to comply with regulations and file fiscal reports efficiently.
2. Some experienced staff members may be hired for a limited time before and during your festival. They can be hired as "independent contractors" or "consultants," thus avoiding the cumbersome bookkeeping required in computing payroll taxes and filing the necessary forms with state and federal agencies. (If any individual hired under this arrangement is paid more than $600 during the calendar year, it must be reported to IRS on Form 1099; see page 43.)
3. If you hire performers, advisers, or workers who must travel, establish credit with a travel agency, and prepay airline, train, and bus tickets. It will simplify your financial records and give you more control over travel schedules.
4. Write checks for participants' honoraria in advance, and take them to the festival site so that they can be delivered at the time specified in the contract or letter of agreement.
5. If you pay transportation costs to performers who drive, obtain a road atlas and use it for computing mileage so that reimbursement checks may be written in advance of the festival.
6. If your contract or letter of agreement with participants specifies reimbursement for meals to and from the festival, request receipts and mail checks later.
7. Require invoices before paying bills, note the invoice number on check and check number on invoice.
8. You will need some petty cash at the festival site. Even though you have informed participants and staff that you cannot cash checks during the festival, there probably will be some emergencies. Insist on receipts for all petty cash expenditures, and record such expenditures in a notebook.
9. The final financial report of your festival should follow the outline of your budget. We recommend preparing two versions:

one reporting income and expenditures under basic headings and another supplying the kinds of details that will help you budget for the following year's festival.

The administrative staff should be prepared to deal with persons and organizations who request permission to sell items at the festival. It should first be understood that such requests are *programming* requests, as such offerings become part of the total impression of the festival. The persons in charge of programming should set guidelines in advance and make decisions regarding each request. Such requests can be held until the program committee has made its decisions and a sales coordinator has been appointed. The same applies to would-be performers and craftspersons. Once your festival is announced, your office will be deluged by letters and telephone calls from potential participants. These requests should be held and referred to the program committee chairperson.

In the early stages, the administrative staff will become involved in almost every phase of festival planning and production—and it will all go more smoothly if the advance work is handled efficiently and relevant information is passed on to each coordinator.

STAGE STAFFING

Each stage will require at least three full-time staff persons, and you may find it worthwhile to have as many as six staff for each stage. The three essential staff members are: a *manager* responsible for the stage; a *sound technician*; and a *person (sometimes called a "gofer") who can assist the stage manager,* go to headquarters for items needed on stage, find out why a band has not arrived for a workshop, etc. (If you are able to link your stages to festival headquarters and mobile personnel through the use of a local CB radio club, the gofer becomes a radio operator who has charge of communications with the headquarters base station and mobile personnel.) Others may be: an *assistant stage manager,* a *recording technician,* and a *recording log keeper.*

VOLUNTEERS

Volunteers will be needed to do some of the work in most aspects of festival planning and production. One person will have to be responsible for making a list of each coordinator's volunteer needs, recruiting the workers, screening them, and coordinating their actions both before and during the festival. A questionnaire can be helpful in gathering the information you'll need to work with. A sample letter to volunteers can be found on page 205.

Volunteers, like participants, should be notified in writing before the festival as to what they will be expected to do and where and when they should report. They should also be told what, if anything, their volunteer status entitles them to—food, lodging, free admission if yours is a paid event, or an invitation to festival parties.

It is a good idea to have each coordinator evaluate the work of volunteers assigned to him or her. You have an opportunity to build a group of hard-working persons who consider it a privilege to be involved in the production of a folk festival and want to return in subsequent years. Even one year of experience helps; if this is your first festival, keep lists of volunteers, invite them to participate in a festival re-cap session, and you may come up with a group of experienced volunteers for the following year's festival.

Site, Date, Budget

SITE

You now have an idea for a festival and a group of persons interested in working on it, presumably persons with experience in the fields of work outlined. Your first decisions are festival site and dates—prime considerations in determining who and how many people come to your festival. Do you want to hold it indoors or out? Are potential sites accessible and convenient in terms of transportation and parking? Do they have electricity, water, and other facilities you may need? Is there a possibility of donation of a site, or will you have to rent it? If the festival is to be held outdoors, is there a time when good weather will be more likely? Can you arrange an alternative site in case of rain? (Postponing a festival to an alternative date is impossible in most circumstances.)

If you wish to attract many different kinds of people to your festival, there is an important but subtle consideration in site selection: *a need for neutral turf*. Simply put, some people do not feel comfortable in locations which appeal to others, so in selecting your site you are making a decision about the composition of your audience. Assuming that you aim for cultural pluralism in audience composition, each site you consider will be less than perfect. The task is to find the one most suited to the audience composition you desire and which can fit the needs described above.

Some sites have an elite or academic connotation which can be a disadvantage. For example, truck drivers, waitresses, and other working-class people rarely attend events held on college campuses; therefore, campus locations are a disadvantage to planners who wish to have a significant number of working-class people in their audiences. This disadvantage can be overcome by festival publicity and community relations, and at least one college-based festival has dealt with this problem with exemplary results. But this event is held on the campus of an institution with an unusual history of commitment to community, and festival organizers assure working-class people that they will be welcome by aiming much of their publicity at them.

Some historic sites are similarly disadvantaged due to their association with famous people or supporting organizations that are not economically or culturally representative of the area. Again, the disadvantage may be overcome, but if it exists planners should be aware of it and make allowances for it in selecting participants and in publicity.

In attempting to counter such disadvantages and make festivals more accessible to working-class people, some urban festival organizers have held festivals in downtown streets, in shopping malls, and in urban parks adjacent to working-class neighborhoods. Such strategies may or may not work, and the conventional wisdom of "taking the festival to the people" should be rigorously questioned during your planning. For example, an urban park may be the turf of some working-class people or even of a specific ethnic group, but if you wish to attract working people from a broad area or many ethnic groups, it may not be the best location. How far do you intend to reach? And whom? In planning, avoid stereotyped analysis of where working-class people live and where they are willing to go. In most cities working-class people and ethnic groups tend to live in more than one area, and a downtown location can have the effect of making an event inaccessible unless it is convenient to highways or freeways and provides adequate parking, safety, and other amenities.

Shopping malls and downtown street locations bring free services to many festivals, but such sites are seldom aesthetically pleasing. The issue of whether or not it is possible to present traditional folk culture in such locations is automatically raised, because the subject matter of a folk festival is the antithesis of commercialism. While it may be possible in theory for a festival organization to present traditional folk culture while promoting business, it is notable that, from among the many hundreds of such festivals which now exist, no examples worthy of emulation have emerged.

Among the sites which best combine accessibility, neutral turf, adequate space, the possibility of site donation, and perhaps even some supporting services are the local, state, and national parks. A common problem is that it is not possible to charge admission at many park sites because of a lack of enclosed space or because it would not be appropriate in a particular park.

The sites most commonly used for folk festivals are privately owned. Farms, campgrounds, and performing arts parks are favored iocations for many successful festivals. If you are inclined toward using a private site, your need for security services may be greater than at a public site, and the questions noted at the beginning of this section should be given added analysis.

You may be able to borrow tents, portable generators, a water truck, portable latrines, and other facilities from the National Guard, your state fair authority, or state parks director. You may wish to rent some tents, but they are expensive. A tent large enough to assure a "rain or shine" festival is usually a poor investment as it will probably cost more than you would lose in gate receipts in one day of rain.

In selecting a site, you may find yourself engaged in a discussion of what people are likely to do in a given situation. Can you expect Polish people to come out of town to a state park? Will Afro-Americans come? Will steelworkers from the east side come? These questions involve far more than site selection, and such matters as participant selection and the directing of publicity are at least as important as the site. One way to predict whether a group will come to

ADMINISTRATION 33

a specific site is to know whether or not the group now travels to sites outside its immediate area for programs which appeal to it. Where do black gospel and "soul" performers, country and western performers, and major ethnic artists now appear in your area? Do their supporters travel to see them, and how far?

DATE

Because people who like and attend an event are its best potential future audience, establishing a recurring specific date for a festival is an important consideration. Some of the best-supported traditional festivals occur on predictable, easy-to-remember weekends. For example, the Old Fiddlers Convention in Galax, Virginia, is held the first full weekend in August; fans and contestants who have moved away from the area know when it will be held and make vacation and travel plans far in advance. Many do so without seeing any advertising for the current event.

In general, holiday weekends are good for festivals where most of the audience must travel considerable distances or where homecoming themes are important. Conversely, holiday weekends are usually poor choices for urban events because city people of all socioeconomic levels tend to use such weekends for out-of-the-city leisure activities and visiting.

Although weather is unpredictable far in advance for specific dates, some areas have predictable spring rains and periods of intense heat. It is a good idea to choose dates in a period when weather is more likely to be pleasant.

Almost any date chosen is likely to produce a conflict with some other local event, but you can avoid troublesome conflicts by reading back issues of newspapers for the time period you have chosen. Are any local traditional folk events usually held in the period you are considering? If so, you can ask organizers what dates they have chosen for the coming year and minimize the possibility of conflict.

Some new festivals have been integrated with older community traditions through cooperation with the organizers of other community events. For example, one Southern festival is held during a period traditionally used for local church and family homecomings.

Another way to show respect for local traditions is to choose dates that were once used for a traditional event which has been discontinued, or dates of local historic significance. Such dates can bring local support if the tie to local tradition or history is made clear. Some festivals are named for dates. For example, Arthur Middleton's Birthday Party is a South Carolina celebration which honors a historic figure associated with the area in which the festival is held.

Giving careful, analytical attention to these and other local considerations at the outset will prevent the changing of dates after they are announced and the extra work and confusion which inevitably accompany date changes.

BUDGET

In formulating a budget, you must balance festival costs with estimated income. If you depend on grants and contributions, make your application for funding well in advance of the event. If admissions will be your main source of revenue, you may have to arrange a loan to carry you through until the money comes in. Cash flow is one of the principal problems of festival planning and must be thought out carefully early in the planning stage. Planning your budget will involve a lot of ground work, probably on the part of several people. There are various ways to set up a budget, and you should consult an accountant or someone well versed in festival finance to make sure you're taking all necessary precautions. For our purposes, we'll set up a budget based on the five categories we've discussed — administration, programming, publicity, hospitality, and production. The figures used are arbitrary and should not be taken as any sort of indicator. Costs in any category can vary from zero to $$$$ depending on the circumstances. Take every area of the budget into consideration, however, as each item must be accounted for; if it doesn't involve cash outlay, it will involve time expended securing a donation and a certain amount of administration.

Let's examine how a budget is formulated. The festival director, possibly with advice from budgetary experts, defines budget categories, estimates what each area might cost, and itemizes possible income sources. How does one determine what to budget for each

ADMINISTRATION

First Annual Folklife Festival Anticipated Budget

Expenses

Administration	
Staff & consultants — salaries and benefits	$ 2,000.00
Rent, supplies, phone, postage, etc.	1,000.00
Participant Costs (Hospitality)	
Participants' honoraria	3,200.00
Housing & food	750.00
Transportation	500.00
Publicity & Public Relations	
Newspaper, radio, advertising	250.00
Posters and brochures	300.00
Program book or leaflet	750.00
Production	
Facility or site costs	free
Sound, lights, equipment rental	500.00
Stages, tents & booths, signs	500.00
Documentation — recording & photographing	250.00
Miscellaneous	
On-site emergencies, insurance, permits, fees, etc.	500.00
TOTAL EXPENSES	**$10,500.00**

Income

Grants & Donations	
National Endowment for the Arts	$ 2,000.00
State Arts Council	1,000.00
Local contributions	750.00
Revenue	
Program & poster sales	500.00
Admission charge	6,250.00
TOTAL INCOME	**$10,500.00**

Total Expenses	$10,500.00
Total Income	10,500.00
	–0– or a balanced budget

item if a fixed income is not known? Obtain as much solid information as you can, then estimate what each item will cost on a hypothetical basis and apply for funds based on this hypothetical budget. If you are applying for grants the figures should be reasonably sound estimates, as a proposed budget is always required.

Obtaining budget figures involves determining what you want to present and translating those ideas into costs by carefully examining every potential cost area. How many participants are you inviting? How much are you paying them? How many will come from the immediate area? How many will you have to transport, house, and feed? What arrangements will have to be made to prepare the site for the festival? Is power available, or will it have to be brought in? Do staging areas exist, or will they have to be built or borrowed? Will you need tents or booths? Will you need paid advertising to supplement public service coverage? What do you plan in terms of posters, brochures, and program books? Make a painstaking survey of each cost item, come up with a realistic cost estimate, and you should have a fair idea of what your festival will cost.

Legal Considerations

The presentation of some folk festivals involves complex legal problems which can be solved only after careful analysis of each set of circumstances. It may be necessary to consult a local attorney who can provide sound advice covering your particular situation. Problems discussed here are not the kind which should be answered by speculation, and laws vary from state to state. Search for an attorney who has an interest in the folk arts and might assist you for a minimal fee, or none at all. The discussion which follows covers the general areas to be examined in each individual circumstance.

THE LEGALITY OF THE FESTIVAL

The initial question is whether the festival is lawful in your particular state or county. In many parts of the nation, the legacy of Woodstock and other rock festivals has fostered certain kinds of prohibitions or restrictions on music festivals. The first step should be to ascertain whether there are any state or local laws pertaining to

the proposed festival. In many cases the law pertains to what is termed an *outdoor music festival*. In determining whether the festival is prohibited, certain questions need to be answered:
1. What is the definition of *outdoor*? (A permanent covered stage and audience area may be excluded.)
2. What is the definition of *music*? (Does it relate only to pop or rock? Does it apply to classical as well? Does its standing as an "art form" modify the terms of the statute?)
3. Does the term *festival* mean a gathering of over x number of people? Can this be overcome by limiting the audience, advance sales, etc.?

REGULATIONS, RESTRICTIONS, AND BONDING

Sometimes there is a requirement that bond be posted to cover any possible damage which could result from the event. The bond may be substantial ($100,000 is not uncommon) or it may be modest. The important element to determine is whether such a bond requirement is *discretionary*. The local government officials may have authority to waive the bond requirement or to set the amount of the bond at a lesser figure. Facts commonly taken into consideration in setting the bond figure when it is discretionary include: (*a*) the history of problems involving the organization sponsoring the event, (*b*) the type of music presented, (*c*) the reliability of the members of the organization, (*d*) the type of organization (profit or nonprofit), (*e*) type and size of audience expected, (*f*) financial standing of the organization concerned, and (*g*) the location of the event. It is imperative, therefore, to make the most effective presentation possible to the authorities — demonstrating the significance of your festival, the kind of music you are presenting, and the nature of the expected audience. It is usually advisable to speak personally with the administrator handling your application. This may eliminate misunderstanding, and it will enable you to describe more graphically the type of function intended. Bureaucrats tend to generalize applicants, and you will need to be persuasive in pointing out that Sacred Harp singing is not the same as rock music.

Be certain that *all* city, county, and state regulations are satisfied. Often a permit is required to use land for other than its normal use.

Sanitary facilities must be approved in advance. Also, the statute or administrative regulation may limit the number of spectators.

FORM OF BUSINESS ENTITY

A large festival can be a considerable financial undertaking. A festival producer assumes responsibility for performers' fees, land rental, advertising, and exposure to risks of personal injury or property damage. For this reason the producer should consider carefully several possible legal forms of doing business and their respective advantages and disadvantages.

A group interested in putting on a folk festival can adopt one of two forms of doing business. These are the *corporate form* and the *partnership* (assuming that more than one person is involved; if there is only one, the form is known as *sole proprietorship*). Each form has certain benefits. The advantages of a partnership over a corporation are that each partner retains a veto power over the decisions of the partnership and each partner is an agent of the partnership and, as such, he or she is able to legally bind the other partners. Each partner is legally liable for all the obligations of the partnership business. Finally, the partnership is subject to dissolution contingent upon certain events, such as the death of a partner or the decision by one of the partners to withdraw from the partnership.

The corporate form of doing business has several distinct advantages, particularly if your event is to be annual. The most important advantage is that you can apply for tax-exempt status. Once you have elected a Board of Directors and officers and have formed a corporation, you should have a lawyer help you draw up by-laws and submit them to the Internal Revenue Service along with an application for tax-exempt status. If the IRS approves your application, you will receive a tax-exemption letter and be assigned a tax-exempt number. Thus equipped, you will be legally qualified to receive funds from businesses and individuals who can deduct their donations for income tax purposes and from such art-oriented governmental agencies as the National Foundations for the Arts and Humanities, state arts agencies, etc. This process takes a minimum of six months. If you plan to apply for grants or receive donations before your organization has tax-exempt status, find an organization that is already tax exempt and is willing to receive and administer your funds until your request has been processed.

The corporation is a separate legal entity and, as such, it acts as a buffer to prevent personal liability of the individuals in the corporation. For example, if someone in attendance at a music festival is injured in such a way as to make the promoters responsible, within the corporate structure the injured individual cannot sue the principals in the corporation but is able to appeal only to the corporate treasury for recovery. Another benefit sometimes attributed to the corporate form is that management can be centralized. Unlike the partnership form, in which all members are equal, a separate Board of Directors can be created that gives continuity to the organization and does not depend upon the continued participation of the partners. Thus, the death of a member of the Board does not have any significant legal effect on the ongoing nature of the corporation.

The only substantial disadvantage in doing business under the corporate form is that it is far more important to adhere to certain formalities, such as having periodic meetings, keeping minutes, and filing certain documents with the state and federal authorities.

The corporation form of doing business is preferable to the partnership for organizations of the type under discussion. However, if only a small number of persons is involved, the partnership form is worth considering.

INSURANCE

Regardless of the form of business entity chosen, insurance is usually a necessity for any festival production. Often, adequate insurance is demanded by local or state statutes or regulations. The producer is exposed to liability for personal injury and property damage caused through any one of several conditions such as defective equipment, terrain condition, or negligence. There is not adequate space here to detail the complex terms of insurance policies. However, a list of the risks you anticipate and the maximum possible protection desirable will enable you to compare policies intelligently. Special event insurance is costly, and the rates vary drastically. Therefore, it would benefit you to obtain a wide sample of premium quotations.

There is, in addition, the possibility of rain insurance to protect you in the event of bad weather. However, premiums for this type of insurance are expensive. Folk festival fans tend to be a hardy bunch who will brave wind, rain, and snow.

COPYRIGHT REQUIREMENTS

Public performance of copyrighted material requires payment to the publishing houses holding these rights through a licensing group (B.M.I., A.S.C.A.P., S.E.A.S.A.C.). These restrictions do not apply to traditional material, but even at the most traditional of festivals a large portion of the material performed is subject to copyright. Many songs become traditional long before their copyrights have expired and they have entered the public domain. For example, the following songs are still copyrighted: *Happy Birthday, Red River Valley,* the common version of *Black is the Color,* and *I'll Fly Away.* Also, there is the additional problem that some folksongs have been copyrighted.

Enforcement of copyright provisions varies considerably from state to state and even from county to county. A check with local musicians or musicians unions might prove helpful.

PARTICIPANTS' CONTRACTS

Informal contracts (e.g., an exchange of letters) usually are sufficient for most performers. Occasionally, professional musicians will require you to execute a standard union contract. In this case, examine the provisions carefully. Check to be certain that the names of the specific performers you expect to appear are on the face of the contract. Frequently the name of the band will appear without designating individuals. Given the constant shifting of performers in some bands, you should realize that legal obligations extend only to those specifically named. The time of performance each day is also usually specified. Be sure such time coincides with your plans. If you prefer that the performers not perform within a certain geographic area of your festival within a certain period of time before and after your festival, be sure to include this provision in the contract. Contracts may also prohibit recording of the event by sound or videotape. Realize that you are free to negotiate any and all terms of the contract (even if on a printed contract form) — but once details are agreed upon, be sure all of the agreed conditions appear on the final document.

As formidable as the problems may appear, they are easily dealt with by careful planning and legal assistance. The rewards from presenting a folk festival are great, and you should not be discouraged by the need to protect all those involved. Attention to legal considerations will ensure greater enjoyment and preserve the festival as an ongoing event.

IRS Requirements for Non-Profit Organizations

If your festival organization applies for and receives tax-exempt status, you will be required to comply with certain Internal Revenue Service regulations. It is not necessary to hire a professional accountant to do this work, although you would be wise to obtain the services of a person well versed in general bookkeeping, IRS requirements, and payroll reporting if applicable.

This section is intended not to replace published IRS instructions but rather to provide a simple guide for requirements for tax-exempt organizations.

EMPLOYER'S IDENTIFICATION NUMBER

1. If salaried employees work on your festival, you will need an Employer's ID Number. It is not the same as your tax-exempt number; the ID is the number which IRS computers use to keep track of your records, while your tax-exempt number proves your status to grantors. If your organization's gross receipts in any year did not exceed $10,000, you would not have been required to file IRS Form #990, and you probably would not have an Employer's ID Number.
2. Apply for an Employer's ID Number on Form SS-4, which you can obtain from the IRS. Check first with your local IRS office to see if a form is available.
3. When you request an Employer's ID Number, request the IRS to send all other forms which relate to federal income tax plus Circular E, the IRS instruction booklet.

4. Once you get your Employer's ID Number, it should be typed on all forms transmitted between your organization and the IRS.

FORM 501 — WITHHELD INCOME AND FICA TAX

1. The deadline for filing Form 501 varies depending on the amount of income withheld and FICA taxes you pay, but you are safe if you file form 501 by the 15th of each month for the preceding month's payroll.
2. If total payroll taxes due are under $2,000, compute the amount to be withheld and the FICA tax from tables in IRS Circular E booklet. It will be the same each month unless your salaries vary.
3. Take your check along with Form 501 to any bank. Request the teller to photocopy your check and the form, and retain this for your records. (The teller stamps the form when your check is accepted, which is the reason you should not photocopy it yourself before presentation at the bank.)
4. Banks will not accept payment of payroll taxes without Form 501. If the IRS does not send the form to you on time to file your withheld income and FICA taxes, send your check with a cover letter to the Director of Internal Revenue at the region in which you file. Be sure your letter bears your Employer's ID Number and is postmarked by the deadline filing date or earlier.

FORM 941 — EMPLOYER'S FEDERAL QUARTERLY TAX RETURN

1. Form 941 must be filed by the last day of the month after the quarter to which it applies.
2. Form 941 is simple to prepare. It is a compilation of withheld income and FICA taxes filed in each of the three months in the quarter.

FORM 990 — RETURN OF ORGANIZATIONS EXEMPT FROM INCOME TAX

1. If your organization's gross revenue is over $10,000 during the year, you must file form 990 whether or not you have salaried employees.

ADMINISTRATION 43

2. Form 990 is due after the close of your fiscal year. It is more complex than any of the other required IRS forms but simple enough if good books are kept.

FORM 1099 — MISCELLANEOUS INCOME

1. Form 1099 must be filed for any consultant or independent contractor to whom you pay over $600 in a given year. It must be completed and mailed to the IRS and the consultant/contractor by January 31 for the preceding year.
2. If you do not have a professional accountant, keep a card file on persons hired as independent contractors or consultants and enter each fee as it is paid. This will enable you to readily compute the total paid to persons you have employed under this arrangement.

STATE TAXES

Write or call your State Department of Taxation and ask them to send you forms and instructions governing state income tax withheld. Procedures for filing vary with each state.

STATE UNEMPLOYMENT COMPENSATION

Write or call your State Department of Taxation and request information. You will probably be referred to another agency, but Taxation can inform you of the requirements.

SALES TAX

If you offer sale items at your festival, write or call your state department of taxation to determine local sales tax requirements.

Funding

This section pertains to festivals that either have nonprofit corporate status or are part of the program of a nonprofit institution.

Of course many folk festivals are directed as fund-raising ventures by clubs and organizations, and some are profit-making ventures of individuals. Most folk festivals operated for profit fail to produce much, if any, revenue; those who assume folk festivals are profitable frequently encounter deficits. Any investor who has purchased this book with the thought of conducting a festival to turn a profit is hereby advised that this is a risky business—even highly successful festivals are usually rewarded with minimal returns.

What should an organization do if it does not have tax-exempt status? This subject is discussed in the section on legal considerations (pages 36–41), but a word of caution is in order here. If you do not have tax-exempt status and plan to use an "umbrella" organization, determine in advance what that organization expects from you. Nonprofit institutions sometimes charge overhead for handling funds and assuming risks, and many private philanthropic organizations and some government funding agencies do not allow such charges. Be sure you know the procedures of any allied nonprofit institution before you undertake fund raising under its aegis.

TO CHARGE OR NOT

Obviously, one way to pay part of the cost of producing a folk festival is to charge admission. You'll note we say *part* of the cost. Most of the better festivals which charge admission do not realize a sufficient return at the box office to pay all costs and are dependent on free services, sponsors, and grants for a portion of their income.

Basing the payment of costs upon anticipated box office income is risky, as bad weather or a disappointing attendance for any reason can wreak havoc with your festival budget. It is wise to estimate the paying audience conservatively and to have sufficient funds to pay performers, workers, and contractors *before* holding the festival. This reserve (called *the nut* in show business terminology) assumes the worst and makes provisions for it.

An admission charge is an eminently fair method of meeting the costs of an annual folk festival. Those who enjoy and learn from the event contribute to its continuation, and box office proceeds for one year relieve the pressure of raising funds for next year's events. Such returns are a tangible indication of the festival's success in communication and community acceptance. An admission charge also demands more and better publicity and adds an element of purpose to this activity which makes it a serious undertaking.

There is some evidence that an admission charge does not necessarily result in a smaller audience. From 1971 through 1975, the National Folk Festival charged no admission for daytime activities, although there was a charge for evening programs. A two-dollar daytime charge was initiated in 1976 and resulted in little change in audience size. Daytime charge was increased to four dollars in 1979, and the daytime audience was the largest ever. This reflects the festival's improved publicity and implies that whether admission is charged is not nearly as important as good communication and the quality of the program presented.

It is worth noting that the lack of an admission charge does not guarantee an audience. One "free" three-day 1978 festival had a budget nearly as large as the National Folk Festival and more well-known performers, yet despite good weather it attracted a small daily attendance—in the 800-1,000 range. Like the National, it was located in a suburban area near a major city, required auto transportation, and provided adequate parking. No invidious comparison is intended here; the point is that other factors were more important than the admission charge.

A festival admission charge complicates site requirements and increases the need for security measures. Sometimes it is impractical to charge admission at sites where crowd control cannot be effected (some festival goers inevitably try to evade admission charges if possible). The cost of building fences and other crowd control devices should be estimated carefully. Construction costs for one-time or even annual events can be prohibitive when compared to financial return.

If there is a common mistake among festivals which charge admission, it is a tendency toward overreliance upon "name" performers who are expected to attract an audience. Even "name" folk music performers tend to be obscure or unknown to the larger public; such a strategy directs festival publicity at the relatively few who are knowledgeable of folk music rather than at the many who know little or nothing of folk music but who are interested in local and personal heritage, local crafts, interesting "home" folks, and local arts in general. The former strategy puts the festival in a position of competing for publicity with other forms of traveling show business, while the latter causes it to be unusual in a way which is appealing to thoughtful reporters and editors. We do not mean to imply that it is wrong to present performers who have gained a reputation for quality performance, but this single factor does not ensure the financial success of a festival that charges admission. Developing a conceptual approach to publicity may be difficult when there is a festival admission charge; however, it can be more rewarding than copying blurbs from press agentry and incorporating them into press releases.

Although most established folk festivals raise a portion of their production costs through admission charges, some of the new ones rely solely on grants and sponsors for financial support. These often are directed by persons who feel that the folk arts and folklife should have broad exposure and that eliminating admission charge accomplishes this. Many of these festivals are directed by state and local arts councils which feel a responsibility to showcase the folk arts of their area as part of their regular programming.

It is difficult to argue with such reasoning. Some established festivals reflect an element of cultism and are more likely to attract the faithful than the uninvolved public. But as our earlier example shows, it does not follow that free admission will attract an audience; poor attendance is just as embarrassing at one kind of festival as at the other and endangers the continuation of the festival in much the same way. Clearly, the festival that attracts a representative audience must have a convenient, attractive site, intelligent programming, and good publicity — and these factors are far more important than whether or not admission is charged.

In the final analysis, whether or not a festival charges admission is likely to be determined by opportunity. Festivals sponsored or subsidized by state or local arts councils can ignore the box office, but this can be a short-term advantage, since such support is usually determined on an annual basis. Festivals dependent on gate receipts have long-term security if they are able to build a solid core of supporters which carries over year after year.

THE NATIONAL ENDOWMENT FOR THE ARTS

Two NEA programs are possible sources for funding a folk festival: Folk Arts and Expansion Arts. This confuses some applicants who do not know whether to apply to both or to one of the two. It is *not* a good idea to apply to both, but which program is preferable depends to a considerable extent on the program content, scope, and financial status of your festival. In any case, you'll need federal tax-exempt status and someone knowledgeable of folk arts as director of your festival.

It is often useful to discuss your proposal with NEA staff *before* submitting it. The Folk Arts Program also asks that a one- or two-page letter be sent describing the event you plan, how much it will cost, a summary budget, and how much you will ask the NEA to fund. Most Endowment grants are matching amounts (50-50 or less) and you should know where you will obtain other funds for your festival.

Allow at least eight months for an application to the Arts Endowment, as schedules of reviewing panels vary. After discussion and preliminary correspondence, formal application is made on forms provided by the NEA. Give close attention to the NEA guidelines; read guidelines carefully, noting the scope and interests of the panel to whom you are applying, and pay particular attention to deadlines for applications. All this may sound complicated, but applying to the NEA is actually rather simple if you follow this pattern:

1. Obtain and read the guidelines.
2. Have a preliminary conversation or engage in some preliminary correspondence.
3. Apply within deadlines.

Be direct and explicit in explaining what you intend to do and its probable effect. For example, if yours is a multiethnic festival, do not say that it will aid in preserving folk culture. There is no evidence that folk festivals have any effect upon the preservation of folk culture. In fact, because some remove folk culture from its natural context and present it in an alien setting, where reactions to it differ from those of the culture in which it was produced, it is more reasonable to say that folk festivals *alter* folk culture. Of course, all culture is subject to constant alteration by internal and external forces, and the effect of a given folk festival is comparatively benign. But the all-too-common claims of applicants that they can bottle folk culture or preserve it like a bug in amber is an indication to the Folk Arts Panel that the organizers do not know much about the dynamics of community and culture.

NEA panels look with special favor upon applicants who, in their presentations, honor senior traditional artists—persons who have held to the folk traditions in which they were reared and are excellent performers. Every part of the nation has such artists, and the NEA panels are more concerned with local honoring than with importing artists from afar. Any festival organization which engages in even a little bit of fieldwork and serious study of its area will find such artists nearby.

If you intend to pay anyone (coordinator, director, fieldworkers, consultants, or others) and request such funds, you should also make provisions for the payment of folk artists. NEA panels tend to look askance at applications which make provisions for the payment of others while folk artists are expected to deliver free services. That artists should not be paid is a widespread and bewildering assumption which hints that the sensitivities of many of those who prepare applications are geared more toward organizers and institutions than toward folk artists.

If you feel that you need a consultant with training or experience to assist you in planning your festival, do not hesitate to ask the NEA for support in acquiring such assistance. NEA experience is that bringing more experience and knowledge to the planning phase results in better festivals.

There are other common mistakes to avoid when applying to the NEA. Don't hire a grants writer or grantsmanship expert to deal with the NEA. The program directors, staff, and panel members were chosen because of their expertise in folklore and local and regional culture. What you propose is far more important than slick packaging, grants language, or a background of successful dealing with other federal agencies. Panel members live in all parts of the country, and you should assume that they'll know other experts in your area and will be well acquainted with what you propose. Expect nuts-and-bolts questions such as the names of performers you intend to hire, how you selected them (or intend to select them), the qualifications and experience of those advising you, your own experience and qualifications, and other practical, important questions. To summarize, your folklore skills and experience and the quality and authenticity of what you propose are far more important than proposal writing skills.

Kyle Creed playing banjo in a Reels, Jigs, and Breakdowns Workshop at the 39th National Folk Festival. Creed also demonstrated banjo-making in the crafts area. Photograph © NCTA.

A few more warnings. Avoid asking the panel to ignore its own guidelines. Don't ask for far more than you need or expect to receive. NEA panels have dealt with many festivals and know at least as much about costs as the average festival director. Above all, don't ask for funds to make a movie of your festival. Festivals are poor sites for movie making, and the NEA is aware of this shortcoming.

But how do you decide *which* of the two panels should receive your request? Here are some suggestions.

If you plan a festival which will draw its performers from those who perform within their tradition (e.g., the Appalachian fiddler who learned to fiddle from his dad in Appalachia rather than from records while in college), apply to the *Folk Arts Program*—the NEA's major program in folklore. Its staff and panel consist of persons with extensive academic training and experience in the folk arts. A portion of this panel's definition of folk and traditional art appears on page 24; every phase was carefully weighed before it was incorporated into this definition.

If you plan a festival which incorporates a folk festival within the larger framework of a non-folk community festival, celebration, or gathering, consider applying to the *Expansion Arts Program*. This panel is concerned with much more than folklore but has funded some festivals.

You can obtain more information from the guidelines of each program by writing to the National Endowment for the Arts, 2401 E. Street, N.W., Washington, D.C. 20506.

STATE ARTS COUNCILS AND HUMANITIES COMMITTEES

State Arts Councils and Humanities Committees have a mandate to support programs in folklore, folklife, and the folk arts. Many state arts councils have folklorists or folk arts specialists on their staffs, and some have been generous in supporting folk festivals.

One of your first steps should be to meet with representatives of these agencies. Their application procedures usually require months of lead time, so don't expect a quick reaction. Obtain guidelines and give particular attention to the types of performances funded and to application deadlines—and then schedule a meeting.

State arts and humanities officials vary widely in their knowledge of folklore. At worst, you'll meet a person so uninformed that he or she confuses folk arts with commercial country music. If this should happen, accept it as a challenge: many state agencies began with staffs ill-informed concerning folk arts and folklife. At best, you'll meet one of the new breed of state cultural officials — a professional eager to help showcase the indigenous folk arts and folkways of your state and with knowledge of a network of persons who can help you.

Whatever the reception, funds dispensed by these agencies are raised largely through state and federal taxes, and programs in the folk arts are as worthy of support as other forms of cultural presentation. Make application. If your application is denied, reapply after discussing it with agency officials. If the agency has no category under which you may apply, discuss the need to initiate one with the elected officials in your state who appear most likely capable of influencing the agency.

FOUNDATIONS AND CORPORATIONS

A common misconception about fund raising is that foundations and corporations are the most likely source of donation to any cause. The fallacy of this assumption is shown in some recent statistics: individuals give 74 percent of all funds raised through direct gifts and another 12.5 percent in bequests and other deferred gifts. Foundations give 9.6 percent, and corporations provide only 3.9 percent of all funds given in the private sector of the economy. Yet foundations and corporations are the major target in most fund raising efforts, especially those directed by people inexperienced in fund raising. It is the area of fund raising in which competition is stiffest, and knowledgeable individuals carefully ration the time they invest in it.

There is another important consideration in soliciting corporations and foundations: few give to programs in the arts. During the past decade, some major corporations and a few of the larger foundations have begun supporting such arts organizations as symphonies and dance companies, but support of the folk arts has been meager. Not one of the major general welfare foundations has a program in the field. Corporate contributions have tended to be small and have been given through community programs administered at local plants.

If you solicit corporations and foundations, carefully choose those where you can deal personally with management or persons handling such contributions. Corporations with home offices or major concentrations of employees in your locale are likely to be the best targets. Sending a solicitor who has a tie to a foundation's donor or board member is a good idea in soliciting foundations. In either case, you must be able to receive funds as a nonprofit organization or have them dispersed through one. Have a specific and detailed budget; be prepared to put your proposal in writing if the foundation or corporation should indicate interest. Letters requesting appointments and outlining the project in a page or two are okay and save your time as well as that of those being solicited. However, don't spend unnecessary time writing a lengthy proposal in response to a comment such as "we don't have time to see you but send a proposal" from a foundation executive. More than likely, this is simply a brush-off.

The widespread idea that a foundation or corporation giving program is an impersonal entity, staffed by specialists who objectively select and support good projects, is only partly true. These institutions reflect the personal interests of donors, the self-interest of corporations and special interest groups, current trends, and the relationships of their donors or owners to others in the community. Although the directors of such programs usually contend that selections are made with objective professionalism, anyone with long experience will tell you that the adage "it's *who* you know that counts" is almost invariably true of foundations and corporations. Look at it from their point of view: people who deliver are more important than individuals who happen to have good ideas. Ideas alone don't always sell themselves.

SUBSCRIPTIONS

If you have other events during the year, consider selling subscriptions featuring the festival as one event in a series. Organizations long devoted to the arts have found subscriptions to be a highly effective way of selling tickets. Much less effort is involved in selling a single subscription than to sell, say, six individual tickets. We know of only one organization which has sold subscriptions to a folk series, but since this example was successful we feel that others should try it. The organization is rural and has sold more than 300 subscriptions at $60 each.

If you sell subscriptions, start early—at least six months in advance. Direct solicitation is the best way of selling. Try to see potential buyers face-to-face; if this is not possible, use the telephone. Using this method, a subscription committee of twenty-five members should be able to sell 250 or more tickets by calling fifteen to twenty persons each.

Potential subscribers will be most interested in what and who you plan to present. Plan your programs ahead so that you can provide performers' names, skills and other details. Put it all in writing for your less articulate subscription committee members, and consider printing a brochure. As you become better known, the task will become easier and you'll find many repeat customers. In this endeavor, you'll find that mailings and announcements are not nearly as effective as direct sales. Also, your results will be far better if your committee is large, active, and aggressive. The chairperson or co-chairperson of the committee should call all members once a week, asking what results they have and urging them to complete their calls. If you are so successful that you sell all tickets through subscriptions, you'll insure a good season the next year—a threat of a sold-out performance is enough to move even laggards.

An obvious attraction of a subscription series is that it removes much uncertainty from your event. A driving rainstorm is much less a threat if half or more of the tickets are sold in advance.

3. Programming

Establishing a Programming Concept

It is often useful to examine what you and your community are getting into by looking at what folk festivals are and what they can do. Once you have an overall concept, it can be featured in your festival programming. A common complaint about folk festivals is that those who organize them are obsessed with folk music to the point of excluding equally important forms of expression. Other criticisms are that producers fail to engage their audience in a meaningful way with folk culture or tend to present a skewed, quaint, and dressed up version of folk culture which has little relationship to the real article.

Such criticism is often valid. However, the festival format itself brings together two phenomena which are nearly incompatible: folk culture and show business. An examination of the listing of common genres of folklore in any survey text shows that many are not suitable for presentation on stages or even in the small-group gatherings possible within a festival. In fact, many would not be suitable for presentation in *any* context other than the one for which they were created.

But surely other genres of folklore can be presented. Program committees developing festivals should consider other folk forms and the presentational strategies appropriate to them. The problems are great, but the potential payoff is worth it. For example, religious song has long been a part of festivals, but such a simple device as asking local churches to move their services to festival grounds for a day devoted to folk religious expression apparently has never been implemented successfully.

Your program committee should give attention to basic questions such as: What are we celebrating? Which local forms of folklore best demonstrate this? Which local folk artists best render these forms? Are we celebrating multiethnic cultural survivals? Should evolving and new forms of folklore be considered?

A particular focus may be obtained by paying attention to the way in which the presented folk forms are grouped. For example, look at the challenge the forms of "just talking" present, trying to highlight riddles, tales, sayings, or toasts. What happens when you attempt to put such forms on a stage or move the audience into an intimate area? Could you add a lying contest to this? Are such things traditional in your locale? If not, what kinds of good talking could be substituted?

Could you build a section of your festival around folk medicine and remedies? local folk architecture and building? If you have a children's area, can it be devoted to games and activities based on local traditions in children's folklore? What forms of work and work lore, food preparation, clothes making, and weather lore might be amenable to presentation? Do you have water witchers who could demonstrate their art?

Although there may be several ethnic groups in your area, you may open interesting possibilities by focusing on one group at a time. For example, in 1976, the Mississippi Valley Folk Festival (in St. Louis) was largely devoted to the arts of the French who have retained their language and a rich folk culture in Southeastern Missouri. Their foods, crafts, mining techniques and tools, music, and gambling (betting upon crawfish racing) were presented. The festival's planners also brought to the festival a sampling of other isolated North American groups which have retained rich elements of French folk culture: Cajun musicians from Louisiana, Mitchif French-Indian dancers and musicians from North Dakota, Zydeco (black French) musicians from Texas, and an excellent Northern Quebec fiddler.

Another focus could be the exploration of some major phenomenon taken for granted in the larger society which may not be viewed similarly in some folk cultures. For example, the idea of progress could be explored. Folk cultures do not necessarily agree on such an ideal, but it is so deeply ingrained in contemporary Western culture that it is difficult (but rewarding) to think about featuring it in your presentation. To do so, however, is to risk adopting a purely sentimental approach. The challenge is to find a balance between the two views.

As attractive as they are, such concepts do not necessarily sell themselves. This is especially true if you try to present them through storying or other forms of talk. It is a mistake to place them in direct competition for audience with music, dance, and other performing arts. Such discussions have been featured at folk festivals for more than forty years and have always fared poorly when placed in competition with performing arts, especially if "experts" lead the talk.

A useful idea is to highlight local talent, for then you better serve yourself and your community. Even when this talent reaches outside the locale, a larger local purpose is served, as it was in the Mississippi Valley Festival's bringing together isolated French cultures.

Identifying Festival Participants

In choosing participants for your festival, you are determining far more than what will be presented. At this point your concept is put to a test. If you are celebrating the survival of a particular form of folk culture, will you be able to persuade persons who personify such survival to participate in your festival?

Choice of participants is a major factor in determining what type of audience you will attract. It will help determine the degree of respect your festival receives from your peers; furthermore, since your peers may include those who provide your funding, it may determine whether or not yours is a one-time festival.

Unfortunately, choice of participants is also the one area of your festival which will bring you the most unsolicited advice. People with very different perspectives about life, work, and even aesthetics may feel that they know best what *folk* is and thus what a *folk festival* ought to include. Knowledge of the range of folk forms of expression and of the many different kinds of folk artists is needed at this point. If you do not have such knowledge or your knowledge is limited to folk music recordings, seek the assistance of a person who has training in folklore or experience in festival planning. If you seek assistance, carefully and objectively assess the skills of the consultant you are hiring. It is often useful to find a trained folklorist, of course, but such an individual doesn't necessarily know how to present traditional arts and artists. On the other hand, there are lots of consultants with credentials in festival production who know little about the fabric of traditional life. Learn something about the festivals your prospective consultant has worked on. The term *folk festival* is widely used, and not all events so described deal in the culture of traditional peoples.

FIELDWORK

One of the most interesting facets of festival production is selecting the participants. To set the tone for the present discussion and to get a sense of the importance of fieldwork, you might read the conversation between Ralph Rinzler, Frank Proschan, and Dewey Balfa in the section entitled "A Performer's Point of View" (pages 162–72). We are not suggesting that every fieldworker will have the experience of discovering a Dewey Balfa, but every energetic fieldworker finds new friends who are able to teach him and others, as Balfa has since he and Rinzler first met.

The amount of original fieldwork to be done for your festival should be determined by the festival director and program committee early in the planning stage. Funding will play a role — budgeting for this phase of your festival requires careful planning of the number of fieldworkers involved, distances traveled, and the amount of time spent in the field.

Fieldwork that has as its purpose finding performing participants suitable for presentation in a folk festival differs from the fieldwork of folklorists, anthropologists, and other academics interested in the comparative analysis of an item in folk culture or the long-term study of a folk community. The festival fieldworker's options concerning what can be used are circumscribed by the festival format, time pressures, and the concepts and themes to be presented. The festival fieldworker should have some training or experience in observing in folk communities and should be able to differentiate between genres of folklore and non-folk material. But these performers and craftspeople will be taken from their home community and placed in a strange situation. Thus, while the fieldworker should

Master potter Vernon Owens of Jugtown practicing his craft at the 1978 North Carolina Folklife Festival. Photograph by Bill Boyarsky.

have some of the skills of a booking agent, finding good potential participants is only half the task. The other half—persuading traditional people to present their culture in a folk festival and letting you set the stage for them so that the audience will understand what is going on—can be a difficult task.

Perhaps the most important element of successful fieldwork is the collector's sensitivity to the feelings and values of other people. When trying to persuade members of a folk community to exhibit their talents in a folk festival in the "outside" world, be aware that many of these people may be wary of strangers. Fieldworkers will be wise to learn from the work of previous collectors and attempt to establish relationships of trust with those whose cooperation they seek. Remember, however, that the only way to learn how to do fieldwork is to do it, for each situation is potentially different.

Sources available to fieldworkers are many and varied. This section outlines some possibilities to festival producers who intend to include original fieldwork in their plans.

Academic Collectors and Other Fieldworkers. Colleges, universities, and local libraries have many collections of regional and local folklore which are likely to be used by collectors and fieldworkers in the area. Ask the librarian in charge of folk collections for names of collectors or fieldworkers working in the locale or in your particular sphere of interest.

Once you have located your potential source, keep in mind the following simple guidelines for your approach:
1. Describe the nature and concept of your festival and *ask for guidance.*
2. *Allow time for personal interaction.* Most conscientious collectors and fieldworkers will want to evaluate you and learn as much as possible about your festival before they are ready to cooperate.
3. *Don't expect collectors to turn over their files, tapes, or lists of informants.* Networks of sources, built up over months or years, are the heart and soul of the collector's life. Few researchers are ready to open their project files to strangers because they have an investment in their material and in the relationships of trust they have developed with their informants.

4. *Don't assume that a collector will feel that he or she owes you anything.* Few folk festivals have been of benefit to the members of the folk community, and many serious collectors have reservations about them. The complaints you hear about festivals probably will be justified; the burden will be on you to show that your purpose and your festival are to be taken seriously.
5. *If you don't spark interest or gain cooperation on a first visit, spend time in the field and try again.* Tell the collector what you have learned and share your hopes about your festival. Once you have demonstrated that you do not wish simply to raid his collection, he may provide valuable leads and suggestions.

Even the smallest community college is likely to have at least one faculty member who is interested in local folklore, and larger institutions may have several. The interest may be peripheral—for example, a language professor who has studied the dialect of local ethnic groups, or a historian who has studied local folk communities from a historical perspective—but you may be lucky enough to find an ethnic studies program or a professor who teaches a course in folklore with some assigned fieldwork. Obtain a copy of the catalogue and look for courses which have some relationship to your interests.

The following list of classes selected from a University of Maryland adult curriculum schedule is an example of courses which appear to have sufficient relationship to warrant further investigation:

Black Culture in the U.S.
Culture and Society in American Humor
Regional Character and Culture in Maryland
Recreational Crafts
Beekeeping

Other Collectors. Folklore has always been a field in which the inspired amateur has played a central role. Sometimes such individuals go back to school and get academic credentials in folklore. But just as often you'll find excellent resource people in record collectors, writers who collect local tales, collectors of artifacts, and others compiling information about local folklore.

For example, most of the best collections of recorded folk music in the United States are owned by private collectors rather than institutions. The men and women who have compiled these collections are gifted collectors, and in most cases their knowledge of folk music extends far beyond records. The owners of large collections of 78 RPM recordings frequently are well informed about local artists who recorded for obscure companies years ago and who may still be around. Record collectors usually have a network of peers — and a collector of jazz recordings is likely to know collectors of ethnic recordings, blues recordings, or rural music. Don't begin with the assumption that such record collections are commercial and hence worthless. The large recording companies recorded ethnic and rural white and black musicians for decades and sold the recordings to the communities from which they were drawn. Later, specialty companies replaced them, and today there are scores of small companies which specialize in folk music and commonly press 500 to 2,000 copies of an LP. The best folk recordings come from these sources.

Also, individuals and musical groups often hire a custom recording company to press and package recordings. Many such recordings are of poor quality, but there are exceptions which find their way to collectors. Recording by this method is common among ethnic folk musicians. Limited pressings are inexpensive and are usually a self-liquidating expense, even if the artist sells no more than 500 copies.

Be persistent — explore every means of locating academic and non-academic collectors of every type. We have used record collectors as an example, but they are only one type of collector. Collectors of material culture artifacts are just as zealous in their work, and collectors of local color stories often will guide you to storytellers in the folk community.

A Network of Musicians. One common experience of festival fieldworkers is the discovery of networks of musicians. Folk artists and artisans are likely to know the other artists and artisans in their locale. When you find one fiddler, if you can win his confidence you may have a key to a community of fiddlers. Performers who have played with and have learned tunes from other performers usually have definite opinions about the others' abilities and repertoire. So when you meet your first fiddler, ask him or her about other performers. More often than not, you will be referred to the best fiddlers in the community. A good fiddler is also likely to know a lot about other musicians. In many communities this will include guitar and banjo players — in some ethnic communities it may include the cello and hand drums.

Regional and Local Collections. Colleges, universities, and local libraries sometimes house collections of regional and local folklore which can save you steps in the field. The use of such collections will require some preparation. Begin by reading the history of the area, concentrating on local settlement patterns. For example, if Dunkards settled the area, learn about Dunkards. Are there local histories which trace Dunkard families to modern Brethren churches in the area? Are there any traces of old order Brethren there? What Dunkard names are preeminent in your locale? Do some genealogical research at the local courthouse. Is there a distinctive Dunkard architecture, and is it evident in some local houses? Could you form a tour of local houses to show the local folk architecture of Dunkards? Look for presentation ideas in the early phase of your study. Search out the distinctive historical features and settlement patterns of the area and develop ideas of what you should be looking for in the field.

Folklore as a culture study means that work by anthropologists and sociologists may prove important in gaining the broad knowledge of your performing or producing community. Other relevant disciplines which may help ground you in the locale, its practices, and products, are studies in religion, occupations, education, oral history, politics, and the economy. Such "backgrounding" is incredibly helpful when you turn to the main body of regional and local collections. The stories, songs, beliefs, and other details of life provided by folk informants can be fully understood only when you know how they mesh with the fabric of life as lived by real individuals within real communities.

If regional or local collections include disc or tape recordings, reserve time for them. It is more time-consuming to listen to tapes than to read written accounts, but sound recordings may transport you to the scene of the collecting in ways written accounts cannot. Especially among collectors who keep their mikes (as well as their eyes and ears) open, the collections are bound less by the aesthetic choice of the collector than by the tasks of the performers and craftspeople. Moreover, tapes can provide clues about the collector's techniques not reflected in written accounts. After listening to tapes for several hours, you'll find that you have gained a degree of experience in how to interview and collect and how not to—for every collector, even the most experienced, makes mistakes (usually by talking too much). Striking a balance between asking questions and just letting your informants talk is difficult but essential.

The most practiced fieldworkers take elaborate notes and make account of the recording situation. Important information will be found in such field notes—information not included in the sound recordings themselves: a description of the social and physical setting, economic conditions of the informant or family, matters not discussed because of potential embarrassment, the collector's analysis, and other information of value. Some of this kind of information was not consigned to written form by early collectors. Younger folklorists tend to be more thorough, carefully documenting the conditions and contexts in which they collect. Consequently, you will hear many questions on tape such as "Where did you learn this?" "When did you tell stories like this one?"

Check to see if the college or university has material collected during the late 1930s and early 1940s as part of the Federal Writers' Project activities. Some of this material may provide clues as to what is traditional in your locale and where informants may be found.

It is important always to keep a file of the names and locations of informants, just as you will find any such previously made files useful. You can't know for sure who will be working on the festival five or ten years later and might want to run down old leads or rediscover performers or craftspeople interviewed. They may still live where they did when the collection was made, or perhaps a son or daughter has carried the tradition forward another generation.

Do the collections include information about more recent immigrants and their folklore? Recent immigrants are making important contributions to the nation's folk traditions, and their folklore is just as interesting as that of the earliest settlers. By including this dimension of local culture in your festival, you can help dispel the erroneous notion that folklore is something found only in Appalachia, French Louisiana, the Mississippi Delta, or in other remote or isolated areas.

Newspapers. County weeklies and ethnic newspapers chronicle cultural life that is much closer to the folk than what is found in the urban dailies. When you've located such a newspaper, read back issues. "Local color" and "human interest" stories are often to be discovered, as well as descriptions of entertainments, family reunions, and "life stories"; in many cases, local poetry and craft tips submitted may provide potential talents for your festival. Does the newspaper have one writer who specializes in feature articles about unusual and interesting events? Seek him or her out and explain your interests carefully. Has the writer written about a local person who makes gourd dolls or bakes peanut pies from a grandmother's recipe —or someone who heals by the laying on of hands? If you present such examples, the writer will know that you are interested in more than only music or crafts.

Music Stores. All musicians need supplies. Frequently, music store managers have broad knowledge of the musicians in their community, including folk musicians. Again, explain your interests with care or you are likely to be sent to visit a singer-songwriter who calls himself a folksinger.

Places Where People Get Together to Entertain Each Other. In all communities you will find one or more information centers— gathering places of considerable importance in the gossip and entertainment networks of the community. For instance, it is not unusual to find music sessions on Saturdays in the local barber shop, just as there may be a saloon, a good-times place, a juke joint, a gymnasium club (very important among Central Europeans), and even a funeral parlor as the important places where people get together. Don't forget the beauty shop, for this is precisely the kind of place where lively talk is to be found—after all, that's where you go to let your hair down.

Senior Citizen Clubs and Old Folks Homes. Retired people can provide important resources and other benefits. Many old people's clubs, church groups catering to older congregants, or even old folks homes are already in the folklore business, running special storying situations or talent shows. It is these people, after all, who preserve traditional folk arts and skills handed down in their community or family. Retired people often have networks of peers and the time to pursue their interests.

If a local group has a bulletin, you may wish to have your needs and interests discussed in it, giving your address and telephone number. You may wish to request volunteer help both for your fieldwork and at the festival. You're likely to encounter great appreciation for what you are doing and perhaps some willing guides who know what is traditional in the community from years of living in it.

Celebrations. Every community seems to have some folk celebrations, although the word *folk* usually does not appear in their titles. These include annual picnics, religious holidays and commemorative events at ethnic, minority, and subculture churches; celebrations of national independence days by some immigrant groups; local meetings of musicians and musical contests; harvest celebrations; ethnic festivals, gospel singing, and even the reunions of large families. Notice of such events may or may not appear in local newspapers, since many of them occur at a specific time such as the first Sunday in May or on a holiday weekend. Summer events calendars published in local newspapers sometimes include notice of these events.

Craft Groups and Organizations. Practically all of the craft groups you are likely to encounter will be dedicated to contemporary crafts. Even when an interest or skill in traditional crafts is claimed, you are likely to find that the craftsperson did not learn the craft in a traditional community or family and does not practice the craft in a traditional way. There are hundreds of city-bred makers of "Appalachian" dulcimers, many artists who produce pseudofolk paintings and sculpture, potters who create folklike pottery, persons who have learned "traditional" weaving at a crafts school, and others who produce folklike art. Many of these are good pieces and some are excellent, but such items are *not* folk art and such artists are *not* folk artists.

Yet it is sometimes possible to find traditional folk craftspersons through craft associations. Be alert to terms such as *primitive crafts* and *country crafts* which are occasionally applied to folk crafts. Do not be misled by your experience with craft organizations: the absence of folk artisans from most craft associations does not mean that they do not exist in your area. It simply means that few join such associations.

Folk Art Galleries. Of all the terms which are abused and incorrectly applied in this field, *folk art* in referring to painting or carving probably ranks highest. Daubings and carvings which are in no way traditional are passed off as folk art simply because the painter or sculptor obviously had no academic training in art. Galleries supposedly devoted to folk art often are filled with many different types of non-academic art which could be better called naive, pioneer, primitive, popular, or by some other more accurate term.

The self-trained artist who functions primarily at the level of folk culture may be as creative as those who produce academic or popular art. But art produced by an individual who is a member of a folk group is *not* necessarily folk art. Folk art emerges from shared traditions and a community aesthetic. Many artists who live and create in folk communities nevertheless follow individual concepts in creating art. Is this hairsplitting? Not really. On the one hand, you have the talented individual artist who creates primarily according to a personal definition of art. On the other, you have a community definition of art based upon shared traditions.

Many of the artists mistakenly labelled as folk artists have created in isolation from their communities, with their art becoming well known only after their death. Their communities have admired the work of others as the work of talented individuals. The clear distinction between these artists and folk artists who reflect community aesthetic and share traditions has been confused in the marketplace.

Most folk art is an elaboration upon the functional. For example, a quilt may reflect the group aesthetic for proper quilt making and its making may be a pleasing creative outlet, but its function is to warm its owner. The weathervane pleases the eye, but its function is to show the direction of the wind. The pie safe may be decorated with intricate and beautiful designs, but its function is to prevent

PROGRAMMING   67

flies from settling upon pies and pastries while they cool. A Santos may be attractively carved and painted, but its function is to bring its owner closer to a supernatural being.

In seeking out folk artists—or in separating them from others—ask yourself, "Is the object this person produces one that was traditionally produced in this community? Is the skill used in producing the object one learned from family or in the community?" In asking such questions, you will find that functions change. A basketmaker may make baskets in exactly the same manner as her grandfather, but she sells them to tourists who will use them as decorative art, rather than to farm women who use them to gather eggs. The form has continued, but function has changed. In time, form may also change; decorative art does not need to be as sturdy as a strictly utilitarian object.

Folk art is not necessarily crude, untutored, "cute," or primitive. Such terms come from outside the culture which produces folk art. The creation of many forms requires a high degree of skill or has resulted from many years of traditional training in a folk community. The line between folk art and some forms of popular decorative art can be a thin one. But it is easy enough to reject the more blatant examples of popular art, for they are the products of manufacturing. They are out of place in a folk festival which emphasizes traditional culture.

State Arts Agencies. Some states have state folklorists or state folk arts coordinators; others will be able to lend assistance by directing you to recognized folk performers, and they may know scholars or collectors who have worked in your locale. A few states have undertaken folk arts surveys. If you are located in one of these states or in one with a full-time folklorist, you are fortunate. In either case, discussion with these persons should be a good place to begin.

Directory of Organizations. A local Chamber of Commerce or library may have a directory of organizations in your area. Such directories often list very diverse organizations: antiquarian groups, place name societies, fiddlers' associations, ethnic societies, and architectural associations, which could possibly provide leads to potential participants.

National Organizations. The Smithsonian Institution and the National Park Service have cosponsored the Festival of American Folklife since 1967, and thousands of participants from throughout the U.S. and its territories have been featured. Similarly, the National Council for the Traditional Arts has directed the National Folk Festival and cosponsored other festivals since 1934, bringing participants from throughout the U.S. The American Folklife Center at the Library of Congress has conducted surveys of folk culture in some sections of the U.S. The Archive of Folk Song at the Library of Congress is the repository of materials collected throughout the U.S. Most of the Archive's collection is music. It is the single most important collection of folk music in the U.S. and is therefore an invaluable resource in learning the genres and subgenres of American folk music. The Archive also houses recordings of traditional religious services, children's games, folk tales, and interviews with traditional performers.

One can also locate informants in the Archive of Folk Song. Listen to field recordings made in the area of interest and track down performers or their families.

Occupational Groups. Important contributions to collections of folklore have come from occupational groups such as coal miners, fishermen, lumberjacks, Appalachian farmers, and cowboys. A part of your search for festival participants could be directed at similar occupational groups.

The great majority of the tedious and low-paying jobs in American society have fallen to migrants, immigrants, minorities, and subculture members. The movement of such people to fill these jobs has important cultural repercussions. For example, the best examples of Irish traditional fiddling were recorded between 1920 and 1940 in New York and Chicago rather than in Ireland. Chicago's police commissioner, Francis O'Neill, always had a job on the force for a good fiddler. New York's Irish enclaves allowed fiddlers from widely separated Irish counties to meet and trade tunes and techniques—a situation which likely would not have occurred in the old country. More recently, the spread of bluegrass music in the U.S. resulted in part from the migration of Appalachians who carried their taste for this developing style of music to northern cities in the 1940s and

1950s. The areas where they settled in large numbers became important centers for this music—notably Washington, D.C.; Baltimore; Detroit and Flint, Michigan; southeastern Pennsylvania; and the Dayton-Cincinnati area of Ohio.

Some occupations have become way stations—or perhaps escape valves—for upwardly mobile workers and have been used by several cultural groups, one after another. For example, the jobs filled by "hillbillies" in southeastern Pennsylvania were largely in the mushroom industry. This is dirty, back-breaking work, and workers commonly work seven days a week for the minimum hourly wage. But workers can work as many hours as they like; some hold to a twelve- or sixteen-hour day. Even workers disadvantaged by a lack of education, experience, or a knowledge of English can accumulate some savings under such circumstances.

This mushroom industry was founded before World War I by Italian immigrants. A few became wealthy mushroom farmers, but most moved to easier work after becoming acclimated to the new society. Southern mountain people—mainly from upper east Tennessee, northwestern North Carolina, and southwestern Virginia—began moving to Pennsylvania during World War I, and the flow increased through the 1930s and 1940s. It slowed during the 1950s and ended during the early 1960s. There are a few "hillbillies" still in the industry as owners and managers, but most have moved along. The new workers are mainly Mexican and Puerto Rican, and Mexican appears to be the dominant cultural group. The bunkhouses and cabins which once rang with the bluegrass music of Bill Monroe now feature the Norteña music of the Texas-Mexico border country.

Such examples are not unusual even today. The dry-wall carpenters in the metropolitan area of Washington, D.C., include significant numbers of Lumbee Indians and French Canadians. There are many Gypsy fender and body repairmen in New York. Chicago construction crews include many people from the Arkansas Ozarks. The oil platforms in the Gulf include large numbers of Cajun workers. Manhattan's many open-window gyro sandwich shops extensively employ newly arrived Greek immigrants.

These groups are not always evenly drawn from the societies they left. For example, a large percentage of the older residents of New York's Chinatown originally came from a small area of Canton province. Several thousand Greeks from the Island of Karpathas live in Baltimore—perhaps as many as now live on the island. In Baltimore those who came from various villages on Karpathas form clubs and associations based upon the village of their origin. The Southern mountain people who went to Chicago tended to come from areas of the mountains different from those of the people who went to Pennsylvania.

In collecting folklore, it is vital to understand that family and community relationships of folk society persist amid the steel and concrete of our cities. Changes are inevitable, but whenever folk communities move, they tend to move in groups and many individuals may work in the same occupation. To learn the occupational subcultures of your city is one way to make the folk culture of the area more familiar. Few scholars—and even fewer fieldworkers—have given attention to this.

Dance Associations. There are so many recreational dance groups (clog dancers, Balkan dancers, Morris dancers, and the like) that one might assume that finding good folk dancers is no problem. Nothing could be further from the truth. Finding dancers who learned their art in the folk process, from family or in a folk community, is every bit as difficult as finding excellent storytellers and musicians.

Here the fieldworker is faced with some of the results of the acculturation process. Dance is a common social activity that acculturating ethnic and folk groups seize upon whenever they wish to demonstrate an element of their culture to outsiders. This usually involves the creation of a performing group that revives the wearing of earlier work or holiday costumes of the group and adapts its styles of social dance to group choreography taught by instructors. The results may be colorful or even spectacular, but these "folkloric" groups are already once removed from the folk community and are part of the larger national culture.

Moreover, there are choreographed recreational dance groups, without links of any kind to folk communities, which imitate one or more types of acculturated "folkloric" dance. These groups tend to stress the authenticity of their costumes and dances, in much the same way that non-folk singers of folksongs assert that they are performing traditional music.

Because such groups are created for presentations outside the folk community, the emphasis is upon material (the costume or dance) rather than upon the person who wears the costume or the context of social dancing. Many groups even dispense with musicians and dance to music on tape recorders and records. (It would seem as reasonable for a group of musicians to project a movie of dancers while playing, but we've yet to see such an artificiality.)

The situation faced by the fieldworker is delicate. If a need for folk dancers for a festival is announced, recreational groups will apply because they seek an audience and because they call their dances folk dances. They may even be folk dances once removed, but they have been festivalized too long to maintain a folk connection; the fieldworker who wishes to depict this facet of folk culture in a reasonably accurate way has to avoid the recreational groups while seeking out more private presentational forms. One way to do this is to attend dances and traditional events at which dancing is common. Two of the best folk dancers we've seen were recruited at a Greek wedding and had never before been on a stage.

Perhaps the most common choreographed groups today are clog dance teams—an outgrowth of high school folk dance classes taught as a part of the physical education curriculum. These teams began in the 1930s in North Carolina, when high school physical education teachers allowed students to use the local clog or flatfoot dance steps in the western squares formation being taught. This soon became a local fad and was widely diffused during the early 1950s when a North Carolina clog dance team was used to open filmed segments of Grand Ole Opry shows on many Southern television stations. Choreographed Appalachian clogging is not traditional in any community.

Yet some dance groups may have individual members who learned buck dancing, jigging, flatfoot, or hotfoot from family or community. Where do traditional people dance in your community? Go see them. Ask traditional musicians who regularly play for dances about the dancers they know.

Journals and Bulletins. In your visits to libraries and regional collections, become familiar with the regional folklore publications which serve your area. On page 261 of this book is a list of publications with a national circulation which may be of use. Along with these, you should give attention to other publications of historical associations and bulletins of local anthropology groups.

Folksong Societies. Some local folksong associations have knowledge of traditional folk artists in their area and invite such artists to perform at their functions. A few have done fieldwork.

Churches. Church members, ministers, and other religious leaders in folk communities frequently have a view of religious belief and practice which is fundamentally different from that of festival organizers and others outside the community interested in the cultural aspects of the church. The person from outside may be interested mainly in the styles or performance dimensions of the service: gospel songs, the chanting style of the preacher, or perhaps the handling of snakes as an act of faith. But these are a part of an elaborate system of belief, so interwoven into the fabric of cultural life as to be nearly impossible to unravel for viewing in performance terms.

Problems arise when members of folk churches feel that they have been treated as freaks or their acts of faith have been scorned. For example, a festival organizer can easily create such a situation by inviting the members of a rural evangelical Baptist Church to a festival to sing gospel songs to an unruly festival audience. Festival organizers can deal with such problems in the planning and execution of a presentation, but some initial judgments and sensitive groundwork are responsibilities of the fieldworker.

It is particularly important that the fieldworker know more about the church and community than merely the songs or other manifestations of the religion to be presented. For example, will the minister want to interrupt the song service with a brief sermon? If so, what can the festival presenter do to prepare the audience in a way which will not insult the minister or his congregation? What kinds of behavior are church members likely to witness at the festival, and are these forms of behavior likely to cause the group to withdraw? How can we appreciate without destroying? Are there types of religious behavior that might best be left alone?

PROGRAMMING

INTERVIEWING

Let's assume you've succeeded in finding an important potential participant and you now are knocking on his or her door. How do you introduce yourself, explain your mission, obtain photos and tape recordings for others to consider — and at the same time handle the interview in such a way that this person will not be insulted if he or she is *not* chosen for the festival?

Most of the people who have preserved the custom of their people are courteous and hospitable. Most will welcome you into their homes and listen to all that you have to say. If you show respect for their art, most will perform for you.

You are as much a product of your culture as the persons on the other side of the door are of theirs, and it is important to remember that social rituals differ. Your culture may respect the person who looks you straight in the eye, but some Indians feel that direct eye contact is aggressive behavior. Our business-oriented society claims respect for those who "get down to brass tacks," yet businesspeople often transact their most important business in carefully planned social rituals such as the business lunch. In your culture, talking fast, directly, and aggressively may be prized. Your culture may value explanation that is conceptual, impersonal, and theoretical. Terms common in your speech may be jargon in the ear of your host.

Stick to basics in cross-cultural situations. Explain who you are, what you are doing, and the names of persons who referred you to the potential participant. Allow time to get acquainted. Don't push for immediate answers regarding possible participation or anything else. If you wish to make notes, photos, or tape recordings, ask permission. If you cannot commit your festival organization to hiring the person for your festival, be candid about your position and admit that you are gathering information for others who will make these decisions.

Expect questions about money. Many people, particularly musicians, tend to confuse festivals with show business. Many of the people you will visit are financially insecure. Be prepared to say how much they will be paid in honorarium and expenses if chosen for participation.

If travel to an unfamiliar place is involved, be prepared to offer special assistance — a person who will accompany, possibly someone of the potential participant's selection. Worries about such details often result in refusal to participate. Explain the selection process, give an approximate date of when the potential participant will be invited, and how soon after that you'll need their response.

Planning Workshops

The term *workshop* has been used for various kinds of presentations: music, storytelling, dance, academic discussions, interchange among various types of participants, and other presentations. But *get-togethers* might be more useful if you want to emphasize informality. *Workshop,* then, isn't the only term you could use for these small groups. There may be local terms that would personalize those sessions.

At the National Folk Festival, five stages are used for these presentations; thus the audience is dispersed between the stages and the crafts area. But to put a workshop on a stage may formalize it more than you want. In other words, it's just as important to think about smaller get-togethers as about larger events.

Because crowds at any one stage are smaller than at the larger evening concerts, workshops and other informal gatherings frequently are cited as the most fun and the most educational feature of festivals. They allow the performer and audience to interact in the same way that "the folks" at home or at a community gathering do.

WORKSHOP POSSIBILITIES

After choosing a theme for your festival and selecting the participants who will present the various traditions, you should be able to list these people and their skills. Your list should include *all* of their skills. Does Mr. Jones, scheduled as a singer, also tell stories learned from his family? Does the guitarist who provides accompaniment for a singer also play old-time banjo? If your participant information is complete for every performer, you are ready to begin.

Each featured soloist and group could present one concert, then be fitted into appropriate workshops. Take stock of the skills and arts for which you have more than one representative. Do you have

Mandolin Workshop at Tucson, Meet Yourself. Tom Jennings, workshop leader, listens while Joe and Mary Venuti play and Richard Dungan (*background*) records the session for future use. The Venutis play mandolin and guitar instrumentals at a variety of neighborhood and community functions on Tucson's west side; Jennings is a member of a musical family from the Gila Valley in eastern Arizona. The workshop setting allows a more relaxed, intimate presentation than does the concert stage. David Barr photograph, 1978.

two or three ballad singers? If not, do you have one ballad singer and two musicians who can sing ballads? If so, you have performers for a comparative ballad workshop. Do you have two or more fiddlers? If so, you can have a fiddle workshop. (In this process, it is not important to keep bands together. While the fiddler is playing on a fiddle workshop, the band's guitarist can participate in a guitar workshop in another area.)

It might be useful to see some of the workshops which we have developed for the National Folk Festivals as examples of the mix-and-match sorts of themes you can generate from surveying all of the abilities of your participants:

Children's Songs and Stories
Singing the Blues
Clog Dancing
Brother Style Songs
Blues Guitar
A Pot that Never Melted (discussion of cultural pluralism)
Unusual Instruments (participants, others, bring uncommon instruments)
Old-Time Bands
White Top Reunion (musicians from a particular area)
Folk Piano
Bones Workshop
Unaccompanied Ballads
Barroom Songs
Virginia Banjo Styles
Fiddle Workshop
Blues Piano
Reels, Jigs, and Breakdowns (fiddlers, pipers, banjoists)
Hammered Dulcimer
Chinese Opera
Old-Time Banjo
French Music Workshop

Gospel Songs
Finger-Picked Guitar
Military Songs
Acadian Accordion
Harmonica
Folk Dance
Old Ways in the New World
Family Traditions
Bluegrass Banjo
Stomach Steinway (accordion)
Mandolin Workshop
Buck Dancing
Bass Workshop
Rhythm Workshop
French Canadian Music
International Dance
Song Swap
Mining Songs and Stories
Children's Games
Songs of the American Indians
Whistles, Flutes, and Harps
The Folk Process
Cajun Fiddle
The Emerald Isle (Irish music)
Understanding Shape Notes
Depression Songs

PROGRAMMING 77

Tales, Stories, and Bald Faced Lies by Experts
Coming to America (a discussion by immigrants)

Folk Genealogy
Starving on the Family Farm (a discussion by participants who are farmers)

The National Folk Festival attempts to engineer storytelling sessions and academic discussions in its workshop schedule—in other words, we have tried to encourage informal formal discussions. The Mississippi Valley Folk Festival has taken people on bus tours of folk architecture sites. The Festival of American Folklife has featured a genealogy workshop. The North Carolina State Folklife Festival has had a workshop featuring discussion of policy matters affecting folk culture. The possibilities are vast. What are your concerns, and what are the concerns of your community?

Common types of workshops are the following:

Collecting. How do people find people, getting the folk together with those who like to listen, and maybe even learn?

Comparing. What can you do once you develop an audience with an eye, an ear, amassed from different kinds of traditions? Variations or similarities in cultures may be compared. If you have Appalachian, Texas, French Canadian and Serbian fiddlers, you have the makings for a comparative workshop in fiddle styles. You can show how different cultures meet a common musical need with, for example, a rhythm workshop showing how hand drums, a bass, a guitar, or bass drum may be used to provide a rhythmic framework. You can compare the vocal stylings of various cultures or how they approach the relating of an anecdote. You can compare the decorative art which some cultures bring to small textiles—handkerchiefs, small rugs, doilies, and the like. You can compare riddles, jokes, or even gestures. This is one of the areas proven to be among the most appealing and most capable of stimulating a good interchange between announced participants and the audience.

Another kind of useful comparison is a demonstration of historical point, such as how a style or form developed. Such workshops should be approached with caution; all the antecedents of a form may not be obvious, and it is easy to oversimplify complex processes. Also, it is easy to fall into the trap of treating older, simpler forms as steps to more complicated renderings when the process, in fact, may have gone the other way. (Consider, for instance, some of the incredibly complicated wonder machines of the nineteenth century which promised to make lard rendering or soap making easier.)

Participatory. There is a wide range of workshop types, only some of which call for strong audience participation. Audience involvement may in some cases further your purposes and be enjoyable, but it is easy to overstress the casual back-and-forth qualities of workshops when that may not be the tone you want to establish at all. You may wish to allow some questions from the audience—perhaps at collecting or comparing sessions—but this is usually most successful when it is strongly guided by the presenter directing the workshop. Here again we cannot stress too strongly that the kind of place you pick for the workshop may be the most important determining factor. Using a stage brings about a different kind of interaction than sitting on the ground together in a grove or working within a small tent. If you want to have a mini-concert, for instance, make sure that everyone present is able to see and hear who's performing.

Discussion workshops, on the other hand, call for other arrangements. If they involve just folk, that is one thing; but if they involve performers, a presenter, academics, and other persons you feel should be heard, that is another. You should not expect or want discussions to attract audiences as large as those for performing workshops.

Then there are the special problems you may encounter if you want to have workshops for one segment of the audience—children, for example. Don't assume that you must have such kinds of workshops. Children's areas remove children from the larger festival which they might enjoy more than a children's area, making a distinction that most folk groups don't make. Granny Riddle, the traditional singer from Arkansas and veteran of folk festivals, claims that adults are the only ones who really enjoy children's songs. Most of the "babes" she's dealt with would rather hear "Barbara Allen" or "The Death of the Drunkard's Blind Child" than "Go Tell Aunt Rhoda" any time.

SCHEDULING

Once you have a list of your possible thematic workshops, a list of possible concerts by groups, and all possible discussion-type workshops, you are ready to begin scheduling. It is not an easy task, so allow at least a day for it—more if yours is a large festival.

Do you have as many as twenty-five groups? If not, do you have twenty groups and five performers who work solo but not as a part of the bands? If you do, you may be able to run as many as four workshop stages continuously.

At this point you should transfer your workshop information to file cards. The planners of the National Folk Festival use a large bulletin board and different size cards to represent workshops of different lengths: a 3″ × 5″ card = one hour; a 3″ × 2½″ card = thirty minutes, and a 3″ × 3¾″ = forty-five minutes. (This may appear tedious, but the task is difficult when several stages are used and you will find visual cues helpful.)

Throughout this process, you will be making decisions. A band of high quality can give a one-hour concert, while a solo performance possibly should be held to thirty minutes. If you have five fiddlers in your fiddle workshop, they will need at least an hour and possibly even an hour and a half. Ask yourself, What is the optimum time for this particular group? Can you put these four different performers on this workshop in forty-five minutes? Remember to allow time for discussions and introductions.

If you are using three or more stages, a large cork board and a supply of thumbtacks can aid you at this point. Be careful: the guitar player from a band can't participate in a guitar workshop while his band is giving a concert. The key is to use participants to their maximum. You'll probably find it necessary to shift some of your cards to prevent having one person in two places at the same time.

If your festival is more than a one-day affair, you may wish to repeat some of the more appealing workshops. Also, check to be sure that you've allowed each participating group at least one concert of their own. It is *not* necessary to give each group the same amount of concert time, but if you have chosen well, each group should be capable of at least a thirty-minute concert.

PRESENTATION

The format of a folk festival makes use of the devices of popular and academic culture—staged presentations, sound systems, publicity, introductory speakers, and program guides. Yet the material and performers presented came from a very different milieu. Most folk arts are suited to presentation to relatively small groups: the family circle, the community gathering, the meeting of friends. To move such material and such performers to the large stage, using sound equipment, lighting, and other devices of popular and academic entertainment, is to create a distance—and perhaps a tense experience for the performers—between *what* is being presented and *how* it is being presented.

For example, bringing an Appalachian farmer to a Manhattan concert hall creates an instant need for analysis, and possibly interpretation, to ensure audience appreciation. The scope of the farmer's knowledge may be as rich as that of his audience, but his skill in communicating with urban people may be as fumbling as theirs would be in attempting to shoe his horse.

Folk culture is thus much like other culture in its need for interpretation and sensitive analysis when presented in a cross-cultural context. When grand opera takes to the road, its companies are well equipped with introductory speakers and program books offering explanations of context, plots, details subject to misinterpretation, and the background and training of leading performers. Even the portraits and landscapes in major art galleries are nowadays liberally interpreted by guide books and cassette recordings. Shouldn't we accord our folk artists the same respect and attention?

The problem is not so much that folk performers are not able to cope with large stages; it is one of removing folk performances from their usual context. It is difficult to demonstrate folksongs usually sung in sitting rooms or kitchens when the ballad singer must use the stage format developed for great operatic divas. By tradition, the diva is an inaccessible and exotic personage who does not inhabit the same world as her patrons. We need not mention that this is not so with "the folk."

To cope with such problems, any well-produced festival features a wide range of performing areas: large outdoor stages, small stages, multiple staging to spread crowds, participatory areas, intimate areas, and places devoted to work and work skills. Easing the transition of folk material and forms into a popular culture format is not the only reason for the use of different types of performance areas, but it is a primary one.

The directors of folk festivals usually err in not providing enough informal interpretation. The absence of intelligent communication with audiences is evident in many ways at presentations of traditional folk culture. For example, the beginning of a traditional folk fiddle tune on a stage anywhere in America is usually greeted by a significant portion of the audience with rhythmic hand clapping. Fiddlers tend to intensely dislike this practice because it disrupts their timing and destroys the subtlety of their performance (which is the way *their* contests are judged); clapping, then, is *not* part of the traditional context.

The custom of hand clapping may derive from the pop-folk fad of the late 1950s, when television producers attempted to show participation by studio audiences in such "folk" programs as "Hootenanny." If it didn't begin there, that certainly encouraged the idea that clapping adds a folksy flavor to a performance. But the folk themselves tend to hate it, either because it is not traditional or the audience doesn't really know how to clap their way. Continuing the practice opens up the danger of being insensitive in presenting folk fiddlers and other musicians to festival and concert audiences. Festival presenters who include in their introduction of fiddlers and fiddle styles a request that the audience *not* clap hands will win approval of the musicians. It may appear to be a small matter—but not if you are a fiddler.

The following is an example of an introduction which a presenter might use in introducing a Mississippi fiddler:

Our next musician, Mr. _____, is a fiddler born and reared near the town of Rolling Fork, Mississippi, in the west central portion of that state. Mr. _____ learned his tunes from his father, older brother, neighbors, and from early hillbilly recordings and local radio performers. Mr. _____'s fiddling is a good example of an important regional style of fiddling first recorded during the 1920s on hillbilly recordings by such Mississippi performers as Narmour and Smith, Will Gilmore, and The

Freeny's Barn Dance Band. During the 1930s, Library of Congress collectors found much the same style played by such excellent Mississippi fiddlers as Stephen Hatcher. If you'll listen carefully, you'll hear some notable differences in this music—the use of high notes and high sharp slides and a quality which some students of this fiddle style have called "wild." If it is wild, it is a controlled and joyous wildness. This wild quality may be native to Mississippi and it marks this important and intricate regional style of folk fiddling. Those of you acquainted with the more common American folk fiddle tunes will also note that Mr. _____'s repertoire differs from what you usually hear. Yet the tunes he plays are common ones among older Mississippi fiddlers. Mr. _____ has been playing for 31 years; he has played at a local VFW square dance for 15 years, and he plays with two of his friends at his home most Sunday afternoons. His son, _____, will be playing the guitar accompaniment.

Finally, I'd like to ask a favor of you. Please don't clap your hands. Hand clapping is not part of this or any other fiddling tradition. It sometimes disrupts a fiddler's timing, and it prevents others from hearing this music as they should. Thank you.

This brief (two-minute) introduction informally establishes the following information:
1. The presenter is well acquainted with the traditional folk item he is presenting. This is important. No performer should be subjected to an introduction by a presenter who is uninformed and unappreciative of the finer points of the tradition being presented. This requires a careful matching of presenters and performer/participants, and a presenter may have to study a tradition before presenting it.
2. The presenter is respectful and knowledgeable of the performers and tradition being presented. Without making a big thing of it, he refers to respected antecedents of this performer. Many presentations of similar forms in the national mass media, especially such television programs as "Hee Haw" and "Beverly Hillbillies," have treated folk art forms condescendingly. Folk festival audiences have been exposed to such attitudes and without guidance may adopt and bring their preconceptions with them to their interaction with folk performers.

3. The presenter advises the audience to listen for a unique aspect of this music.
4. The presenter mentions the context in which this music is played (for example, at dances, at home) and makes clear that the performer learned this folk art by listening to and observing other performers.

Stages and Heightened Expectations. The concert or workshop format involves situations familiar to most festival goers. While the music may be unfamiliar (in fact, we hope it often is), the concert stage is familiar. But though audiences are comfortable in such a setting, they also carry into it heightened expectations. They expect to enjoy themselves and be entertained, among other things. Therefore, those who perform on stage are supposed to meet certain performing standards.

There is only a limited number of forms which lend themselves to being presented from a stage; folk tales, music, and dance are among these. Because stages create a heightened expectation in audiences, festival planners should think ahead about whether a form or a specific performance is appropriate to stage presentation. In some cases the personality and forcefulness of an individual performer may justify a stage presentation, whereas another less forceful performer might better present the same tradition in a more intimate circle. A cappella singing often dramatizes this problem, for example. Exceptional performers can hold the attention of an audience for a thirty-minute concert of, say, a cappella shape-note singing or other such traditional art forms. But others cannot and are better presented in a seated circle on a lawn or in a concert format which intersperses the a cappella singing with instrumental music or even a puppet show.

Cross-Cultural Sensitivities. Urban middle-class folk festival audiences who expect to witness "quaint" customs can be shocked and even repelled by certain traditions dramatized at folk festivals. A good example is butchering. A vital and important part of many folk cultures, food lore can enrich a folk festival. (In fact, many festivals rely on the variety of traditional foods as a way of maintaining crowd interest and involvement.) Yet the attitudes of farm people and some urban ethnic people toward butchering differ greatly from those of some persons who have attended folk festivals.

An experience at a Virginia folklife festival shows how this common folk activity can shock and horrify a portion of an audience and cause unnecessary social division. A complete butchering and the preparation of veal was to be demonstrated. Signs and announcements proclaimed that a butchering was to take place. Yet some of the audience allowed their children to pet the calf which was led to the site, as if they were at a zoo. When the animal was suddenly pulled aside, shot, its throat cut, and hoisted for the skinning, some of them were outraged. An explanation that such an event preceded each veal cutlet and baby beef steak they had eaten did not still the emotional objections: the event was "awful" and "barbaric."

The preparation of a meal of goat for an Iranian folk celebration in New Jersey was halted by police; three persons were arrested when neighbors protested the impending butchering of the goat. A humane society intervened, and reporters arrived to interview the hero instrumental in averting the dire deed.

A pony pull — a traditional folk event in which ponies and horses compete in pulling sleds heavily loaded with weights — was objectionable to some of the audience at the Virginia folklife festival mentioned above. At the height of the contest, owners strike the animals with whips or guidelines to produce greater effort. This was seen as abusing the animals.

This Virginia festival attracted significant numbers of rural people. They admired the skill and speed of the man butchering calves and found excitement and betting opportunities in the pony pull. They were dismayed by the objections of their fellow attenders.

Most urban dwellers are removed geographically from contact with food and work animals, and this has affected their views of other traditional folk events. Catching the greased pig has also been considered an objectionable event, to say nothing of cockfighting, greyhound races (in which the dogs run after a rabbit), and even the more high-toned horseback fox chase.

Does all this mean that butchering should be omitted from food demonstration/presentations at folk festivals, that greased pigs should not be caught, and that demonstrations of work with draft animals should be ended? It does not. Rather, it shows such events should be clearly and forcefully described in advance so that those who may find them objectionable don't have to attend. Such events also must be in strict compliance with the law, particularly if the meat and other food products made at festivals are to be sold. Discussions with local health authorities should precede any preparation of food intended for sale at a festival.

Urbanized and modern people sometimes are disturbed by other common folk traditions. At a Tennessee festival a tourist was upset by a folk preacher who had been invited to preach during a part of the event which featured religious music. The tourist found the preacher's chanting style of delivery strange and thought that his fire-and-brimstone message "could disturb the children who are here." No objections were heard from the children, however, who seemed to enjoy the preacher. Let's face the fact that we are seeking to present strange ways and singular, out-of-the-ordinary styles. There will be a lot of people who are put out with us for doing so. But it's worth the effort.

CONCERT SEQUENCE

We all sympathize with the quiet and subtle performer who has to follow the flamboyant group that has just received a standing ovation. Poor fellow; why didn't they put him on first?

Indeed, why not? Your fieldwork should tell you which groups or persons will be most accessible to your audience. Save the big bang until the end. If you have two hot groups, have one perform just before a short intermission. Then when things have quieted, you can present another quiet performer or two and then have another flamboyant ending.

Some concert planners prefer letting it build—beginning with quiet performances and building to the hottest group at the end. This is a tactic borrowed from popular presentations, and we note that folk concert planners who attempt to use it frequently misjudge which group is hottest. Anyway, we like to mix it up, keeping the performers happy and the audience a bit off balance with unexpected treats for those who can hear and understand.

Other kinds of juxtapositions also require planning sensitivity. One would not wish to present Arab and Jewish groups in close sequence without a prior discussion with each group about how they feel about this. This example is obvious enough, but there are many others: Armenians and Turks, Greeks and Turks, Cambodians and Vietnamese, Japanese and Koreans, Kurds and Arabs, to name a few. More than presentation sequence is involved: one does not put such groups together without knowing if it is acceptable. The sensitive planner does not make broad assumptions, even when groups speak a common language. There are Indian tribes who live in close proximity to each other but do not care to be presented together. The French Canadians and Cajuns are sure to like each other, but it does not follow that the Puerto Ricans and Mexican-Americans will wish to be housed together.

What does the planner do who knows little about such matters? He asks others who know more, and if major presentational cooperation is involved—as in a Hispanic area or Balkan area—he discusses his plans with each group well in advance.

STAGE CUES AND DIRECTIONS

Stage anxiety can be mitigated to a considerable extent if the persons presenting folk performers are sensitive to their on-stage needs. The instructions for stage managers in Part II of this book cover the major needs, but at least one matter should be decided far in advance by the fieldworker or festival director: the amount of on-stage presentation the performer will need. Some performers require a presenter on stage at all times, introducing each item, while an introduction will suffice for others.

Even those who have much experience will be grateful for instructions that are simple and easy to follow. For example, if the songs in a singer's repertoire are normally about two and a half minutes long and you want her to perform for fifteen minutes, ask her to do four songs. Then tell her, "I'll be standing off stage at your left. Look at me when you've sung four. If there's time for another, I'll hold up a finger." If her sound set-up is brief, her introductions for the songs short, and she does little tuning, she'll have time for the extra song.

An obvious benefit is that you have better control of stage time.

More importantly, the performer can concentrate upon her performance and not worry about time. This is much better than saying, "You have fifteen minutes." Also, she knows where you are if she needs you for other reasons. You can further reassure her by saying, "I'll be there all the time. If you need me, just motion." Never leave a performer on stage without a person in sight who can help. We'll repeat that once for emphasis: Never!

The finger trick is also a good one for longer performances. If a group has forty-five minutes, tell the leader, "I'll catch your eye and give you a finger when there's time for just one more." Without this, she will have to look at her watch several times or ask, "How much time do we have?" or perform beyond the allotted time. Either of these is worrisome for her, and the stage manager or presenter should assume this responsibility.

Many folk musicians are so intimidated by large stages that they will play out of tune rather than stop their performance for tuning. This is a problem that the presenter or stage manager can address in "I'll be over there" before-performance comments. Tell those who appear even mildly insecure, "If you have any problems with tuning, just stop and tune until you are satisfied. I want you to sound good." Folk musicians also tend to be intimidated by both sound systems and sound engineers. The before-performance comments should include some mention of sound: "If you have any problem in hearing yourself or if things don't sound right, stop and tell the man back there. His job is to make it sound good."

4. Publicity

Forming a Committee

The amount of time spent on getting publicity for your festival will vary according to the size of your community and the nature of its media. If your festival is a comparatively modest, regional event held in a small community, it is likely that the local media will consider it newsworthy, and getting their attention may not be a problem.

If you are launching your first festival in a larger community — or one which has not received notable attention from the press in previous years — it will usually be wise to form a small publicity committee at your first planning meeting. Ideally, if you plan to make your festival an annual event, the same people should handle publicity each year and should consider it a year-round responsibility.

A publicity committee can include an advisory group of professionals who work in television, radio, and the newspapers or magazines. Such persons can make a valuable contribution. *One* person should be designated as the press contact person. If this appears to be too onerous, an alternative plan is to designate one person as contact for each segment of the press: TV, radio, newspaper. (Members of the press sometimes are confused if a number of different persons contact them regarding news stories, television appearances, and so on.) A publicity committee composed of persons with expertise in the various media serves as a back-up to the selected contact person, especially if you do not hire a professional publicity or public relations expert. At the National Folk Festival we have tried it both ways and have found it just as effective for a member of our staff to handle publicity if that person has advice from an active publicity committee.

Prefestival Publicity

The nature of your prefestival publicity will in part determine the kind of audience you attract. The kind of festival you have chosen to present — traditional, regional, ethnic, and so on — should constitute the theme of your publicity. If you want your festival to appeal to families, this can be encouraged through lower or free admission for small children. In any event, all persons dealing with publicity should be fully aware of the scope and purpose of your festival and should be capable of communicating its appeal to the press. It is essential to pick one or two themes and constantly emphasize them in your publicity.

MEDIA CONTACTS

Your first task is to make a list of media contacts to whom you will send press releases. In some metropolitan areas, a "media factbook" is published which lists information on radio and television stations, newspapers, and other publications serving that area. Often these publications become outdated in terms of persons; however, they usually provide helpful listings of news media outlets.

Next, telephone each publication, television, and radio station to determine the names and titles of persons who should receive your press releases. This will vary from one publication to another, although there is a general pattern for TV and radio. The following is a general guide:

Newspaper:
1. news editor
2. performing arts editor
3. special sections editor
4. calendar editor
5. music critic
6. art critic
7. feature writers

Television:
1. news editor
2. public service director

3. feature or "talk" show producers
4. calendar or event programs (these are generally a section of a regular news broadcast)

Radio:
1. news editor
2. calendar editors
3. feature announcers
4. hosts of related programs

Once these contacts have been established, it is good practice to determine a key person at each publication or station who is genuinely interested and is in a position to get your story into print or on the air.

PUBLICITY CAMPAIGN

A publicity campaign can begin as soon as the dates and location of the festival have been established. The first press release should contain general information outlining the history of the festival and its cultural objectives. Press releases should be written to dramatize the theme or tone of your festival. For example, if you are stressing cultural diversity, your press release can accentuate this by noting contrasts in individual performers and ethnic groups.

Press Releases. It is a good practice to address press releases to persons (not titles only) if you have made personal contact with specific press representatives. A short personal cover letter sent with the first press release often helps establish rapport; at least it will distinguish your press release from others received the same day.

Six weeks before the festival, send another general release, including the same information plus descriptions of the participants. Follow-up releases should be sent every week until the festival, featuring stories about individual performers and groups, craftspersons, and interpretive sessions. If your festival includes workshops or simultaneous performances on a number of stages, this provides good material for a press release. An artist's sketch of workshop schedules accompanying the press release will add visual interest which is difficult to capture in words.

Yaqui Deer and Pascola dancers, Border Folk Festival, El Paso, Texas, 1978. Photograph by Kathy James.

If your budget allows, photos of participants (5" × 7" glossy black and white) should accompany press releases. Attach an identifying caption on the back of each photo; do not print or type on the back of the photo itself.

The same press releases should be sent also to television and radio contacts, again addressed to *persons*. It is wise to establish contact with TV and radio public service directors and producers of talk shows as soon as festival dates have been set.

Public Service Announcements. Public Service Announcements (PSAs) are ten-, twenty-, thirty-, or sixty-second spots, similar to paid advertising, which radio and television stations make available to public or non-profit institutions on a first-come–first-served basis. Many television stations allow limited time for producing public service spots, so time should be reserved well in advance. You may have to provide carefully timed copy. If you can arrange to record the spot at the TV studio or radio station, be prepared to furnish recordings of music to be featured at the festival along with all the information concerning your festival location, dates, and times. Some stations will tape a PSA using a performer you intend to feature with a voice-over about the festival. If you have such an opportunity, select the performer carefully and you will have a spot which says much about your festival.

Publicity Features. Booking your participants on TV talk or feature shows usually requires more aggressive action. Begin as early as possible. Send press releases, personal letters, photos, biographies, recordings, and tapes. Time on talk shows and feature shows is in demand (particularly in larger cities), so begin early and be tactful but persistent.

If your area has a state or area public television network, you may be able to persuade those in charge to videotape your festival for showing on the network. This will have little effect upon the current festival, but it will help you build an audience for subsequent years by exposing some of your offerings to a broader, uninvolved public. We do *not* recommend that you pay any part of the production cost for videotaping; public stations have a miniscule audience when compared to commercial television, and such costs are high. Also, we do not recommend that you allow videotaping by anyone unless there is a concurrent commitment to air the material. See the section on documentation for more on this subject (pages 115-116).

Advance news or feature stories are, of course, advantageous if they can be arranged. If any of your performers happens to be giving a concert in the area near the time of the festival, you might be able to persuade a critic to review the performance and, in the course of doing that, promote your upcoming festival.

Most newspapers have an entertainment calendar. Make a careful survey of dailies, weeklies, local magazines, and folk-related publications for calendar deadline dates. Many larger urban dailies have a section in the Sunday edition which features upcoming area events. Publicity possibilities will, of course, vary from one community to another. Familiarize yourself with the overall habits and idiosyncrasies of publications and radio and television stations in your area, and supply press releases accordingly.

Talk to the hosts of radio folk music programs in your area. Can you take a stack of records or tapes of people you'll feature over to the station and go on the air with them? How often? Will they do a feature on the festival for three or four successive programs?

Check local radio guides for specialty music programs which you may be featuring. For example, if there is a Polish hour or an Irish hour and a Polish or Irish group will be at your festival, take recordings to the host of these programs and ask for an opportunity to discuss the festival on the air. Bluegrass and old-time music audiences for local radio programs are attracted to folk festivals and can become a very supportive audience.

Morning and afternoon rush hour driving audiences are enormous. Every city seems to have one or two popular programs which feature traffic reports, jokes, and a discussion of events. Can you book one or more of these shortly before the festival? As in the case of other popular programs, you'll need to work far in advance.

First-Day Coverage

A week before your festival begins, telephone your media contacts and invite them to attend the festival, regardless of whether or not they have been cooperative on advance publicity. First-day press coverage can be vital to the success of your festival in terms of attendance. Keep a list of those who accept, as you will want to leave complimentary passes for them at the press room. You should also offer to make special parking arrangements for television crews.

Press kits to be passed out at the festival should contain:

1. Duplicate copies of press releases mailed previously or, if you feel there is too much repetition, the last wrap-up release plus another which covers special features (workshops, children's programs, etc.).
2. A program book.
3. Fliers, newsletters, or special publications which relate to your festival.

Your publicity chairperson or a staff person who knows or has had contact with the media persons attending should supervise the press room during the festival. Any person who is designated to manage the press room should be well briefed and capable of making instant decisions which will facilitate coverage of the festival.

Follow-Up Publicity

Write thank-you notes to all press persons who have been helpful and cooperative. Now that you've made the initial breakthrough, it's good practice to stay in touch with your media contacts. Keep your press clippings, releases, media lists, and notes from the completed festival in good order and filed carefully. Most important, don't wait too long to pull them out again and start planning your publicity campaign for next year's festival.

Festival Publications

The publications related to a festival fall naturally into the realm of the Publicity and Public Relations Committee. However, we consider it important that the Program Committee share the responsibility for getting biographical information and good photographs as soon as participants are selected and contracts are signed. This material is needed for dealings with the media and should be available as early as possible to allow time for writing, rewriting, editing, designing, and publishing the program book.

PROGRAM BOOK

A printed program book offers festival planners an opportunity to describe in some depth the traditions presented at the festival. This can be particularly beneficial in explaining the work of artists whose culture is unfamiliar to most of the audience. An excellent example is Clydia Nahwooksy's sketch of Zuni Indian craftsman Randolph Lalio, which is reproduced in Part II of this book (pages 258–59). It is reprinted from the 1972 program book of the Festival of American Folklife, sponsored by the Smithsonian Institution.

Ms. Nahwooksy deals clearly with a problem Native Americans encounter at festivals: the insensitive comments and lack of understanding exhibited by some of the audiences. She puts Randolph in context: he is Zuni, scion of a people who have built, herded, and harvested in the Southwest for over a thousand years. He has learned from watching his parents and grandparents, and he is keeper of their traditions. Their religion and their way of life are important to them. Randolph will function in a broader society, but he is Zuni and part of "the sinew of continuance that is Zuni Pueblo." Ms. Nahwooksy combines one photo of Randolph with three taken at his pueblo in the nineteenth century, reinforcing visually what she says about Randolph and Zuni Pueblo.

Other sample pages reprinted in Part II are taken from program books of the thirty-eighth, thirty-ninth, and fortieth National Folk Festivals, held in 1976, 1977, and 1978. Descriptions of performers vary in length, but each attempts to make the performer and his or her art more familiar. Because the National uses four or five stages simultaneously, the program book also helps festival goers select which performers they want to see at a particular time.

POSTERS AND BROCHURES

Brochures and posters are helpful publicity tools. Both take about a month to produce and should be distributed two months to six weeks before the event. Copy must be written and a layout designed and prepared for the typesetter, who will probably take two weeks to deliver the finished product.

The most important information on any festival poster is the name of the event, the dates, and the location; and any design you choose should focus attention to these items. Again, the theme of your festival can be emphasized through the design of your publications. At the thirty-ninth National Folk Festival, we selected a photograph of Emett W. Lundy of Galax, Virginia, and used it on both our program book cover and poster. Mr. Lundy was an important traditional musician who left a precious legacy. We felt it was in keeping with the traditional nature of our festival and especially meaningful because Mr. Lundy's grandson was performing at the festival.

Brochures are useful when you have mailing lists of persons you wish to inform about your event. They're also handy to distribute in stores, schools, libraries, and other outlets as a take-home reminder of your festival. They usually contain more detailed information about the program than the poster and are particularly important if the festival has a large scope of activities — music, food, crafts — and lacks featured performers or names familiar to the audience. Sometimes a brochure can double as a throwaway, or small poster, with essentials printed on one side and program details on the other.

DISTRIBUTION

Distribution is, of course, the key to effective use of posters and brochures. Begin working on this several months before the festival. Check out all possibilities: stores, businesses, schools, libraries, Chambers of Commerce, tourist bureaus, and so forth. Be sure to enlist plenty of volunteers to handle distribution; assign each person to cover a certain area, furnishing them with a list of places to go and how many to leave at each stop.

5. Hospitality

Prefestival Communication with Participants

From the time participants are chosen until they arrive at the festival, adequate advance work and communications will enhance the chances that your festival will run smoothly in terms of crucial logistics such as transportation, housing, food, festival site operation, and overall coordination. (In this section we assume that you will provide housing for participants and that some will travel long distances.)

Once a participant or group is chosen by the program director or committee a formal letter of invitation should be sent, even though there probably will have been telephone or personal contact previously. This letter should contain:

1. confirmation of previous commitments and arrangements including festival location, dates, and fees;
2. at least a partial list of other participants who have been invited; and
3. information about the nature and intent of the festival.

When a participant or group has agreed to perform at the festival, send:

1. a signed contract (two copies);
2. a participant information sheet; and
3. a welcoming cover letter requesting the participant(s) to return one signed copy of the contract and the information sheet plus biographies and photographs (for publicity and the program book).

In composing letters and information sheets, strive to be direct, clear, and concise. Avoid jargon and words which may be obscure to persons with little formal education. Ask yourself, "Will a person who is barely literate understand this? Will a person who speaks little English understand it?"

Although it may seem superfluous after the first communication, repeat important information in subsequent letters to your participants. It is wise to include the name, location, and date of your festival in every letter you send. Make it clear that you must have names of family members or friends accompanying participants to the festival, and state clearly your guidelines for housing and feeding extra people.

Two weeks before the festival, send another mailing to participants which includes:
1. information on check-in, housing, food, security, recording;
2. a performance schedule; and, for participants driving to the festival:
  a map of festival and housing sites;
  information regarding parking restrictions, if any;
  a reimbursement arrangement for mileage; and
  a reimbursement policy for meals during travel.

Relay the above information by telephone to persons who have had little formal education or who don't do much business via letters.

Prepare a file folder for each participant or group and keep copies of all correspondence, contracts, information sheets, bios, photos, and call slips with telephone messages between staff and participants. You may wish to make a checklist to determine who has returned what. This will be helpful for ready reference as deadlines draw near. The files will contain participant information needed by staff members, so it is a good practice to have a duplicate set of participation information sheets—one set to remain in the office files and one set to be made available to staff members as needed.

The participant information sheet is your guide to much of your prefestival planning. Following is a simple procedure which makes good use of this form and saves time for festival staff coordinators.
1. Prepare a transportation chart and transfer information as each form arrives. Your transportation coordinator will need to know the airline flight number, railway or bus number, arrival and departure time, number traveling in the group, and how much equipment they are bringing. If you are making reserva-

tions for your performers, use a travel agent. To make reservations, you will need:
   a. last name and first initial of each person for whom reservations are made;
   b. place, date, and time of departure and arrival; and
   c. a telephone number where participants can be reached. If you purchase tickets and send them to participants, send them by registered mail. Tickets can be prepaid through a travel agent, in which case your office is billed and participants pick up a paid, non-transferable ticket at the departure point. Work as far in advance as possible to take advantage of economy fares and less expensive night flights.
2. Prepare a housing and food checklist and transfer details from participant information forms. This will provide your housing and food coordinator with appropriate information for making room reservations and planning meals.
3. Compile information for your on-site coordinators regarding what equipment will be needed:
   a. electrical and sound equipment;
   b. equipment needed to assist participants in moving musical instruments, crafts displays, etc.; and
   c. tables, chairs, stools, microphones needed by each performer, group, and craftsperson.

Participant information kits should be presented to each participant or group when they arrive and check in according to previous arrangements. These kits can be prepared as soon as the information needed is definite. They should include:
1. badges or other means of identification to be used on the festival site;
2. duplicate copies of performance schedules;
3. a map of the festival site;
4. a copy of the program book;
5. a meal schedule and meal tickets where applicable;
6. a release form for any recording which is planned;
7. special information or regulations which apply to the festival site or housing facility; and
8. complimentary tickets to performances which participants may wish to attend when they are not performing.

Transportation, Housing, and Food

TRANSPORTATION

Transportation of participants to and from the airport, train, or bus station to the festival or housing site should be handled by friendly, courteous persons familiar with the geographical area. They should, of course, drive reliable vehicles. Back-up drivers should be available in case of late arrivals.

Transportation between housing and festival sites will vary from one festival to the next. Make arrangements as far in advance as possible, and be sure to have back-up drivers for participants who miss buses. If the housing facility is a long distance from the festival site, have drivers available to transport older participants back to their rooms for rest periods when they are not performing.

HOUSING

For festivals lasting more than a day, housing accommodations for participants and staff will be necessary. Modest, comfortable rooms, nourishing food, and a quiet atmosphere should be provided — particularly for older participants.

Preparations for housing and food should be made as far in advance as possible. If the number of participants is not large, it is possible they can be housed with local families. Larger groups ideally should be housed in one facility. Besides making transportation logistics simpler and less expensive, such an arrangement offers festival participants the opportunity to become acquainted and more at ease with a new situation. The best facility is usually a boarding school, conference center, or college which can provide dormitories, a dining hall, and spacious grounds for everything from solitude to spontaneous late-evening jam sessions. Such a single-location facility also offers a bonus for your festival staff, who are given an opportunity to meet participants informally and learn more about their lives and culture. At the National Folk Festival, late-evening gatherings have become a tradition. Normally a midnight snack is served in the dining hall, after which participants and staffers gradually drift into groups and enjoy conversation, music, and dancing.

Contract. Once a housing site has been selected, a contract between the festival sponsor and the landlord must be negotiated. The person in charge of housing should be an amiable, competent person capable of interpreting to the landlord not only logistics but a feeling for the occasion as well. If this is your first festival, it is likely things will occur which are not covered in the contract. The rapport between the housing coordinator and the landlord will be critical in dealing with such matters.

Besides such obvious items as cost of lodging and food, advance payment and liability deposit, security, and insurance, the contract should anticipate difficulties and cover such issues as the following:
1. the use of alcoholic beverages;
2. late-evening parties;
3. off-limit areas;
4. the provision of sheets, towels, washcloths, etc.;
5. the hours meals are to be served; and
6. clean-up responsibilities when the festival ends.

It is good practice to allow at least two weeks for negotiating the contract before it is signed. Someone should visit the housing site several times. Designate a room to be used as a festival staff office, and make arrangements for telephone installation. The telephone number should be assigned well in advance, even though installation is not necessary until a day or so before the festival. Participants will want a telephone number where they can be reached during the festival.

Take a walking tour of the housing site to determine, from the participants' point of view, where signs should be placed to indicate directions to dormitories, the dining hall, the festival staff office, and other facilities. Discuss the preparation and installation of signs with your landlord, and follow through accordingly.

Room Assignment. Assuming you are dealing with a large number of participants and have negotiated a contract for a suitable site, the next important task is advance room assignment. Obviously, large ethnic groups should be housed together in one dormitory or one area of the facility, as should groups of musicians. Try to foresee compatibilities. For example, craft participants might appreciate being housed together but not necessarily isolated from musicians. Older participants should be assigned first floor rooms near the dining hall but in a section of the housing facility where they are least likely to be disturbed by late-evening activities. There is no guaranteed formula: a little foresight and sensitivity to the needs of your participants should achieve agreeable results.

Expecting the Unexpected. Never mind that you have corresponded with your festival participants and have reminded them again and again about reservations for assistants or family members who might accompany them. *Some* are bound to show up with spouses, children, friends, or an extra musician whom they failed to mention before their arrival. Last-minute arrangements will have to be made, depending on relationships, age, and other relevant factors. Obviously, you cannot send a participant's spouse or small child to the nearest campground. Just be aware that this situation is likely to occur, and use your own good judgment.

If the budget allows, plan to house at least two staff members in each dormitory or motel wing to serve as hosts to participants. The benefits are obvious: congenial houseparents will carry through a spirit of hospitality and will be available to handle unforeseen complications or emergencies.

Welcoming Participants. Participants will have been informed in advance to check in at the festival staff office at the housing site. When they arrive and register, give them a participant information kit, which should include duplicate copies of what you have sent through the mail plus any additional information concerning schedule changes or other relevant details. The office should be staffed adequately to allow someone to escort participants to their rooms, to assist with luggage, to answer questions, and to be generally helpful.

A substantial number of participants will probably arrive the day before the festival. The arrival day can set the tone and spirit of your festival. Participants may be arriving in a strange city or area and may be hot, tired, or anxious to get settled and rest—or some may be eager to meet other participants and begin the festivities. They are your guests. Welcome them! Arrange to have a number of friendly staffers at the housing site to anticipate their needs and follow through accordingly. A good evening snack and liquid refreshment will establish a favorable mood for all concerned. If you create a friendly and enjoyable atmosphere, everyone will be pleased, and you will enhance the prospect that those performers you might want to invite again will accept the invitation.

One of the interesting aspects of folk festivals is the potential for cross-cultural interaction. Many folk festivals include participants from various parts of a state or region. There is no guarantee of instant rapport anywhere, but a little time and effort, especially on the part of the reception committee, can help to get people to know one another. As the festival progresses—and as participants and staff become better acquainted—the resulting exchange will show positive results in performances, in staff spirit, and in the tone of the festival.

The festival staff office at the housing site should be manned each day from early morning until participants return after the evening concert. Besides a general bus schedule, it is wise to have a station wagon or van available to transport participants to and from the festival site at irregular hours.

Check-out. Out-of-town participants probably will be checking out over a period of two days. Housing checklists and transportation schedules prepared in advance will ensure an efficient check-out operation. Be certain your drivers are equipped with reliable vehicles and are thoroughly familiar with routes to airports, train, and bus stations.

Follow-through. The housing coordinator should make an appointment to go through dormitories or motel rooms with the landlord immediately after the festival is over to determine whether there has been any damage to the premises. Remember, your aim is to maintain businesslike and friendly relations in case you plan to use the same housing facility the following year.

FOOD

If you are dealing with large numbers of participants housed in a facility equipped to serve food, your best bet is to serve breakfast

Zespol Harnasie, dancers and musicians from the Podhale region of southern Poland living in Chicago, 38th National Folk Festival. Photograph © NCTA, 1979.

and late snacks at the housing site. Compare quality and prices with those of local caterers and restaurants, bargain with the landlord if necessary, and come to an agreement on meals well in advance of signing the contract.

If the festival site is a substantial distance from the housing site, it will be desirable logistically to serve lunch and dinner at the festival site. Consider the possibility of having volunteers prepare and serve one or both meals, but be fully aware of the task you are undertaking. The food coordinator should consult with a person experienced in quantity food preparation. Numbers of volunteers or staff will be needed to handle purchase, preparation, and serving of meals, food storage, and clean up. After years of combining various arrangements, at recent National Folk Festivals breakfast and late-night snacks were served at the housing site, and lunch and dinner were catered and served at the festival site. The food costs were higher than the years when volunteers prepared some meals, but we found it highly efficient—and for the first time we heard no complaints about food.

A few things to keep in mind:
1. Determine whether there are food restrictions at the festival site. Some grounds contract with one caterer.
2. Some of the people you have invited may have special dietary needs for reasons of health or religious proscriptions. Look over your participant list. Are any of these people orthodox Jews, Muslims, Buddhists, or other people with dietary avoidances? Does your fieldworker know of vegetarians among the participants? Should you consider dietary preferences, such as rice for Asian people?
3. Caterers usually require a guaranteed minimum number of servings and a final figure reported forty-eight hours before each meal.
4. It is a good idea to over-order slightly. Extra food is usually consumed by the staff.
5. Go over menus, prices, and meal times carefully and put all decisions with the caterer in writing.

In addition to meals, be prepared to quench the overwhelming thirst of your participants and staff. Abundant quantities of soft drinks, water, and iced tea should be available at the festival—in the performers' lounge or rest area and at each stage and craft area. A substantial back-up supply should be stashed at a location known to stage managers and other staffers who will transmit requests for beverages.

6. Production

Festival Site Preparation

The first step in preparing your festival site is to take a good look to determine what is already there that can be used and what will have to be brought in. This should be done early in the planning stage. If your prefestival communication has been thorough, much of the information you need for site preparation will be on participant information sheets and should be made available to the festival site coordinator as soon as he or she joins the festival staff.

You will need stages, tents, booths, or other housing for crafts areas, work and food facilities, an area for general administration ("base operations"), sanitary facilities, ample parking, electricity, water, and telephones. Compile a list of these needs and see where you stand. Does some staging exist on the site or will you have to rent or borrow it? Some cities and towns have stages which they use for special occasions and may be willing to lend you. Staging can be rented or it can be built relatively easily if you don't require a large platform. Of course, take into consideration the size of the groups that will be performing.

If you are in an area where rain or intense heat is a problem, consider providing covering for the stages. Tents can be rented in a variety of shapes and sizes, ranging from 10' × 10' to 90' × 150' or larger. Most rental companies will set up and dismantle them. Plan what you will need to accommodate performers, craftspeople, concessionaires, administration, and a participant rest area; order well in advance, scheduling precisely the days and times for setting up and dismantling.

Tables and chairs will be needed, so determine what is required and find a source of supply. Churches, schools, and funeral parlors sometimes lend tables and chairs. Check out such sources before making inquiries about rentals.

If sanitary accommodations are not available on the site, you will have to rent portable facilities. Does your county or city require a specific number of portable toilets for each 1,000 estimated audience? If parking is a problem, you may want to consider auxiliary parking and busing to the festival site.

Power and water are so elementary that they sometimes get overlooked or taken for granted. Make sure of all your requirements in these areas. You will need to know how much power each sound system requires and which craftspeople need electricity and how far power lines will have to be run to service them. If more than plugging in is involved, you should hire an electrician. Plan to have several hundred feet of cable and extension lines on hand. Sometimes the sound company can provide this if you give them advance notice.

Production goes into high gear the week before the festival with the preparation of the festival site. This may take one day or ten days, depending on what needs to be done. At this point, make up a production schedule, assign duties, and distribute copies to staff and volunteers working on site preparation. If you are erecting a number of structures—tents, stages, booths—stake out the site, marking dimensions and position of each structure so that you can get an idea of the exact geography of the site. Be sure to allow for guy ropes when placing tents side-by-side. They can form a formidable obstacle course for people moving between tents.

Storage also must be considered. There should be a safe and secure place to store sound systems, musical instruments, craft supplies, program books, and other sale items. Maximum security should be provided for musical instruments and craft supplies; if possible, they should be stored in or near the participants' rest area, and a system should be devised which allows musical instruments and supplies to be checked in and secured when not in use. We advise having one group of volunteers or staff responsible for this duty during the entire festival. Participants will become familiar with persons in charge of their valuables—and vice versa.

Signs are another concern of the site preparation crew. Make sure your site is clearly marked for the benefit of both the public and the participants. All stages, crafts booths, performers' areas, administration, dining, information, and off-limits areas should be clearly identified. The bigger the sign, the better. If the site is a large one, a printed map is helpful. Make a list of the signs you will need, and have them printed on durable material so they can be used in succeeding years. All craftspersons should have a sign giving their name, where they are from, and what they are doing. It is also helpful to have a schedule posted at each stage if possible.

It is advisable to have on hand basic tools and supplies such as hammers, saws, hatchets, nails, rules, plenty of rope, stakes, plastic sheeting to cover equipment in case of rain, and gaffer tape or duct tape, which is a festival staple. Poster boards and magic markers also are useful.

The coordinator in charge of festival site preparation should be able to determine how many helpers will be needed, if she begins early and plans carefully. It is a good idea to enlist persons who can work also on breakdown after the festival is over. Taking it all apart quickly and efficiently can be done best by those who put it together.

Because site preparation can be very expensive at a substandard site, before making final decisions in site selection assess carefully the amount of work necessary. Erecting lengthy fences and other permanent structures is especially expensive and hard to justify for a three- or four-day festival.

Sound

Sound reinforcement has two primary functions. The obvious one is to make the performers audible. The second function is more subtle: to create a balance of sound between instruments and vocals, or among members of a group. This is particularly important with non-performance-oriented people (as most folk festival performers are), who often play louder than they sing (or vice versa) or don't realize it if they can't be heard by the audience. This balancing act requires both adequate equipment and skill on the part of the operator.

Before discussing the type of sound equipment best suited to folk festivals, a warning about a common pitfall is in order. Some festival producers make the mistake of economizing by using guitar amplifiers, home stereo amplifiers, cheap microphones, and makeshift bookshelf hi-fi speakers. Others borrow inadequate public address systems from schools or clubs. Don't do it! The sounds that folksingers and acoustic instruments produce are often delicate and must be handled carefully if they are to be preserved and heard by your audience. Even in a small area where a modest powered system is adequate, high-quality professional equipment is needed.

The temptation to economize results from the fact that sound reinforcement costs are considerable, and the first-time festival director may have spent much of the budget before realizing that costs were underestimated. For this reason and others, it is best to obtain such estimates early. The use of inadequate equipment is a mistake that will irritate and alienate both the audience and the performers.

HIRING A SOUND REINFORCEMENT COMPANY

If yours is a fairly large festival, with perhaps an anticipated audience of 3,000 or more and with several stages operating simultaneously, the best bet is to go to a commercial sound company. Practically all moderate-sized cities have at least one, and they are usually prepared to travel a few hundred miles with their equipment. There are two kinds of sound companies: one installs commercial sound equipment in schools, offices, and the like; the other specializes in concert sound reinforcement. Some do both. The former may have equipment for rent, but prices probably will be higher and they won't have the expertise you need. The latter is the kind you want, but be wary. The commercial sound reinforcement business flourished with the growth of rock music concerts, and most companies were established to cater to that trade. This is good for the folk festival because equipment that can handle adequately a rock vocalist can do justice to a folk artist at a reasonable volume level. The secret is to find a company which is sympathetic to acoustic music and won't bring out their heaviest equipment just to show how loud they can make it. Check the Yellow Pages telephone listings and start calling and asking questions.

What to ask? First, find out if they're available (some companies are booked months in advance). Then, tell about your festival and ask if they are interested in the job. Ask about what type of work they usually do and where you can go to hear them at work. Most companies will not have handled an event such as yours, so it is important to emphasize that you are seeking a *natural* sound. Find out if there is someone on the staff who knows anything about folk music and talk to that person. The technical details they'll need include: How many stages? Indoors or outdoors? What size audience at each stage? How many microphones, and what type of microphone stands? Any amplified instruments or drum sets? What type power is available? While it is feasible to operate a sound system independent of main power, having adequate 115 volt 60 hertz power is better. Be sure they can supply plenty of booms for the microphone stands and adequate wind screens for the microphones at outdoor stages.

SOUND SYSTEM OPERATORS

Hiring a company with experience in sound reinforcement is important, but finding an operator with experience in mixing acoustic music is just as important. The National Folk Festival hires its own operators and keeps a couple of people from the sound company around to help out when something goes wrong. Not all companies allow this, however. The National's operators are people who have had experience in running sound systems at folk festivals and are familiar with professional sound equipment and techniques. Knowledge of music is the most important criterion. It is quite reasonable to utilize operators who don't have engineering degrees if they know how the music should sound and understand the basic operation of the system.

Don't try to run your system without operators! Once the sound is set for a specific artist, hands off the knobs is the best policy. But someone is needed to make the initial setup, place microphones, and make adjustments if the instrumentation or performing situation changes. A performer cannot determine from the stage how things sound in the audience, but he does expect to be heard and shouldn't be burdened with the responsibility of adjusting his own sound. A good operator will be aware of the overall sound level, not letting his stage get louder and louder as the day goes on and his ears get dulled, and he will be careful to keep things below the level at which feedback (howling) is a problem.

SPECIAL CONSIDERATIONS FOR ELECTRICALLY AMPLIFIED INSTRUMENTS

Many traditional musicians who play amplified instruments own poor-quality equipment. At the National Folk Festival musicians bring their own musical instruments but leave their amplifiers at home and use festival-supplied amplifiers. Amplifiers are rented for a very reasonable price from a local musical instrument rental company which delivers, picks up, and can also supply spare fuses, tubes, and cords to connect the instruments to the amplifiers. If your area doesn't have this kind of shop, ask your sound company. They might be able to steer you to one or supply amplifiers as part of their package. The stage crew will have to haul the amps to where they are needed throughout the day, so rent high-quality but compact ones.

SOUND CHECK AND MICROPHONE REHEARSAL

If your festival has a feature concert, hold a sound check for it. This is important for two reasons. The first is to allow the sound people to fine-tune their equipment to the hall or stage and to the music, as well as to get a preview of what instruments and voices must be amplified, the best placement for mikes, and volume levels for each microphone for good balance. This is not a simple matter. The best microphone placement for an a cappella choir can be sixteen individual microphones, or a suspended pair, or any of a dozen other possible arrangements. Because the hall, the speakers, microphones, operators, console, and performers all are variables, there are no guides that can be automatically adopted. Nor is there a sound company that can deal adequately with these variables without some time for experimentation. This is done at the sound check.

The other reason for a mike rehearsal, one of primary importance to you, is to acquaint performers who may have never been on a concert stage with proper microphone techniques, allowing them some time to practice in front of a microphone and to become accustomed to how their own music sounds coming back at them from stage monitor speakers. This rehearsal will give the performer the

Carl Martin at the 34th National Folk Festival, July 1972. Martin was a blues guitarist and mandolinist from Knoxville. Photograph © NCTA.

opportunity to argue a bit with the engineers about how he should sound. This is important. Sound is changed and given color by equalization, reverberation control, volume levels, and different types of mikes. Extra time spent here will pay off in far better sound, satisfied performers, and a smoother performance during the concert.

If possible, the concert stage should not be used for workshops so that sound checks can run concurrently with other festival activities. Make a schedule for sound checks (don't schedule someone for a check while he has a workshop) and stay with it. Allow at least thirty minutes for each solo performer and at least forty-five minutes for each group, and don't forget to add set-up time for performers requiring equipment. Also, remember that instrument amplifiers will be needed during the sound check if they are to be used in the concert, and make arrangements to have them at the concert stage at the right time.

Who should be at the sound check? The sound technicians, of course; the stage manager for the concert; a stage crew to handle equipment and microphone stands (a union stage crew is required in some houses); one of your presenters who has a particularly good rapport with performers; and, if possible, the MC for the concert. A good policy is to have as few hangers-on as possible; they tend to make some performers nervous and often get in the way even though they have good intentions.

First, have the performer run through at least one complete song without interrupting with instructions or moving equipment. This helps to overcome initial nervousness and allows the crew to assess potential problems. After the performer is warmed up (take another song or two if necessary—don't rush it), start moving microphones and giving instructions on how close to stand to them. Once the performer is warmed up, it is usually okay to fragment a song to change mikes, but once the placement is decided, have the performer do at least one complete song. If a performer is playing several instruments, be sure to try all of them during the check.

Above all, be sure that your performers have a clear understanding of how they worked the mikes during the checks and can duplicate it during the actual performance. A good test is to have them walk offstage after the mikes are set, then come out and see if they

PRODUCTION

are in the correct position at the end of the performance. Although it may be necessary to adjust a microphone during a performance, the best performances will have it right the first time.

Documentation

If the participants at your festival are well selected, you will present persons who are not regulars on festival circuits and whose art may not have been previously documented. If your fieldwork and selection process have emphasized regional style and cultural survivals, it is important to preserve a record of performances. Conversely, if you have hired mostly travelling festival regulars or persons who are performing outside their culture, effort required to document probably will be greater than any potential benefits, as it is likely that numerous recordings of these groups exist.

Festivals are not usually a good environment for either sound recordings or photography, so stick to the basics: careful sound recording of stage presentations and much good black-and-white still photography along with some color slides.

Sound recordings of relatively good quality can be made from the sound system mix, and this is far better than hiding performers behind two sets of microphones—one for recording and one for sound. Recording from the PA mix will be monophonic. This is okay, but if you must have stereo recordings, either split the PA microphones with transformers (the sound company can provide these) to a separate mixer for recording or attach separate recording microphones to the stands holding the PA mikes (this avoids hiding performers behind extra stands). Don't be tempted to use a simple stereo pair of microphones. These would be adequate if you had time to experiment with placement, but in a dynamic festival situation, you are likely to have severe balance problems using this method.

If possible, professional recording equipment should be used. Nagra, Ampex, and Scully are examples of recorders often used for such work. Semiprofessional recorders such as Revox, Technics, and Teac also are quite good for festival use. If professional equipment is not available, you may have to rely upon higher grade consumer equipment such as that made by Teac or Sony. If possible, tapes should be made on recorders with half- or full-track heads rather than the common quarter-track variety. Tapes should be recorded at 7½ ips or faster — those made at lower speeds are lower in quality and are usually inadequate for reproduction as well as being difficult to edit. The bias for each machine should be set for the specific tape to be used, and the tape should be new and of the highest quality: Scotch 206, 207, or 250; Ampex 406, 407, or 456; or a tape similar in quality to these. Reel-to-reel machines are preferred, since many cassette machines are markedly inferior and cassettes are not as useful as reels for retrieval and storage purposes. Recorders which accept ten-inch reels are an advantage. Recordings should be made *in one direction only* and stored "tails out."

The photography which will be most useful to you in future years is high quality black-and-white stills. Color slides are less useful but are good for some purposes.

Videotaping and filming are far more expensive and are poor choices for the expenditure of funds in virtually all cases. If you have money for such frills, it is better to invest it in upgrading sound recording and hiring an excellent still photographer. The problems with videotapes and films may be stated simply: they are expensive to make, expensive to edit, nearly impossible to distribute, and are seldom seen by more than a handful of people. You may receive an offer to videotape and distribute from a cable TV system. Cable systems are diversifying their programming, and many seek what they call "specialty programs." If such an offer is made, insist on some control. Don't allow camera crews to disturb performances for the live audience. In advance arrangements, insist on being provided a copy of all videotape, including the out-tapes as well as the finished product.

Stage Management

Effective stage management results from thoughtful staffing and the careful division of responsibilities. The ideal stage manager is knowledgeable of each item of folklore and each person to be presented and is authoritative without being stuffy or pedantic. This person keeps the stage operating on schedule, has good relations with persons being presented and with other stage staff, performs introductions at the stage unless there is a guest presenter, and keeps an eye on performers to see that their needs are met and that they hold to schedules. Some training or experience in folklore and presentation is essential for this person.

The stage manager is in charge of other personnel assigned to the stage. These may be as few as two or as many as five:

1. The assistant stage manager is concerned with logistics: insuring that performers due at the stage arrive on time and that microphones, chairs, and the like are in place and are the correct number for each group. This person is in charge of communication with other areas if the festival is radio-linked and if the stage does not have a full-time "gofer" or radio operator. The assistant stage manager substitutes whenever the manager must be absent from the stage.
2. The sound system operator should have no other duties. Even the best of sound systems requires constant monitoring and, other than helping with microphone and cable replacements, the operator should remain at the controls.

If the material being presented is recorded, two additional staff members are necessary:

3. One person should keep a recording log which identifies in order each performer (if a group is performing, each member), his or her instrument, and the name of each item performed. If the material is a story or discussion, it should be summarized for the log. Beginning and ending times should be noted for each performer or group and the log should be headed with the date, the number or location of the stage, and the number of the tape reel (for example, *7/30/79, area 2, reel 4*).
4. The other person needed if material is recorded is the one who operates the recording equipment. It is a task for a conscientious person. Keeping an eye on recording levels and monitoring tapes can be boring at an exciting performance, but good tape requires close and careful attention.
5. The "gofer" becomes the legs of the stage crew, fetching soft drinks, tools, more tape, and whatever else is needed, assisting other stage staff or taking over when they are absent from the stage.

The manager should be given a schedule as early as possible. The manager should have an opportunity to meet and visit with performers well in advance of presentation. Performers should be told how much time they will have on stage, and a backstage signal system should be agreed upon to use as a set draws near the end. In allotting time to performers, a good rule is five minutes less than the scheduled time, allowing for changeover and introduction of the next performer(s).

In spite of all precautions, a stage may get behind schedule. If it runs more than fifteen minutes behind, adjustments should be made to fit the remaining time. As far in advance as possible, participants should be informed of schedule changes and should be requested to cut their time.

When performers or equipment fail to show at a stage on time, it may be necessary to change the order of the schedule. The stage manager should check with base operations before making a change to determine other last-minute changes and avoid the possibility of disrupting another workshop schedule.

Rain is one of the most common problems a stage manager will have to face at an outdoor festival. It is a good idea to go over rain contingencies with stage managers before the festival begins. A few basic rules are:

1. Stage managers should contact base operations immediately regarding communication of rain plans to performers and public.
2. Never attempt to continue a performance on a wet stage on which electricity is present. With the first raindrop, all equipment should be fully covered with plastic sheeting.
3. If a stage is totally covered a performance may be allowed to continue, but power should be cut off if it is exposed to moisture.

Another common problem that stage managers face is controlling access to stage areas for reasons of safety and security. Stages at folk festivals often have no clear-cut backstage areas and can become congested with spectators. In most cases, the areas immediately to the sides and in back of the stage should be limited to participants and staff. It is a good practice to rope off this area to give the public some indication that it is off limits.

Safety and Security

Unforeseen problems and emergencies characterize all large public gatherings, and you should assume you will have some and plan

PRODUCTION 119

for them. *Security* is a word many people do not like, but festival producers have a responsibility and a legal obligation to secure the safety and property of participants, staff, and audience. Meet with your landlord well in advance of the festival to determine the ground rules, decide who is responsible for what, and develop methods of enforcing your decisions.

SAFETY OF PERSONAL PROPERTY

Portions of the site should be off limits to the public. Designate "Participants and Staff Only" areas with signs, and plan to reinforce doors and gates with guards, staff, or volunteers if necessary. Develop a system of identification badges or passes for participants, staff, press, volunteers, and any others who are part of your festival, and determine who is allowed where.

You can best protect personal property by strictly reinforcing regulations made for the areas which are off limits to the public. Procedures for storing musical instruments and crafts materials are covered elsewhere in this book. Beyond that, participants are entitled to feel that their personal property is reasonably secure in areas designated as performers' rest areas and in the festival housing facility. You can make this more likely by designating specific staff members who will check participants in and out of the housing facility and who will remain at the housing facility around the clock. This is probably the least attractive job for volunteers, so it might be necessary to hire at least one person who can provide this continuity. If you are using a hotel or motel as a housing facility, your problems will be fewer. To ensure safety of personal property in participants' rest areas, simply limit the number of persons who have access to these areas and enforce your regulations.

HEALTH EMERGENCIES

There is considerable variation among communities in the handling of public safety and health emergencies. In some cities, police departments dispatch ambulances and first aid personnel. In others, such matters are handled by fire departments, city hospitals, or volunteer rescue squads. Key staff should become familiar with local procedures. If given adequate advance notice, some volunteer squads will bring an ambulance and personnel to large public gatherings and will remain to meet whatever needs arise. If you cannot obtain such services, post telephone numbers of rescue squads on all festival telephones.

You may want to have a clearly marked first aid area at your site with trained staff and the usual supplies for alleviating the discomfort of insect stings, abrasions, small cuts, and other minor injuries. But rely on professionals whenever life-threatening emergencies occur; summoning and guiding the proper personnel to people in difficulty is the best service you can give.

MAINTAINING APPROPRIATE BEHAVIOR

Appropriate behavior is that which does not threaten others or unduly interfere with their enjoyment of the festival. The vast majority of persons who attend folk festivals are considerate people who come expecting to enjoy themselves and to be tolerant of others' enjoying themselves.

Many common problems can be avoided through the use of signs and careful use of advertising. If your advertising hints of a whoop 'em up, rowdy event, you'll attract some persons who wish to behave in that way. If advance publicity or signs note conspicuously that the public consumption of alcohol is banned, you'll have fewer inebriated people at the site and fewer alcohol-related difficulties.

Instruct your staff in methods of handling undesirable behavior. If a festival goer disturbs the enjoyment of others, the behavior should be discouraged as gently as possible and in a way that does not escalate a minor matter into a confrontation. Frequently the person or persons creating the problem do not recognize it as such, and a friendly discussion which informs will bring equally friendly compliance. An approach which leaves egos intact is best; staff should not exacerbate the problem by adopting a belligerent attitude. A staff member should never physically engage a festival goer. In the case of serious and continued aberrant behavior, the staff member should call police or security officers, who should be given the option of ejecting the person or accepting their promise to end the behavior.

If you plan to charge admission, carefully check the condition of the fence or barrier around the site. Will you need to reinforce the fence with volunteers or guards? A word about gate crashers: avoiding problems or confrontations by not dealing with these persons is not fair to those people who supported the festival by paying admission. Also, if the word gets around that it is easy to sneak in, your audience may be filled with gate crashers, and they tend to be the persons who create other problems.

SECURITY STAFF

In the absence of a police force which is already assigned to the festival site, such as in a public park, you can hire off-duty police officers or designate staff members to serve as security guards. There are advantages to having both. Hiring off-duty police officers will of course be an expense item, but you can turn over the problem of guarding property, watching fences, and maintaining appropriate behavior and expect it to be handled in a professional way. If you use your own staff, they can do double duty by answering questions and giving directions and possibly even selling programs. If you opt in favor of using your staff as security guards, we suggest you hire one or more police officers as professional back-up. In any case, engage your security staff well in advance. One person on your production crew should be responsible for overall security and should assign security positions and duties to the staff.

Communications During the Festival

Communications during the festival depend largely on prefestival communication and careful preparation of participant kits and staff schedules. If persons or groups have in their participant kits a schedule of what is expected of them hour by hour, they are more likely to be at the right place at the appointed time. If staff duties are clearly outlined on paper, participants and staff will be more likely to take matters which need to be resolved to the person who can resolve them.

A few snafus and unforeseen problems are inevitable, but they can be handled speedily with electronic communication. Nowadays CB radios and excellent walkie-talkies are commonplace, and they are a boon to festivals spread over a wide area.

Establish a base operations station as festival headquarters near festival telephones. Designate one person to be responsible for communications from "base." Schedule changes, routine requests, and emergencies should be directed to base operations. The base operator should regulate all communications, putting one on hold while talking to another and cutting short gossip or unnecessary detail. FCC regulations concerning the use of transmitters should be studied and followed. CB radio clubs may volunteer to supply reliable communications via walkie-talkie. By law, they are not permitted to charge fees, but free admission, food, and a welcome to festival parties will help in gaining their assistance.

Communication equipment should be available at each stage, crafts area, main admission gate, and other locations where instant communications may be useful. One person should be in charge of radio communication at each station; others wishing to transmit messages should do so through this person.

The festival director and other key decision makers should never be far from a radio during the festival. For this reason, walkie-talkies are preferable to CBs. At the National Folk Festival a CB is used at base operations and walkie-talkies at other stations. The festival director or site coordinator may be anywhere on the festival site and yet instantly available of a decision is needed.

A word of caution. Radio is a useful tool, nothing more. The ability to communicate problems instantly does not mean they will be solved instantly, and radio operators should not become excited or demanding in transmitting messages.

Concessions

The most common failure of festivals is in what they choose to sell. Many offer more junk food than folk food. Some sell items unrelated to their area, region, or folk culture. Many feature rows of booths manned by weekend hobbycraft merchants selling tourist kitsch. Thoughtless hucksterism cheapens the impressions festivals leave in other programming areas. This is unfortunate, as almost as much energy must be expended to mount a poor concessions area as would be required to create an excellent one. As in many other programming areas, the critical factor is planning.

PRODUCTION   123

It is important to understand that concessions *are* a part of programming. What is sold, who sells it, and the physical arrangements for sales are matters to be decided by the program committee and the festival director. We recommend that your criteria for inclusion be as rigorous as those for any other programming area.

FOOD

If thoughtfully planned, the preparation and sale of folk foods will be your most popular craft demonstration. It will bring to your festival the food editor of your local newspaper and scores of other people who may care little for music, dance, storytelling and craft arts other than food.

The inclusion of local foods and the foods of minority and ethnic groups can add a strong local flavor to your festival. Church, synagogue, civic, and ethnic organizations can serve as concessionaires and can demonstrate local and ethnic food preparation while raising funds for their activities. Because some groups require group or board approval of their activities, request participation two or three months in advance. Maintain communications with each group so that you know their needs for equipment and services.

Many areas have traditional food preparation gatherings—apple butter making, corn boils, barbecues, bull roasts, cider pressings, pancake breakfasts, and many others. Do nearby groups get together for such events? Could they be persuaded to have one at your festival? See the section "Tucson, Meet Yourself" in Part II for a description of how one festival handles this.

An alternative is to seek concessionaires among the best neighborhood and ethnic restaurant operators in your area. They have equipment and expertise and may be eager to have a broader public know of their good work.

Many festivals engage professional concessionaires to handle fast-serve foods and beverages. We do not recommend this. The soup beans and cornbread, apple butter, fried chicken, Brunswick stew, homemade cider, and fried apple pies sold at the Blue Ridge Folklife Festival at Ferrum College in Virginia each October are served faster than any so-called fast food we've seen. The church people and civic club members who serve this delicious food do so with good cheer. "This ought to take care of your case," says the fellow who ladles out the Brunswick stew. And he is invariably right. Many festivals are paid a commission on food sales and gain a substantial portion of their income through this method. The common commission is 10 to 15 percent of the selling price. Don't forget to check with local health authorities before scheduling your food concessions. All states and most local areas have health regulations relating to food service.

CRAFTS

If a sales demonstration is part of your festival, selling crafts should be a function of concessions. It is cumbersome and unattractive for a demonstrating craftsperson to handle sales, and if a commission is deducted, computations can be handled more efficiently by concession personnel. Some craftsworkers will resist this and insist that they sell items they make. We advise you to be firm in the policy even if some of them refuse to participate. It removes the element of commercialism and results in a more attractive and interesting crafts demonstration.

SPONSOR'S BOOTH

Most festivals have at least one booth where festival-related items are marketed—program books, tee shirts, memberships, souvenir posters, and phonograph recordings made at previous festivals.

PERFORMERS' RECORDS

If you choose to sell phonograph recordings made only by performers, make arrangements in your prefestival letters, stating clearly your conditions. Are performers required to ship records in advance, or may they bring them along to the festival? If you ship unsold records to them, who will pay shipping costs?

It is simpler to sell records for even dollar amounts—for example, $6.00 rather than $5.75. If possible, establish one price for all performers' records to avoid confusion. We recommend selling performers' records as a service, with no commission deducted. This can add a bonus to a modest honorarium. Festivals which sell performers' records usually handle them only in the sponsor's booth.

PRODUCTION

The sale of additional records can be a source of income at your festival. You might chose to sell a variety of records on consignment from one or more companies. If you decide to sell other than performers' records, we suggest choosing carefully and relating selections to your festival programming. After years of more or less indiscriminate folk music record sales at the National Folk Festival, it was decided that it best serves our performers if we sell only their records and recordings made at previous festivals.

PHYSICAL ARRANGEMENTS FOR CONCESSIONS

The concessions site should be in an area that allows room for traffic flow and vehicle access and is not too near stages. If indoor space is used, use rooms with more than one door—preferably large rooms. Wide corridors may be used for the sale of some items. Outdoor sales areas should be covered for protection from sun and rain. Department store camping equipment departments sell inexpensive coverings that may be used for small sales areas.

Calculate the number of tables and chairs needed, and coordinate obtaining them with obtaining the chairs and tables needed for the crafts area and stages.

Determine what sales items will arrive before the festival and arrange for secure storage. You'll also need a plan for transferring sales items to storage space during the festival and a security plan.

Make a list of items you should bring to the site and include the following: a cash box, receipts, pens and pencils, masking tape, cord, magic markers, rubber bands, a staple gun, hammer, nails, change aprons, and plenty of coins and dollar bills to make change.

CONCESSIONS PERSONNEL AND OPERATION

One person should be in charge of concessions before and during the festival. This person has responsibility for the following tasks: taking an inventory of sales items, obtaining and assigning salespersons, supervising concessionaires, collecting daily commissions from concessionaires, reimbursing craftspersons and performers, settling sales accounts, and preparing a final financial statement.

This person should prepare an assignment sheet designating who is assigned to what tasks and the hours for the entire festival. Workers should also be assigned for the set-up and breakdown of concessions at the beginning and end of each day and the beginning and end of the festival. Arrange to have youngsters roam the site selling program books. Leave a few persons unassigned for tasks you did not anticipate. Selling to crowds is tiring, so plan a rotation system.

Instruct the staff to arrive early the first day and log everything in as it arrives. Issue receipts to performers for their records and to craftspersons for craft items to be sold. Before the festival opens, brief the staff regarding sales procedures, answering common questions, and especially the handling of money.

Often the concession booth serves also as a general information source, so brief the staff in answering common questions (Where are the restrooms? Where can we get refreshments? Is there a first aid unit?). If the festival grounds or building is very large, a map giving this information is useful. Otherwise, make signs as questions become obvious.

Keep a file of names of good workers to ask to work at subsequent festivals. At the end of the festival, close as many financial arrangements as you can: collect from concessionaires before they leave, and return unsold recordings and craft items (obtaining a receipt for cash and the unsold items).

Festival Breakdown

Some staff members are needed to work at the festival grounds until equipment has been removed or properly stored. Problems are minimized if the site preparation crew serves also as the breakdown crew.

Determine deadlines in advance. It is a good idea to specify in your contract the time for clearing the festival site and to stay with it. The groundskeeper will appreciate an efficient breakdown, especially if another event is scheduled soon after yours.

The coordinator in charge of breakdown should devise a schedule and direct the crew. Some things to keep in mind:
1. Know to whom each piece of equipment belongs and where and when it should be returned. It is easy to underestimate the amount of effort this requires; before the festival, assign to specific staff members the responsibility for returning specific items.

2. Keep a list of reusable items which have been made or purchased for the festival, such as platforms, tents, signs, and coolers, and note where they are stored.
3. Arrange for adequate crew and vehicles to accomplish the breakdown schedule.
4. Be equipped with extra trash bags and garbage cans to facilitate breakdown in some areas while other areas are still active.
5. Allow plenty of time to break down the crafts area since it usually takes longest, and follow through on arrangements for transfer of crafts material.
6. Determine which, if any, performers need assistance with costumes, instruments, or equipment at breakdown time, and be ready to give that assistance.
7. Be aware of contractual provisions for leaving the grounds clean, and follow through accordingly.

Festival Recap Meeting

One way to ensure that problems in one festival do not recur in succeeding festivals is to hold a recap meeting a few days after the festival, while problems and successes are something more than a blur. Invite key staff and other knowledgeable persons who were at the event.

Discuss each major facet of the festival in a predetermined order: prefestival planning, site preparation, presentation, communications, security, housing, food, and so on. Do not allow the meeting to deteriorate into gossip and non-constructive criticism.

Ask each key staffer to compose a "how-to" memo for your files. This will be helpful in planning your festival the following year.

Part Two

7. Examples of Festivals

TUCSON, MEET YOURSELF
JIM GRIFFITH

Introduction

Since 1974, Tucson, Meet Yourself, a festival of traditional music and food, has taken place in Tucson's downtown El Presidio Park in early October. It typically consists of three days of music and dance, performed for the most part by local ethnic artists. Visitors to the festival may purchase ethnic food prepared by local cooks. The festival is intended to be a celebration of cultural pluralism in Tucson.

The festival was sponsored in 1976 by the Cultural Exchange Council of Tucson, Inc., and Pima Community College. In October, 1976, about 20,000 people attended the festival, which was presented free to the public. Eighteen distinct cultural traditions were represented by thirty-two groups and individuals, twenty-five of whom were Tucson residents. Food was offered from seventeen ethnic cuisines. The future of the festival, at this point, seems relatively secure. This report outlines the various kinds of decisions which went into the production of the festival.

The Community

Tucson has a population of 452,000 (1975) — up from 45,454 in 1950. The stereotypical Anglo-Hispano-Indian Southwestern cultural mix is overlaid by blacks, Chinese, and Serbians, as well as by many other ethnic and regional groups.

One result of Tucson's large, recent population growth has been fragmentation of the community. Geographically, there is no functional nucleus that one can call "Tucson" in a real sense. The city consists of acre after acre of subdivisions interspersed with shopping centers. Few of the city's immigrant majority are aware of its environment—natural or cultural. The festival was seen as potentially functioning to provide a sense of community for Tucsonans and, at the same time, giving graphic evidence of the ethnic diversity of the larger community. The festival was slanted in the direction of the folk and vernacular arts.

A Festival—But What Kind and for Whom?

In 1974 it was decided that a festival of ethnic diversity, spotlighting local people, would be held. The next questions were, "Who is the potential audience?" "What sort of festival should it be?" "Where and when should it happen?" The answer to the first question was "As wide as possible a segment of Tucson's population." As soon as this was determined, many of the other questions almost answered themselves. The basic problem then became, "What is the best way to dramatize Tucson's plural society for the greatest possible number of Tucsonans?"

Once it was decided what was to be done and for whom it was to be done, all that remained was to figure out *how*. The date was set for October, after the brutal summer temperatures would have cooled enough for people to enjoy themselves outside in the daytime and before either the cool weather or the winter visitors arrived. It was decided that if the festival was to take place outside the tourist season, it would emphasize its local nature. The site was chosen on the basis of access for the most people. A downtown park was selected, near enough to the barrios and the poorer districts of town for their occupants to feel comfortable but close enough to the new community center buildings not to threaten the people from the east side of town and the more affluent foothill areas. The area chosen was well defined, well kept up, only a block from the bus terminal, and provided with grass for sitting plus ample nearby parking space. Having chosen this park, it was then necessary to seek the cooperation of the City Parks and Recreation Department, and officials from that organization were invited to attend planning sessions at appropriate times in the process.

It was decided that something more than stage presentations would be needed at the festival. The intention was to provide a means by which representatives of different ethnic groups could meet other Tucsonans more or less on their own terms and make any statements concerning themselves that they might see fit to make. The idea of ethnic food booths was chosen for the following reasons: (*a*) American culture is to a great degree consumption- and food-oriented, (*b*) food experimentation is an easy form of cross-cultural sampling, and (*c*) the selling of specialty foods to raise funds is a familiar activity for many ethnic Americans. Thus both producers and consumers would feel comfortable with the transaction. A decision was made to de-emphasize crafts because Tucson already has a strong craft fair tradition and it was felt that this would only complicate matters, given the difficulty most people have in distinguishing folk and popular culture. Workshops, often an important feature of folk festivals, were not considered necessary in this case, but space was set aside for jamming, and informal gatherings were encouraged. (In the third year of the festival a local traditional music club offered to organize fiddle, banjo, and guitar workshops in a corner of the park. These were quite informal, approaching jam sessions in nature, and were very successful. Workshops of various kinds are now a regular part of the festival.)

The main entertainment was to take place on a large stage directly in front of the ornamental façade of one of the older buildings facing the park. There were to be two basic types of entertainment: that provided by individuals and groups invited by the coordinator, and that provided by the ethnic interest clubs already planning to operate food booths. Each of these organizations was given an opportunity to present a short program of music or dance.

Sponsors

Sufficient funds to produce the festival had to be sought to put any plans in motion. The Cultural Exchange Council (C.E.C.) is a local organization whose aims are to foster cultural exchanges between Arizona and its neighboring Mexican state of Sonora. In 1974 the C.E.C. was successfully solicited as a sponsor, largely because their aims coincided with those of the festival. Pima Community College joined as a sponsor in 1976, and at that time the following division of responsibilities was agreed upon:

Preparing Papago Indian popovers at Tucson, Meet Yourself. Lorenzo Pablo tends the fire while Frances Manuel kneads dough and Florence Lopez cooks the popovers, a form of fried bread. Visitors to Tucson, Meet Yourself get to observe ethnic food preparations, as well as sample the foods themselves. Helga Teiwes photograph, 1977.

C.E.C. – obtains grants
        raises funds in community
        runs soft drink concession stand at festival
P.C.C. – administers funds
        provides volunteers
        assists with publicity

Funding

In the first year, the festival was put on for under $3,000. By 1976 the total budget had grown to $9,510. Costs included fees for coordinators and musicians and some advertising expenses. Since the festival began, funds have been obtained from a number of sources. The festival has received grants from the Arizona Bicentennial Commission; Una Noche Plateada, a local benevolent organization; and the Expansion Arts Division of the National Endowment for the Arts. Funds were also raised through solicited contributions from local merchants and interested groups and parties in the city of Tucson, and at the festival through the operation of the soft drink concession.

Festival Coordinators

A husband and wife team, Jim and Loma Griffith, coordinated the festival. Their responsibilities included total artistic responsibility for the festival, planning and research, locating and booking of performers and food booth operators, contacting and organizing volunteers, and the general responsibility of seeing that the festival would run as smoothly as possible. Their first major functions were to establish participant selection criteria, select the participants, and contact and communicate with the participants. (Other duties are covered under "Festival Staff.")

Locating Possible Participants

A number of sources were helpful in locating ethnic clubs: The Tucson Chamber of Commerce booklet, *Civic and Fraternal Organizations in the Tucson Metropolitan Area;* Yellow Pages listings, such as "Churches"; and the working list of organizations provided by a local organization interested in international presentations. Also helpful were consultations with friends and acquaintances, the City Parks and Recreation Department, and the Foreign Students Advisor at the University of Arizona. The president of each organization was contacted by mail and later by phone, and the festival was explained. A coordinator attended club meetings when necessary. It was pointed out there were several ways to participate; operating a food booth was a possibility; presenting a short (twenty-five-minute) program was another. Food booths could also be used for the sale of crafts and for dispensing information concerning the groups' interests and problems. The presentation invariably ended with an invitation to attend the festival, even if formal participation was not possible or desirable. In the first two years of the festival, no charge was made for the booths and the activity was presented as a fund-raising possibility for the group. Later, when the City of Tucson initiated a charge for its facilities, this expense was passed on to the participating groups on a voluntary basis. Response to this expense-sharing offer has been extremely positive.

Participation Selection Criteria

During the first three years of the festival, the performing groups fell into three basic categories of programming:
1. *Individuals and groups playing within the ethnic tradition in which they were raised.* Some of these are currently popular groups such as Papago Indian polka bands, whose music can be heard at any Papago religious or secular celebration. Others, like an elderly Czech accordionist, play music going back to an earlier day. All may be termed *folk* or *traditional* musicians.
2. *Groups, often of children or young adults, consciously exploring aspects of their own national or cultural heritages.* Such groups include the locally popular Mexican *folklorica* dance groups. These may be labelled *revitalization* groups.
3. *Young middle-class Americans who are exploring a variety of traditions not their own and are performing in these traditions.* This category includes many contemporary urban bluegrass, string band, and blues performances.

EXAMPLES OF FESTIVALS 137

The third type has always been at least minimally represented at Tucson, Meet Yourself, but the major emphasis has been placed on the first two kinds of performance. In the first year of the festival, performers were almost entirely local Tucson people. The two exceptions were a group from Phoenix and four musicians from a nearby Southern Arizona town. The second year, federal monies were given for the purpose of expanding the festival by bringing in selected out-of-town performers. Because the festival is designed as a celebration of local cultural richness and diversity, it was important to invite artists who relate in some important way to the various ethnic groups in Tucson. An example of such a choice was Lydia Mendoza, a well-known Spanish-language singer from Texas, who was invited in 1975 and 1976. Her appearances led to the "adoption" of the festival by a sizeable number of the Mexican-American community and to the live remote broadcast of Lydia's portion of the program over one of the local Spanish-language radio stations. In this sense, the festival coordinators saw themselves as programmers pure and simple. Care was taken, however, to ensure that out-of-town artists comprised a small proportion of the performers at the festival.

The ranks of the local performers have been divided pretty evenly between those invited by the coordinators and those produced by food-booth sponsors, thus creating a balance between the aesthetics of the coordinator and those of the ethnic groups themselves.

Communication with Participants

From the outset, it was discovered that in dealing with participants and booth operators, a lot depended upon the establishment of a warm personal relationship between the festival coordinators and all the participants. Many of the people who have been involved in Tucson, Meet Yourself do not participate comfortably in mainstream Anglo-American life, and many depend upon personal relationships to function in the greater society. And so it was the job of the festival coordinators to establish credibility and confidence.

It also was helpful and necessary to stay approachable and maintain contact by telephone with everyone concerned with the festival. All letters had to be followed up with a telephone call and sometimes with a personal visit. Over the years the festival has taken place, the coordinators estimate that they have spoken to each participant at least eight times in the course of planning each festival. All changes in plans and decisions on scheduling and planning are checked with the participants involved.

Payment of Participants

Early in the planning process, it was decided that all musicians and dancers who desired it would be paid. The festival was conceived as a community service, and the distribution of funds throughout the community seemed to be a worthy aspect of that service. Also, in keeping with the public education aspect of the festival, paying the festival performers served as a message that traditional musicians should be shown the same regard as other performing artists and be paid for their services. A standard scale was used, with each group and individual being offered a similar amount. Later, when musicians were invited from out of town, they were offered slightly larger sums as travel recompense. Presentations by groups also operating food booths were approached differently. In such cases, the performers were told that they could be paid if they desired, but it was suggested that the profits from sale of food could be considered sufficient recompense. Each group then made its own decision.

Presentation of Participants

Advice on program presentations was given only when it was asked for and was usually on the level of "Why don't you present the most interesting, unique, and important thing about yourselves that you can?" It was emphasized that the unfamiliarity of an art form was an advantage rather than a drawback. It was the responsibility of the coordinator-M.C. to prepare a program that was varied and that presented each group in the best possible relationship to the groups before and after it. The promoters of this festival feel that an audience, properly prepared, will sit through almost any kind of presentation for fifteen or twenty minutes if it knows that the overall program will be a varied one.

The food booths were organized in an equally open-ended way.

EXAMPLES OF FESTIVALS   139

The coordinator offered advice, when asked, on what foods to sell and, after the first festival, what had sold well or poorly in the past. Groups were encouraged to decorate their booths. Booths could also be used as lobbying platforms for ethnic concerns within the bounds of good taste and peaceful relations. Booths were assigned by lot, slightly modified in cases where a specific situation seemed problematic.

Selecting the Audience

After the previously outlined plans for a festival of traditional ethnic food and music had been made, all further decisions revolved around the desire to draw a wide segment of Tucson's population to the event. An important task was to find a suitable name. It was decided that, in the climate of the early 1970s, *folk festival* had too many connotations of youth culture and could be confused with the similar-sounding *rock festival.* (It was not uncommon at that time to hear the two terms used interchangeably.) What was sought was a neutral-sounding name with a certain amount of dignity which would suggest the nature of the event. The title, "Tucson, Meet Yourself" was finally chosen as best describing the aims of the festival.

The advertising was deliberately dignified, if not stodgy at times. It seemed likely that the younger, middle-class Tucsonans would attend anyway, and so the message of the festival was aimed at an older and presumably more wary segment of the population. Slides and music in the Public Service Announcements concentrated on pictures of children and older people and tapes of fiddle music. It was continuously emphasized that the festival was to be a "family day in the park" and that it was "for the whole community." In a further attempt at gaining a diverse audience, the posters were printed in English and Spanish, and Spanish-language interviews were broadcast on the local radio and television stations.

During this period a concept developed which the festival planners labelled *the concept of neutral ground.* Briefly stated, it is as follows. One of the functions of a multicultural festival such as Tucson, Meet Yourself is to provide both audience and performers (or recipients and presenters) with neutral ground—a setting where neither party feels sufficiently threatened to force a withdrawal, but where all parties are sufficiently ill at ease to suggest being on one's best behavior. To give an example of this: Many Anglo-Americans are captivated by the sounds of black gospel music, but a large number of these people would feel extremely uncomfortable encountering this art form in its native setting, the black church, where—in addition to the nervousness created by visible racial differences—the visitor may have to cope with an unfamiliar set of behavior standards and with such cultural phenomena as altar calls. On the other hand, the Afro-American choir may not be comfortable enough to perform well in a totally secular concert atmosphere. Tucson, Meet Yourself attempted to solve this particular problem by creating a sacred setting. Sunday afternoon was given over to traditional religious music, song, and dance. As was the case with the rest of the festival, wide cultural variety was the watchword at this concert, which over the years has included Eastern Orthodox, Swedish Lutheran and Afro-American and Mexican-American small-group singing, and Yaqui Indian sacred dancing. A measure of success in this area was that in 1976 the festival was concluded by a performance of Yaqui Matachini dancers, a group which dances as a devotional act and will not appear on secular occasions.

Festival Staff

There were three major paid positions on the staff of this festival. With the assistance of a large number of responsible volunteers, they covered all the necessary aspects of producing the festival.

The job of *festival coordinator* was shared by a husband and wife team, Jim and Loma Griffith. Jim is a trained cultural anthropologist with over twenty years experience in the area, as well as an active musician, and Loma is equally accustomed to cultural diversity. The festival depended to a great extent upon these two people and on their ability to project the aims of the event and to get along with a diversity of people in the local community. They divided their duties as follows:

    Loma—contracting food selling groups
          allotting booths
          obtaining necessary Health Department permits
          general liaison in food booth area

EXAMPLES OF FESTIVALS

    Jim—in charge of stage
- research and contacting of performing groups
- program
- maintenance of festival publicity—giving interviews, managing press releases
- coordination of volunteers
- setting tone of event through private and public appearances

The approximate working time for the festival coordinators was one and a half months full-time, two months half-time, and the rest of the year on an occasional, part-time basis. It should be emphasized that the load during the actual festival was almost more than two people should be allowed to carry, but these particular coordinators preferred it that way. Post-festival work involved writing personal notes to all the participants and preparing a final report for the sponsoring bodies.

The *publicity coordinator* was a paid position whose responsibility it was to see promotion through the printer, get information to the papers and PSAs to radio and television stations. He also acted as a liaison between the coordinators and the sponsoring bodies. During the festival, he saw that the performers were paid and that they had an opportunity to sign sound recording releases. After the festival, he prepared a publicity report. The publicity coordinator worked half-time for about two months and full-time for about a month.

The other paid job was that of *sound technician*. This was a post of considerable responsibility. Quality of equipment and of sound work was vital to the success of the festival. In the case of this festival, it was fortunate that a friend of the festival coordinators was able to obtain quality equipment free of charge and then oversee its operation. Otherwise, it would have been necessary to rent equipment and get the work done professionally by a top-quality agency. It is an area where one cannot afford to skimp.

The festival has been documented each year by a photographer and a sound technician. The photography was contracted out to a professional and negatives were deposited with the festival coordinators for the C.E.C. Tape recording was done by another professional and tapes were deposited with the Folklore Center at the University of Arizona. Documentation was considered necessary to the aims of the festival and was used in promotion and publicity for future festivals.

Carrying Out the Plan

The last problem was how to ensure that things would go smoothly and that undesirable incidents could be kept to a minimum. The best thing to do is to try to anticipate problems that might occur and have some system for coping with them. The basic coping system at Tucson, Meet Yourself consisted of a large body of volunteers from a wide range of ages and cultural backgrounds. They were recruited by the festival coordinators over a two-month period before the festival. A volunteer meeting was usually held one or two weeks before the festival weekend. At this meeting, the festival was discussed, tentative programs were handed out, and a "need sheet" was distributed. The volunteer was told that his or her first job was to enjoy the festival and that a name tag was to be put on only when he or she decided to become a target — someone who was taking public responsibility for the smooth operation of the festival. Sign-up sheets were not used, except in the case of a few specific, vital tasks. Instead, a list of things which needed to be done was circulated, and the volunteers were counted on to find out if anybody was doing them at any given time. They were instructed to refer problems to one of the two coordinators. A future goal is that someday most people at the festival will wear volunteer tags and it will be impossible to distinguish "workers" from "the public."

All use of alcohol and drugs at the festival was discouraged. This was done partly by the restrained tone of the advertising, partly by word of mouth, and partly by the volunteer force. Here again, cultural mix was vital. Volunteers were asked to look out for alcohol and drug use, but to approach users *only if their cultural style seemed compatible with that of the volunteer.* In other words, to use a coarse example, straights were not encouraged to approach longhairs and tell them not to drink beer in the park. A volunteer who felt comfortable with the people involved wandered up, chatted a little, and finally suggested that there were better places to do whatever it was that was being done. This system has proven to work well.

The event could not have been put on without a large and culturally diverse body of informed, enthusiastic, and hard-working volunteers. The rewards included satisfaction for a job well done and a postfestival party given by the coordinators and one of the sponsors. It became obvious that an atmosphere of intelligent, dedicated cooperation was essential to the festival.

Several off-duty, uniformed police officers were hired for the duration of the festival, but their function was simply that of back-up. Their instructions were first to enjoy themselves and second to be available in case they were needed. They also watched the booths and equipment during the night hours. In the history of this festival, we have had no really unpleasant incidents, and the police officers have requested that we ask them to work on the festival year after year.

A Final Word

The general outline of festival decisions has been presented, but a final word remains to be said. It is imperative at each festival that the coordinators remain open, solicitous, friendly and firm. The coordinators try to seek input from audience and participants, then make a decision and stick by it. A festival is a complex event involving many on-the-spot decisions—and individual responsibility cannot be replaced by community decision making. This fact is reflected in the contract between the coordinators and the sponsoring organizations and is scrupulously observed by all concerned.

It must be emphasized that this report was prepared not so that the novice festival producer can emulate the success of Tucson, Meet Yourself or even avoid its mistakes, but to make clear the kinds of decisions and thinking which go into the preparation and production of one particular community festival. Other festivals will have other aims and other problems, but in many ways the basic questions and decisions will remain the same. The last and most important point concerning Tucson, Meet Yourself is that it has been eminently satisfying to do every year. Were it not for that, no one would be doing it.

MISSISSIPPI VALLEY FOLK FESTIVAL
Jane Bergey

Introduction

The Mississippi Valley Folk Festival was held at the Jefferson National Expansion Memorial on the grounds of the Gateway Arch, St. Louis, Missouri on September 3-5, 1977 (Labor Day weekend). The three-day event brought together musicians and craftspeople from all over the Midwest and attempted to create a picture of folklife on the American land as it exists today, though it reminds us of traditions which are past and sometimes forgotten.

This was a festival of people who enjoy what they do — they have retained the old ways over the years, and they enjoy sharing a part of their lives with others. The festival has had an impact on the community: we have heard many local shopping centers recently using the phrase *folk festival* for their own events, although the phrase had had adverse connotations for years.

The MVFF was presented by the National Park Service (NPS) and the Jefferson National Expansion Historical Association (JNEHA) in conjunction with the Missouri Friends of the Folk Arts (MFFA), a non-profit organization which promotes and preserves the folk arts. Other organizations involved in the MVFF were the National Council for the Traditional Arts (NCTA), a Washington, D.C., organization which cooperates in events such as this when they are held in national parks; and the Missouri Arts Council.

As this was the first year of the festival, the following report attempts to examine some of the events and problems of the MVFF and suggest some possible solutions.

Festival Programming

Early planning for the festival included establishing programming guidelines which would exemplify the common aims of the festival and the Memorial. The purpose of the event was to create a folklife festival dealing with the broad concept of westward expansion as it relates to the settlement and folk cultures of the Mississippi

EXAMPLES OF FESTIVALS 145

Valley. The rich cultural resources of this region were to be represented in a three-day festival of performing and material art traditions. Participants were selected partly according to their representation of a midwestern style of folk music or craft.

The regional emphasis in this festival is unique and affects audience, participants, and folklore collectors. As the audience is potentially a mostly Midwest regional group, the accent on traditions of the Mississippi Valley may help these people to realize that what survives here is truly theirs and is something worth preserving. The performers find that this kind of festival makes them feel comfortable and proud of where they are from and what they have to offer. At the festival, individuals live and work beside others who preserve their own traditions. As they are able to freely share their uniqueness with others, they can leave the festival with a renewed confidence and value in their art. For the folklorist and collector of folkways, a regional festival is the ideal setting for creating a comparative geographic study of folkstyles. Folk material has much greater variation over distance than it does over time and in the workshops at the MVFF these geographic differences could be observed.

We developed a successful policy for utilization of talented local revivalists in the St. Louis area. As we wished to feature mainly traditional performers on the program, many local folklorists and musicians volunteered their time to serve as moderators and participants in daily workshops. In the future, we hope to be able to expand our budget in order to pay these people who commit time and energy to make the workshops run smoothly.

The presentation and organization of the program was based on models of well-established festivals throughout the country—specifically the National Folk Festival held at Wolf Trap Farm Park, Virginia. Daytime activities were to consist of workshops, crafts, and historical demonstrations. The purpose of workshops is to provide a chance for performers to be heard in an informal setting and to interact with each other and the audience. The emphasis in the crafts area was to be crafts in a living tradition, with all of them being demonstrated. Evening concerts were to showcase performers in a more formal setting. These programming objectives were followed throughout the planning and execution of the festival and most of the guidelines were met when the festival program was finalized.

MUSIC

The program of evening concerts and daytime workshops consisted of nationally known feature performers and local and regional musicians. The evening concerts were designed to present a balanced program of traditional music styles. Those performers who were more well known and who had more experience performing on large stages were chosen for the evening concerts. Each act was allowed twenty minutes on stage. Although such a short amount of time did not allow for a close rapport with the audience or demonstrate fully the variety of each performer's talents, many audience members were not well acquainted with traditional music and would have lost interest with a slower-paced concert.

Workshops were held in two stage areas under large tents. Each stage was scheduled in half-hour and hour sessions from 12 noon to 5 p.m. on Saturday, 11 a.m. to 5 p.m. on Sunday, and from 11 a.m. to 4 p.m. on Monday. Each featured performer gave a thirty-minute workshop each day; these were interspersed with workshops on specific topics (such as "The Way West") or on musical genres (such as "Harmonicas, Accordions, Etc."). The workshops included traditional performers from Missouri, Arkansas, and Illinois. Each specialized workshop had a moderator who could relate the music of one performer to another's, provide historical notes, and give the workshop direction. This approach works well when, as in our case, the moderators are familiar with the performers, the music, and the historical background. Most workshops of this type lend themselves to becoming mini-concerts which involve an active performer with a passive audience. Although it is not necessarily bad if audiences are not always in direct interaction with the performer, new ways to actively involve the audience and new techniques for presenting workshops should be researched. We have the opportunity to study this need further in regular programming.

One place the audience had the chance to "let it all hang out" was the Dance Party at the end of each day's workshops, a concept taken directly from the National Folk Festival. Each evening after the daytime activities, everyone got together for one hour for the Dance Party at the main outdoor stage. The MVFF scheduled a Saturday Square Dance, a Sunday Fais do do, and a Monday Blues and

EXAMPLES OF FESTIVALS 147

Boogie Dance Party. The more successful Dance Parties were in a location with plenty of space and had a well-defined structure. We found these dances to be a good way to end a day and prepare for the evening concert.

CRAFTS

The main objective behind the organization of the crafts was to find participants who had learned their craft traditionally, still practiced it in daily life, could demonstrate their craft at the festival site, and were not commercial. Craftspersons were paid about $25 per day and were allowed to sell their wares. The payment policy, different from that of most craft fairs, was designed to encourage the craftspersons to be more interested in demonstrating the craft, yet it enabled them to afford the time spent. A variety of crafts were offered at the festival, including brooms, apple dolls, cider pressing, shingle making, and blacksmithing. No craftsperson made more than $150 and some made no income through sales.

Crafts participants were selected from previously known sources and from the leads they could offer. The demonstrations were generally of quite high quality and exciting to watch; the most popular were the active demonstrations, such as blacksmithing and corn grinding. The highly positive response indicates that we should seek out more crafts demonstrations of this type. We hope to expand the emphasis on crafts so that it is more balanced with the emphasis on music and to foster direct involvement of the crowd, including them in the production of the end product.

FUTURE PROGRAMMING PLAN

As festival planning time was short and did not allow for original fieldwork, actual programming was a process of selection from known sources. As a result, some areas were slighted. Over the next year, potential Native American representation should be researched.

In future festivals, we hope to include more dancing, as much of the music played at the festival originally existed in the context of dance. Traditional dance groups will be looked into.

A revival of the Missouri State Fiddle Contest, sponsored in the 1930s by the Missouri Department of Agriculture, was another pos-

Basket maker, Dale Black, at the Frontier Folk Festival, St. Louis. Photograph by Joe Pfeffer.

sibility discussed. It was decided that the intent and atmosphere of such an event was not in keeping with our concept of the festival and that funding should be sought to sponsor this event independently. We also hope to explore the possibility of presenting a film series prior to the festival and incorporating a film festival into the daily events at the festival.

Although concepts and emphasis on festival programming may vary over the years, the theme of the festival should always be directly related to the concepts of the Jefferson National Expansion Memorial. To make each festival a unique gathering, we plan on a policy in which no participant, except some of the older significant regional performers and some craftspersons, will appear on the program for two successive years. Variation in the festival may include accenting a specific tradition or a certain location.

Publicity

The MVFF was fortunate to receive good publicity for the event, although there were a number of handicaps. A full publicity campaign could not be launched because planning was started late and funds were cut from the budget in this area. The press and other media were quite receptive to contacts made by the festival, even though a festival of this magnitude had not been produced in the area since the early National Folk Festivals were held in St. Louis. There was, however, a basic misunderstanding among the media of the folk festival concept. Such inquiries as "Is this just another one of those neighborhood street fairs?" and "Are you going to have fireworks like the fourth of July?" were not uncommon. Advance contact and publicity could define the type of event and present it in a more favorable light.

A press conference was held which did not receive the response we had hoped for. However, the one TV station in attendance presented a five-minute interview on the evening news. The press release circulated prior to the festival produced several advance articles and calendar listings. A few reporters expressed interest in doing an advance article if information could be received earlier. Some advance features did appear locally. TV and radio coverage was good, and PSAs and interviews were aired on most local radio stations. Several reviews and features appeared after the festival. Frequent calls and letters received after the festival commended the event.

Ideally, programming should be decided upon five to six months in advance so that proper publicity material is available for early distribution. For Labor Day weekend, initial publicity should be disseminated in May. Even without proper lead time, the amount of coverage the MVFF received in its first year is encouraging and sets a good precedent for the future.

Festival Site

The Gateway Arch is an ideal location for the MVFF. Symbolically, the Jefferson Expansion Memorial represents what the festival celebrates. It is a natural gathering place for visitors and is also accessible to a cross-section of the St. Louis metropolitan population. Such events as MVFF encourage local residents to support the park and enhance the experience of out-of-town visitors.

The festival was set up in the area of most traffic flow. The workshops were held on two 12' × 12' stages placed under large 70' × 30' striped tents. The two stages were placed to provide optimum sight lines for the audience and photographers and so that the sound from one stage would not bleed into the other or the crafts area.

One of the two stage areas was subject to a number of distracting noises—sirens, lawnmowers, riverfront sounds, and a local cruise boat calliope. For future festivals we need to see what arrangements can be made in advance to minimize disturbances or else consider choosing different locations. From a technical standpoint, the stages were run efficiently with power, sound and lighting supplied as needed.

The main stage of the MVFF was not as successful. The stage available for loan from the St. Louis Park Department would have been perfect in fair weather, but it could not be used in rain. The sound consultant, lighting consultant, and a member of the maintenance crew assisted with problems of getting enough power and cable to the area. Time was a large factor and we had to call in a consultant to work out details. A union lighting company was called in, despite the cost, to supply and operate the spotlight and stage lights.

Sound for the weekend was contracted to Don and Kathy's House of Music. They were chosen because they had the best appreciation for folk music, we felt they would be easy to work with, and they presented the lowest of three bids. The sound engineers were responsible for making tapes of all performances. Separate engineers were needed to monitor the tape and keep a log so as to produce quality tapes.

The tents for the crafts area were not entirely effective. Five 30' × 20' tents were borrowed from the U.S. Army Reserve; four housed the crafts. They were effective in keeping out rain but were too short to be stood under comfortably and too warm in the sunshine. They also were not large enough for some of the demonstrations, and visitors could not see into them from the outside. St. Louis fire codes designate that crafts using machinery or fire (soap making, blacksmithing, etc.) must be housed together, and this worked well. Water was supplied by a hose across the sidewalk from the crafts area, and buckets were used to haul water. Power, when needed, was received from the center box and was run to the tents with extension cords. Future alternatives will be formulated according to the activities of the craft participants. Larger tents might be used to make this area one cohesive unit. This would make the craftspersons feel more a part of the whole and would help the visitor understand that the crafts are related to one another.

This year, most on-site equipment was rented, which was rather expensive. MVFF is considering the purchase of tents if the initial investment would prove worth the cost. It may also be possible to form a cooperative agreement with other NPS parks that sponsor festivals. The economic feasibility of this must be researched.

Rain created a major and often insurmountable problem because the site did not offer many rain alternatives. The wetness did not, however, dampen anyone's spirits or discourage attendance. So it is accepted as a part of the festival experience.

Festival Necessities

One of the main goals of the MVFF staff was to create an atmosphere of friendliness and comfort for the participants. This took some foresight into the needs of the people and some staff members who genuinely care about the welfare of the guests to St. Louis.

An important service to the participants was a courtesy area on the festival site. A tent was set aside from the mainstream of activity for relaxing, jamming, and visiting. A festival staff member was on hand to give any assistance necessary. Dinner and lunch were served in the tent, and many participants relaxed there for informal jam sessions. As this area was outside, it attracted visitors who wanted to listen to the music and talk with the performers. The ideal situation would be an inside area, but it must be easily accessible to caterers and old folks. The instrument check was located at the courtesy area, and receipts were given for instruments checked. Instruments were stored in a portable van so that they could be easily transported and easily covered in case of rain. This is an important service for the performers. The receipt system works well when carefully run and can safeguard valuable equipment.

The NPS provided a cash pick-up service for the MVFF. Money was collected from the crafts area and concession and was deposited in the JNEHA safe. This was appreciated by participants and staff.

All out-of-town participants and staff stayed overnight at Lewis Hall, St. Louis University. They were provided with clean rooms and linens, friendly service, and a pleasant atmosphere. This was greatly preferred over housing people in individual homes. The performers enjoy being together and sharing music. We were also allowed the use of an old ballroom and the main lobby for after-concert gatherings.

Food was a major expense but well worth the money spent. A large breakfast was provided since many of the participants were accustomed to having large breakfasts. Also, many would not have time to eat again until dinner. Lunch was obtained through the concession, a system which was not as efficient or of very high quality, but it held people over until dinner. A hot dinner was provided on site by a catering service; leftover food was consumed after the concert by performers and staff. Evening snacks were provided at the after-concert gatherings.

Transportation was a three-fold project:
1. Two vans were rented for the entire weekend and were used

constantly. They transported participants to and from the airport, to and from the dorm, to some performers' homes in rural areas, and were on call for emergencies.
2. A charter service was hired to transport fifty people from the park to the university morning and evening but was more expensive and less efficient than anticipated. A larger rented vehicle might serve our needs better.
3. On-site transportation for instruments, heavy equipment, and people was handled by a Park Service-run pargo cart. This cart was used constantly.

Communication problems were avoided because everyone worked well together, but advance preparation would have been a good idea. The on-site festival information booth was to provide first aid, water, and programs and was to be staffed at all times by volunteers. Unfortunately, these volunteers did not have a clear idea of their duties, and we were fortunate that no emergencies arose. Ideally, the booth should have (a) an NPS staff member and a festival staff member at all times, (b) telephone or radio communication to all stage areas and the pargo, and (c) access to a nearby telephone in case of emergency. Phones or communication to them were needed at the information booth and at the dorm. A direct line between the Arch and St. Louis University should be provided for participants.

Visitor services at the festival included portable sanitary facilities rented by NPS and water fountains supplied by the city. A contracted concession was set up, and a percentage of its profits went to MFFA research projects.

Program Implementation

The festival staff had virtually no problems implementing the festival programs — not because they were highly organized, but because we selected the right people. Three experienced festival consultants — Andy Wallace, Jane Wallace, and Al McKenney — were hired for the weekend. One of them was stationed at each stage area and one was a rover. They knew how to run the stages and anticipate the performers' needs, thus insuring a high-quality program. They worked day and night and were willing to participate in every aspect of the festival. Joe Wilson, a consultant from NCTA, arrived a week in advance of the festival to help with publicity and festival activities.

The MFFA staff for the festival consisted of about twenty volunteer workers. Kathy James and Robert Clark coordinated services to participants: transportation in and out of town, food and housing, transportation and scheduling within the area, and operating the instrument check. The crafts area was supervised by Emily Goodson and a committee of three. Craftspersons appreciated the staff's friendliness, fairness, and consideration. The MFFA Board and staff were a supportive and guiding force throughout the festival.

Setting up, cleaning up, and the smooth running of the evening concert were accomplished through the understanding and cooperation between performers and staff. The only area which suffered because of a limited number of workers was the audio and video documentation. We feel that the quality of material presented should make the festival eligible for documentation by public educational radio and television networks.

The NPS personnel were invaluable to the MVFF staff by helping visitors, staff, and performers.

A festival of this nature should have a semi-permanent staff for six months prior to the festival. The director has ultimate responsibility for the staff. Publicity, public relations and graphics need a competent and experienced person who is familiar with the folk festival concept. Also necessary are a program director and a site coordinator. A support staff will be needed to assist the administrators about two months before the festival.

Festival Finances

The original projected budget for the MVFF was $50,000, which depended on a corporate or arts endowment grant and local funds outside the JNEM. However, the project was begun so late that many sources had committed 1977 funds and most grant application deadlines had passed. This forced us to make the necessary adjustments to produce the program for $25,000. At this point, a day was deleted from the schedule, the fiddle contest was dropped, and "name" folk artists were no longer considered. The 1977 festival was eventually funded by JNEHA funds and received some support from the Missouri Arts Council Artist in Residence program.

MVFF Expenses (1977)

Performer fees:	$6,872.00	Lighting:	$ 261.00
Crafts fees:	1,075.00	Publicity:	2,904.41
Travel:	2,678.01	Site equipment:	2,548.90
Lodging:	760.00	Consultants:	809.35
Food:	2,308.67	Misc. expenses:	694.09
Sound:	110.00	NPS expenses:	1,510.01
		Total Expenses:	23,521.44

Monetarily, the MVFF is one of the largest folklife festivals held in a national park. Others are held annually in El Paso, Seattle, San Francisco, and Washington, D.C. A free event has little opportunity to perpetuate itself, but a paid event also presents problems. It must be decided whether the festival is responsible for fostering the philosophy that national parks are for the people and should be accessible to all. Some festivals charge a fee at the gate, but this creates security and logistical problems.

One way money was raised during the festival was through a concession from which MFFA received 20% of the gross income—about $1,000. The JNEHA could contract this and use the proceeds for future events. As well as providing a service to visitors, the concession could be made a more integral part of the festival. Country picnics and barbecues are traditions of long standing that often accompany presentations of traditional music and crafts. A concession of this type could be set up in a special picnic area. Crafts might also be geared to creating income, although statistics from the first year indicate that this kind of venture is not profit-oriented. A souvenir booklet sold at the festival and supported by paid ads and interested folk arts organizations is another possibility. An agreement should be made with funding organizations that any funds not spent from a grant can be put into a special fund for future festivals.

Though a good festival was presented within a short time and with limited funds, more quality programming could be accomplished if more funds are available.

Afterword

Some of the MVFF was not what it could have been, but most of it was better than I could have ever dreamed. I knew the effort was worthwhile when Harley Sinclair, saying goodbye at the end of the weekend, said tearfully, "It's too bad you have to wait until you're seventy years old to find out what you want to do with your life." Let's do it again.

THE OPEN FIDDLERS' CONTEST
Joe Wilson

Introduction

The open fiddlers' contest is truly open. Any fiddler who wishes can enter. Thus, much of the music heard at any contest will be mediocre. Yet some is likely to be of the highest quality, as the well-advertised open contest will bring out some fine musicians who even the best of fieldwork will miss.

Because most sponsors of such events do not pay musicians (other than those who win and then usually small amounts) and assume no responsibility for their transportation, food, or housing, these are low-cost events for producers. Many musicians refuse to participate in contests, feeling that such events exploit musicians for the benefit of commercial producers or institutions. Nevertheless, fiddlers' contests are traditional in many areas of the country.

Because contests in different areas vary so much, this example is not based upon a single event but is a description which draws upon experience gained at contests in all regions of the country, but primarily in the Southeast, Midwest, and West.

Background of Fiddlers' Contests

The history of fiddlers' contests in the United States is yet to be written, but references to them in early journals and travelers' accounts indicate that some were held before the American Revolution. A 1736 Hanover County, Virginia, account tells that among various contests at a forthcoming celebration would be a violin competition in which twenty players would contend for a violin. The 1803 obituary of a sixty-seven-year-old Charleston, South Carolina, resident tells that the deceased was respected for his impeccable dress and "from his youth the taking of prizes for violin music." Since the pre-Revolutionary period they have been combined with other contests: weight lifting, jumping, singing, dancing and, more recently, banjo playing and even contests to determine the "prettiest girl" and the "ugliest man." Prizes have been violins, gold pieces, a filly, sacks of flour, and even a set of false teeth—a prize which says much about the general state of dental care among rural people a few decades ago.

Other than in the brief period between World War I and the Depression, most fiddlers' contests have been relatively small local events catering to local taste and reflecting local style. But during that period, and especially during the mid-1920s, they briefly became a major activity in the hands of such promoters as Henry Ford, who promoted a national fiddling contest with contestants chosen in regional contests.

Ford's motives were more racial and political than musical. He was disturbed by Jewish and black influences in vaudeville and other popular entertainment and hoped to demonstrate the superiority of Anglo-American and "Nordic" culture as an alternative. His contests aimed at selecting the best fiddlers in a contest process amusingly similar to that used for choosing boxing champions.

Ford's attempt to make a national sporting contest from an activity as subtle and intricate as folk fiddling shows that his aesthetic was as poorly developed as his political and humanistic sensibilities. The violin is among the most responsive of instruments, and attempting to choose a national fiddle champion from among the tens of thousands of players and scores of regional and ethnic styles was ludicrous. Would one attempt to choose a single national singing champion from among the singers of scores of styles? The champion singer of opera? Scat? Country? Gospel? The concept is obviously silly.

Ford failed to spark a fiddling revolution, yet he dubbed two national champions during the period in which he sponsored contests. His questionable assumptions endure in a half-dozen fiddle contests in several parts of the nation, each of which claims that the fiddler it crowns is the real national champion. These events have no ties to Ford or his contests, and the directors of these events are usually unaware of the fact that the national championship idea came from Ford's misconceptions.

Fiddlers' Conventions: Galax

Fiddlers' conventions are usually directed by persons of folk origin or persons once removed from the folk, such as small local businesspersons, rather than by academics or other cultural experts. There is much variation in how they are organized throughout the nation.

At the Old Fiddlers' Convention held annually at Galax, Virginia, during the first full weekend in August, the audience and musicians are closely interwoven. It is only the tourists who sit in the stands and watch the stage proceedings. The traditional audience is scattered throughout the fields and parking lots, gathered in tight clusters around groups of musicians, drinking, dancing, and calling out requests.

This event functions mainly as a meeting place for musicians and their friends. Many of the best musicians who come do not enter the contests. They return year after year to play their music and visit with old friends. Musicians who moved from these Blue Ridge foothills to northern cities return for this weekend even though they may not have seen any advertising for it. They know it will be held during the first full weekend in August and that their musician friends will come. This is an annual meeting of a cult of musicians.

In many past contests the judging at this event has been poor. This disturbs some musicians, especially members of the urban folksong revival string bands who have been coming down from northern cities since the early 1960s. But most of the older and better musicians ignore the judging or treat it as a joke. Many of them attend without entering the competition. The dean of fiddlers from these parts, Tommy Jarrell, once commented: "Anybody who would get up there deserves to lose."

The Old Fiddlers' Convention also includes contests in flatfoot dancing (always the most popular contest), bluegrass banjo, old-time banjo, guitar, folksong, old-time string band, and bluegrass band. The contest is sponsored by the Galax Moose Lodge, which uses the funds raised at the event to support its work with underprivileged children.

Contestants register by mail in advance and may enter as many as three contests. Some contestants who do not register in advance are allowed to enter. Electric instruments are barred, and contestants are advised to perform older tunes. Performers play two tunes in each round and are asked not to talk on stage. Musicians are not paid unless they win (prizes are usually $200 or less) and must pay admission; however, the cost of admission is refunded to musicians who enter the contests. The three or five judges are seated in front of the stage and in recent years they have been musicians or others who might be expected to know the forms being presented. The several MCs are usually local country music disc jockeys or local personalities. They assume that the audience knows the music and make few attempts to interpret it for those who do not.

This fiddlers' contest is one of the most respected in the nation. Much of the credit for this must be accorded to the Moose, who continued it when similar events were being discontinued and who make no claims about national champions. But more credit must go to the scores of fine musicians who choose to meet there.

The Moose maintain a mailing list of prior contestants. These persons are sent registration forms two to three months before the contest and are urged to return them. The contest chairman and the members of his committee make all arrangements and are not paid for their services. All are members of the Moose Lodge.

Western and Southwestern Contests

The most respected contests in the West and Southwest differ significantly from those held in the Southeast. The differences are in the regional styles played and the attitude toward contests. Western contestants tend to be highly serious about the quality of judging and very competitive. The intensity of the competition and the concern about judging has led to the spread of what is called *contest style.* This style is based upon an older Texas style in which the players use long bow strokes and complex fingering to produce a highly melodic and "smooth" music. This style has grown strikingly complex, and the level of musicianship required to win one of these contests must be very high. In these contests, fiddlers play one fast and one slow tune (the latter is usually a waltz); the judges are placed in an enclosed room, out of sight of the stage, and they hear the music over speakers. These speakers are turned off when contestants are introduced so that the judges will not hear their names or voices.

At least two unfortunate developments have grown out of these "contest style" contests. One is a flattening of regional and individual style. Rigid judging has led to a quality of sameness in this style that can be disconcerting. An Idaho fiddler will play "Sally Goodin" in a manner virtually identical to the way a New Mexico fiddler will play this tune. There is a "right" way to play, and regional and individual differences are penalized.

The second unfortunate aspect of these contests is that while claiming to promote old-time fiddling, many promoters refuse to allow the cross-tunings essential to playing many of the oldest tunes commonly known to western fiddlers. *Cross-tuning* is a term fiddlers use to describe any tuning of the fiddle other than standard — for example, C#AEA, EAEA, DADD, and others. While any tune can be rendered in standard tuning, these tunings allow fiddlers to add striking flavors to a tune, flavors that cannot be duplicated on a conventionally tuned instrument. In fact, many of the most striking of the old cross-keyed tunes sound commonplace when rendered in a standard tuning.

The excuse commonly given for barring this class of tune is that they are "trick" tunes and that allowing them would be unfair to other contestants as the judges might be unduly influenced by them. This is hardly plausible, as the judges at these contests are invariably fiddlers who know cross-tuning and its effects. Moreover, these are not "trick" tunes but rather are a very old and valued part of fiddle repertoire. The actual reason is that under the guise of preserving old-time fiddling, the associations which promote contest style are bent upon modernizing it.

Fortunately, there are small fiddlers' conventions in the West, Southwest, and Midwest that have not been overwhelmed by the contest style fad and there are local contest promoters who have strongly resisted it.

Open Contests

Some of the open contests of associations actually are open only to members of the association. In some areas of the country where there is no tradition of contests, promoters use them as a cheap and easy way to provide entertainment at an event where admission is charged. The worst examples involve admission fees for the audience, entertainment in the form of contests, ribbons and plaques rather than cash prizes, and an entry fee for contestants. This is exploitation.

Because we feel that fiddlers' contests should retain a local flavor, a set of directions for conducting a fiddlers' contest will not be given here. We believe that organizers can better learn how to organize acceptable events through discussions with local traditional fiddlers who have a background of participation in such events. There are, however, two points we feel strongly about. First, use only musicians as judges — musicians who intimately know the style of your area. Second, if you combine a fiddlers' contest with other contests (singing, string band, etc.), mix the contestants. In other words, a fiddler may be followed by a singer, buckdancer, string band, and banjo player before another fiddler is heard. This prevents a benumbing parade of similar items. The usual excuse for the parade of similar contestants is that it helps judges. Our opinion is that it bores and alienates judges, contestants, and audience while adding nothing to the quality of judging.

There are local contests in many areas of the nation. The April issue of *Bluegrass Unlimited* and the NCTA's annual *Calendar of Festivals* lists many of these events. (See Bibliography.)

8. A Performer's Point of View

A CONVERSATION AMONG DEWEY BALFA,
RALPH RINZLER, AND FRANK PROSCHAN

The Newport Folk Foundation sponsored a field research project in the French-speaking areas of Southwest Louisiana in 1964 at the suggestion of Alan Lomax. Ralph Rinzler, then a director of the Newport Folk Festival, traveled to the prairies and the rice fields of Cajun country in search of the best musicians who would be able to participate in the festival that summer.

The first presentation of Cajun music before a large Northern audience took place in July, 1964, and was a success which had positive effects that continue to be felt throughout French Louisiana. The Newport experiences and the later participation of Cajun musicians in the Smithsonian Festival of American Folklife, the National Folk Festival, and other festivals and concerts have influenced the people and the culture of Acadiana in many ways. These interviews with Dewey Balfa, violin player and singer with the Balfa Brothers and an important cultural spokesman in his home and throughout the U.S., were conducted by Frank Proschan on February 23, 1977 in Basile, Louisiana; and by Ralph Rinzler on July 30, 1977 at the National Folk Festival.

FRANK What was the first festival you played?
DEWEY The first festival was Newport, Newport '64. Ralph [Rinzler] had come down here, I think in '64, and had interviewed some people. He hadn't interviewed me then because, somehow, I was supposed to have gone to Revon Reed's show to be interviewed, but I couldn't go that day. Then things happened so that I got to go to the '64 festival.

FRANK Was that just you, or your brothers too?
DEWEY No. It was just me with Vinous Lejeune, Glady Thibodeaux, and Revon Reed.
FRANK Were you playing around here [Louisiana] then? Were you active?
DEWEY I played for gatherings, but I was kind of rusty because I more or less had given it up.
FRANK You didn't play dances at all?
DEWEY No, I didn't. See, I think the thing about this type of music is that anytime a person would have wanted to become famous, or maybe make a living at playing music, I think that the performer thought that he would not get anywhere by playing Cajun music because it was looked down upon here as isolated, regional music, you see.
FRANK Were there as many dances back then? Were they playing the same type of music?
DEWEY Yes. Within Acadiana itself, they had always had a strong feeling for their music. But for the performers, I think that anytime a performer got to be pretty good, he got the feeling that if he stayed with Cajun music, he never would go out of Cajun country. That's why many people couldn't understand why groups like our group, the Ardoins, Adam and Cyp Landreneau, and others were invited to go to festivals repeatedly. The people down here couldn't believe it. I couldn't believe it at first, till I finally accepted it.
FRANK The first time you went to Newport, did you expect at all what you found?
DEWEY I didn't know what to expect. I was very pleasantly surprised. I was also very moved by the other performers that were there that year.

* * * * *

RALPH How do you think young people feel now about French music in Louisiana?
DEWEY Well, I must tell you that it's not the music that they prefer listening to, but I can see a great change in the last ten years. From the time that we went to the first festival, people thought it was more or less an occasion to bring the Cajuns up to be laughed at.

RALPH People at home did?
DEWEY Yes, I'm really telling the truth. I can remember people saying, "Why are those boys going up there? Nobody wants to listen to that chenka-chenk music!" I've had friends tell me that a lot of musicians from other groups down there just couldn't understand me. They said, "Dewey is a good musician, and we can't understand why he goes and plays with a triangle." They thought that it's so backwards, so old, that it shouldn't be done.

And I was so moved, performing for an audience of about 17,000 people that year, and almost getting a standing ovation. It gives you a different feeling. I wanted to do something about it and I didn't know what to do. I didn't know how to go about it. But then I was fortunate enough and had good enough friends to sort of open up the way for me. To go back home now, I find that the young people are feeling somewhat different about the music, because I see them coming to gatherings and festivals. The young people are starting to have an interest in their music.

RALPH The first year you were at Newport were you there with Vinous and Thibodeaux?
DEWEY Glady Thibodeaux, Revon, Vinous and I. And of course, Mr. Paul Tate was there. And then the following year it was, I think, the Ardoins, and then the Landreneaus. It just kept on. There's quite a few groups that have been participating in the festivals. And one thing my brothers and I have tried to do is that if we need a substitute, we try to get a different person to substitute, just for them to really see what it's like to perform for a thing such as last night. It's just great. Over the years, I've learned to accept that the people like Cajun music, but I haven't really understood why. After all these years of being isolated in such a small community, and then oftentimes I'd tell my brothers, "This has got to be a dream. We're only dreaming and one day we're going to wake up and find out that it's not really happening."

* * * * *

In the Newport Folk Festival program book in 1965, Paul C. Tate, a lawyer and civic leader from Mamou, reflected on the changes that had already been felt as a result of Newport's involvement with Cajun music:

> [Before 1964] Acadian music had lost all semblance of status. It lay captive, isolated and dying, hedged in by a "subtradition" of mediocre imitation of country or western or popular music. Cajun music held itself aloof from the traditional musician, and was rejected as inferior by the current hip generation. Its traditional instruments—the accordion, violin, and triangle—were drowned out and outclassed by the steel guitar, drum, and brass horn. That this condition existed is not subject to serious dispute. That one can write today about Acadian music in the present tense is little short of miraculous.
>
> The Newport Folk Foundation, through its work and recognition, has liberated traditional Cajun music, has given it status, individuality, and identity. The Cajun has begun to see his music not as a poor imitation of other traditions, but as an independent tradition needing no justification outside itself.

* * * * *

RALPH When I met you on the street in front of the Hotel Cazan in October of 1965, you sang "Parlez Nous à Boire." That was fifteen months after you had first come to Newport. There was a lot of Cajun music on records, but people felt that for Cajun music to be acceptable, it had to be played only in the modern style. And you told me that you knew a lot of music that was not on records, that was just in your family tradition, but that you weren't playing it, because you were playing in a band.
DEWEY I don't know what band, but we were playing the nightclub sounds. We weren't playing the family sounds anymore.
RALPH I don't know how I happened to ask you. Maybe I just asked you if you knew any old songs.
DEWEY Yes you did ask. I hadn't even known you were in town. I was working as superintendent for an insurance company and one of the boys and I had some things to do in Mamou. And we went there and I saw your old station wagon, and I told that fellow, "This is the guy from New York." Somehow, you got out and we got to talking. We went up to your room, and I think you asked

me if I knew any old songs that we didn't do anymore. And "Parlez Nous à Boire" was one of the songs I talked about. Later on, we went to eat, and I remember you writing the music to it, singing it, whistling it.

RALPH I wrote the notes down. It was that same day you told me that you had brothers who played, because I'd never met Rodney, Will, Harry and Burke. Then you told me that your brothers had a band, and you didn't know if you could do it, but you'd see if they could get together. It was that same night. I can remember I wrote the notes down and mailed them in a letter to A.L. Lloyd in England and I looked at my watch and said, "In six or eight hours I'll see all of Dewey's family, and he says they know a bunch of other songs like that." I was amazed, because the only people I'd heard sing old-time songs were the Deshotels brothers, and I liked them a lot, but they sounded very refined. They didn't sound real to me; like they were trying to make the songs sound prettier. And I was very much taken with your musical style. We sat down and recorded. I don't remember why we recorded "Parlez Nous à Boire" without the guitar and accordion, but I think it was because I asked you how people played it in those days, when your father was growing up. You said that they probably didn't have accordions for some of these songs because the notes for the songs don't fit on the accordions. I think that's what it was.

DEWEY You asked me what instrument was used, and naturally it was first the fiddles. That particular night, I don't think we had an accordionist with us. It was just Will, Rodney, Burke and I. So you asked us to do it with the fiddles only and with the triangle. We also did the Mardi Gras the same way that night. Then on Sunday, we all went to Harry's. Momma was still living then.

RALPH What was your feeling about recording then? You knew that people made fun of the music, but you knew that I didn't.

DEWEY After going to Newport and having the experience I had with the response from the audience, I knew that it was serious, that it was something that should be worked at, and I knew you weren't kidding around. And then, I realized that I wasn't ashamed of playing my music.

* * * * *

DEWEY I just came back here, and I felt that there was very little that I could do, but still I figured I was going to do what I could. I felt like I could put my feeling across better with the people I played together with all the time, like Will, Rodney, Harry and Burke. I felt that I could put across my feeling better with those people because I musically corresponded better with them than with the others. Then one day I told Ralph, "I'd like to travel. If you're going to have me, I'd like to work with my brothers." That's when we were invited to the Newport Festival in 1967, and from there we've traveled now in pretty near every state in the Union. I've also done some work over here [Louisiana] towards putting people to the awareness of the treasure we have down here. I started doing a radio show, like Revon does.

FRANK When was that?

DEWEY I guess that was about ten years ago. And then I did work with the Southern Folk Culture Revival Project with a whole bunch of people who had been working through a grant from the National Endowment [for the Arts]. I did, I think, three spring tours with these people. They were very moved by the way I felt, the way I tried to explain the existing of the Acadians here in Louisiana, and that I was afraid that the music and the culture were eventually just going to fade away. I said I would have very much liked to have been able to bring the music and the story of the Acadians to the young people in school. When the Southern Folk Revival Project renewed their proposal the following year, they proposed a small grant for me to start doing this here in Louisiana, and the same thing for John Shines in Alabama. I must say it was very well-spent time and money. It was just amazing to see the student and faculty response. What I would do is ask the faculty and the students in the school to write to me and really tell me what they felt about the project. Did they feel that it was worthwhile? Did they receive any educational information? Did they think that I should not do this, or maybe they had suggestions of what I should do. You'd be surprised reading the letters. Even some of the faculties were impressed by the project.

FRANK Out of that has grown your position on the NEA panel on artists in the schools?

DEWEY I think the position on the panel was by the state agency that had a meeting in New Orleans. Our good friend Alan Jabbour, who was with the National Endowment then, asked if it was possible for some of the people to come down to see this part of the country. We arranged for me to make a gumbo. I can remember some of the officers . . . I didn't know who I was talking to, but we got into a discussion about the regions. I must have been very convincing because I can remember telling the chairman afterwards, "If I was to go in your part of the country and you were going to feed me gumbo and sauce piquante, why I'd just as well stay down here." I said, "If I had the same culture you had, and vice versa, chances are you'd have never come down here." It was just a very nice discussion, and after they went back to Washington I was invited to be on the panel. And I accepted it. I'm not sure I'm doing my job, but I'm doing the best I can.

FRANK I remember in Chapel Hill somebody mentioned your talking on stage; how you explain the music as you go along. You said at the time that sometimes you felt like you were talking too much, but at the same time you didn't, because you wanted people to know.

DEWEY See, when a group of people travel together, like I travel mostly with my brothers, they hear me say basically the same things over and over, and I guess they get bored. I sometimes wish, well I still do wish, that another one in the group would sometimes talk instead of me talking all the time. I guess they get bored and at times they would tell me, "You talk too much." Sometimes I would say to myself, "I'm going to try not to talk so much." But when I get into it . . . I think that if a group is to go and just play music without explaining how it came down here, how it survived over the years, and something about the people, I personally feel that it may not be enjoyed as much. I feel the people need to know who you are and what you're doing, and why you're doing it. And once you've learned that, then I can accept you, and I can enjoy you, because I know where you're at.

FRANK What you said at the time was that your parents hadn't even been able to write their names, and you were so proud that you could make yourself understood, and even prouder of the opportunity to do it.

DEWEY Frank, it's hard for me to explain. But it's like some time back I can remember going to the University of Illinois at Champaign-Urbana, and I had figured I was going to try to jot down the songs I was going to do, and what I was going to say. I'd catch myself looking at this little piece of paper I had, and I just can't work that way. I just work from the feeling I get when the audience responds. It just throws me in a mood and I work from that. What you said about my parents not being educated, and I myself am very limited on the education, book education. But I was never so proud to have had the little bit of education I've had as when I went to France. All the signs except the stop signs were written in French, I guess, and you walk into a store and everything's written in French. You walk into a cafe and you want to order, and pretty near every place it's just French. And I didn't know how to read the French, I just couldn't order. At that time it made me realize how very fortunate I was to have had this little education, and it made me think of my parents, how they have gone through life not being able to read or write. It's a big disadvantage, I guess. However, their life was beautiful anyway, you know.

FRANK If they had had all that fifty or a hundred years ago, you might not still be playing the music. You'd all be talking English. I told that story to Barry Ancelet, and he had talked to Will once, and asked Will the same thing. Will said that once you start talking, he would be content to not play again all night and just listen to you, because he's so proud to be there with you, and proud to be there on his own.

DEWEY One thing I wanted to say. You were talking about being on stage and talking about my culture and so forth. The thing that I could never do until this past year was to be interviewed in front of a camera and really keep my level. But I thought last year, at the [Smithsonian] Festival, I was able to do more in front of cameras and interviews than I had ever done before. I think the greatest thing that has ever happened to me, since I've been at the festivals and working for the culture, was to have been the MC for that afternoon when they filmed all the French-speaking people—from different regions in France, the Quebecois, people from Haiti, the Cajuns. . . . It was really a great honor for me to be MC that afternoon, I think the greatest honor in my life. I'll tell you the truth, these festivals are to me the thing; the thing to get the people to meet, to get the regional cultures to realize that they aren't the only people in the small region or the small isolated place. It wakes the people up to the fact that you should be proud that you're from your section. You have your little way of life, your way of cooking your meals, your way of doing things, and you should preserve that. To me there's nothing like a festival to bring the people from these different regions to learn from one another, and to respect one another. I should respect your culture and your way of life, and in turn, you should learn to respect mine. And I think the festivals have, to an extent, accomplished this: to respect the other type of music. Many people in my region like the Grand Ole Opry type of music, or they may like the rock sound, or something other than Cajun. But the old-timers, if it's not Cajun music they don't care for it. But I think they need to be exposed and told about how the music is played, why it is played. That's why I think that it's so important when I go to play this music to tell the people who we are, where we're from, and why we play this music, and how dear it is to us. Like my music is as dear to me as yours is to you, and if you want to give me half a chance and listen to what I'm doing, you might learn to some extent to enjoy it, and vice versa. If I open an ear to your music, then I can enjoy your music, and that way it's just great.

FRANK I guess even more than finding out that there were English-speaking people who liked Cajun music, it must have been good to be with the other French-speaking people last summer.

DEWEY I mentioned that because, Frank, for many, many years, as long as I can remember, people always said that my French, or Acadian French, wasn't even going to be understood by a person from France, from Quebec, from Haiti. And to see that all these people were there, and we were talking French. It wasn't exactly the same French, just like you would compare a Scotsman with a person from Mississippi, or a person from Arkansas, or even a person from Boston. There are little phrases that we use that they don't use, and vice versa, but basically it's the same language. And as far as being glad and appreciating that people who don't speak French enjoy Cajun music, that is a great thrill to me too, but I had been exposed to that before. Like I said, I would keep

telling my brothers, "It's a dream, we're dreaming, and one of these days we're going to wake up, it's going to be finished."
FRANK What difference has the French language in the schools had? How long has that been really making an effect?
DEWEY Eight or ten years or so, I'm not sure. Some children are learning to speak a little and write. You know, at one time people had the idea that if you were going to be successful and better yourself, you'd be better off not speaking French. I think they're finally realizing . . . I wish I could speak two more languages.
FRANK Someone told me about a picnic at the home of Mr. Domengeaux [chairman of the Council for the Development of French in Louisiana — CODOFIL — and responsible for establishing the French instruction program).
DEWEY We were invited over to the camp of Mr. Domengeaux by a fellow from Quebec. Later on a fellow from France came in and said, "Oh, they are welcome to come, but you have to be very careful how you talk to Mr. Domengeaux. One thing for sure, don't talk about music." So I said, "If you don't want to talk about music, we're not going to talk about music," and we went over to the camp. Mr. Domengeaux must have read some articles about what we had been doing, because when I was introduced to him he said, "Yes. You're one of the guys that are traveling with Cajun music." I said yes, but I didn't try to go into it any deeper. Then later on when we were all talking outside, the subject came up again. He was saying that he thought it was important to preserve the language. I said, "Well, it is very important to preserve the language, but it is also important to preserve the culture such as music." He said, "Music? Cajun music? I despise it." We kept on talking and I said, "Mr. Domengeaux, you don't seem to realize that I think Cajun music has been eighty percent responsible for the fact that our culture has survived over the years. "Ah," he said, "No way." I replied, "If you ever want to see what the people believe, what the people think of music, you put on a festival." "A festival of Cajun music? No." Then a little while later they decided they were going to have a festival. They had made some arrangements to use a room at the University [of Southwestern Louisiana]. When the word got out, they realized they didn't have enough room there. So they went and got the municipal audito-

rium, which is a bigger place. Later they found that the auditorium wasn't big enough either, so they got the Coliseum which seated eight or nine thousand people. I want you to know that it rained the night before, it rained all day and was still raining that night, and they had to turn down about five thousand people. And that man couldn't believe what he saw. He was walking up and down and saying, "I never would have believed it." That really sold him, and now he's really working to preserve it.

FRANK He had done so much for one aspect of Cajun culture through the French language in the schools program, yet he despised another aspect. Some things could be done at one time, and others had to wait. Ten years ago, he could go to school boards and say they should be teaching French. But you couldn't have gone in then and said we're going to play French music.

DEWEY I'll tell you the truth. I think five years ago if I had gotten a grant and tried to do what I'm doing now, it would have just been impossible. People looked at Cajun music as honky-tonk sound—that it was so bad it shouldn't be heard by the young people. Now it is very well received. Some of the students wrote back and said, "Cajun music is not my favorite, and I can't say I ever listen to it. But I must say I enjoyed the program, and I must say that I enjoyed the music." I wish I could remember the words that one high school student wrote. She was thinking and hoping and wondering why it was, especially in history, that there wasn't some combination of teaching history with music that would stick to your mind better than reading out of a book. I thought that it was one of the nicest letters I received, and it went right along with my thinking about music.

* * * * *

RALPH So now where do you think Cajun music can go? What is your feeling about it?

DEWEY Ralph, I don't think that it ever will become as popular as bluegrass, or Nashville country music. But I'm very pleased now. If I was to die, I'm very pleased to know that it has its place in the country now; that the people accept it. And I think that the people will look forward to hearing more of it.

9. Samples of Festival Communications
FOR PARTICIPANTS

National Council for the Traditional Arts

1346 Conn. Ave., N.W. - 1118
Washington, D.C. 20036
Telephone 202/296-0068

Dear Fred:

I understand that Dick Spottswood, a member of our program committee, has spoken to you about your availability for the NATIONAL FOLK FESTIVAL, August 1-3, 1975, at Wolf Trap Farm Park in Vienna, VA, and that your group has agreed to come. This, then, is an agreement for the Trio San Antonio to appear as a spot on one evening concert plus participation in some workshops during the daytime (11 am - 5 pm). It would be most convenient for us if you could arrange to be here Friday and Saturday, August 1 & 2, when Lydia Mendoza will also be performing. Room and board, while you are here, and travel expenses are furnished. The group will be paid $_____.

Please let us know immediately if you have any questions concerning your appearance. Publicity materials, such as records, tapes or articles that could be used for promotion, should be sent to us <u>immediately</u> so we may begin to advertise your appearance. We particularly need <u>biography material</u> and <u>good black and white photos</u>.

If you don't have publicity material, we would appreciate it if you would write, or have someone write for you, a short piece (200 words at the most) telling about the type of music you play, where you've performed, any unusual facts and whatever else you'd like people to know about you. Be sure to <u>list the instruments</u> which <u>each member</u> of the group plays. We must have this material by APRIL 1ST!

Formal contracts will be sent out in May which will include
detailed information plus your concert appearance date.
Meanwhile, this will serve as a letter of agreement for
your appearance for two days at the Festival. Please sign
the carbon copy of this letter and return it to us immediately with any questions you may have.

We are very much looking forward to having the Trio San
Antonio at the Festival and will appreciate your early
reply.

The best,

Agreement signature_____

Date _____

SAMPLES OF FESTIVAL COMMUNICATIONS

National Council for the Traditional Arts

1346 Conn. Ave., N.W. - 1118
Washington, D.C. 20036
Telephone 202/296-0068

39TH NATIONAL FOLK FESTIVAL AGREEMENT

_____ agrees to appear on a Friday or Saturday evening concert during the 39th National Folk Festival at Wolf Trap Farm Park for the Performing Arts in Vienna, Virginia, July 29-31, 1977 and on daytime workshop concerts during the days of the festival (Friday, Saturday and Sunday).

The National Council for the Traditional Arts agrees to pay $_____ as an honorarium plus travel expenses and to supply room and board during the festival at a location chosen by the NCTA. Payment is to be made by NCTA check at the festival on the day of your evening appearance.

The National Council for the Traditional Arts reserves the right to make recordings of said programs for the National Council for the Traditional Arts' use only, and herein agrees that any other use of such recordings shall be only with the expressed written consent of the artist(s).

The National Council for the Traditional Arts will NOT be held responsible for personal injury, loss or damage to property or belongings of participants. The NCTA will not provide liability insurance coverage for participants and craftspersons or their property. While a locked room is available for overnight storage of instruments and crafts, it is suggested that each individual arrange for his own liability coverage.

_____   _____
Participant   National Council for the
                                     Traditional Arts
                                    Joseph T. Wilson, Exec. Dir.

_____   _____
Date   Date

Note: Sign and return one copy to NCTA and retain other for your files.

National Council for the Traditional Arts

1346 Conn. Ave., N.W. - 1118
Washington, D.C. 20036
Telephone 202/296-0068

Dear Festival Performer:

We're very much looking forward to seeing you at the 39th NATIONAL FOLK FESTIVAL at Wolf Trap Farm Park in Vienna, Virginia, July 29-31, 1977. This letter is to tell you how to get there, when you're scheduled to perform, and other information you'll need to know. Here goes:

TRANSPORTATION

1. Participants whose reservations were made by this office; according to our records you are scheduled to:

   Leave:

   Arrive:

   Leave:

   Arrive:

   You can pick up your tickets at the airport. You will be met at the Washington airport when you arrive. Please call your local airport to confirm your reservations and let us know if there are any changes. If the above reservation is not convenient for you, let our office know immediately.

2. Participants who are driving: We have enclosed a map of how to reach Madeira School, where all participants will be housed, and a map of how to reach Wolf Trap Farm Park.

HOUSING

All participants will be housed at Madeira School on Route 193 in Greenway, Virginia. Upon arrival at Madeira, follow the signs to CHECK IN where your room assignments and keys will be waiting. Bill Kornrich or one of his three assistants will be there to take care of you.

Late night arrivals can pick up room assignments and keys from the guard at Madeira gate.

According to our records we are housing and feeding:

If you have not already done so, send us IMMEDIATELY the names of all persons being housed and/or fed. Our housing arrangements are limited, so we must know about any extra people in advance. We must also make arrangements with the food service prior to the festival. We MUST know the exact number of persons in your group who will be eating meals at Madeira School and Wolf Trap Farm Park. Prices for non-participants for whom housing and food is arranged are $8 a night for housing, $1.75 for breakfast, $2.75 for lunch and $5 for dinner. The money for meals is due in advance.

No dinner will be served on Thursday evening, July 28, so if you plan on arriving then, eat dinner first. Ordinarily, we cannot provide food or housing for participants on Sunday night. If it is necessary for you to stay on Sunday night, please let us know immediately, and we will make housing arrangements. Otherwise, final check out at Madeira will be 6:30 p.m. on Sunday the 31st.

FESTIVAL PARTICIPANT KITS

We hope you will arrive in time to register at Madeira and pick up your room key before coming to the Park. If this is not possible go directly to Wolf Trap and go to the parking lot (Lot #1) behind the Filene Center. If you are driving, you may be stopped by a ranger, but give your name and say that you are a Folk Festival Participant, and you will be admitted. Go to the participant area in the basement of the Filene Center where you will be given a kit containing your festival schedule, badge, bus schedule between Madeira and Wolf Trap, parking pass, eating schedule, etc. We have a limited number of parking passes to the parking lot in back of Wolf Trap and an unusual number of people driving themselves to the festival. Once you have checked in, we encourage you to leave your car at Madeira and use the bus service between Wolf Trap and Madeira.

PAYMENT

You will receive a check for your honorarium and travel (if applicable) from Lee Udall in the Green Room at the Festival. Evening performers will be paid on the day of their evening performance. All other participants may pick up their checks on Saturday. We will not be able to cash checks for you at the festival so please plan to have enough money with you to cover your expenses for the weekend.

RECORDING

As in the past years, National Public Radio (NPR) will be recording the evening concerts for possible use on Folk Festival U.S.A., broadcast on 114 public radio stations throughout the country. With your participant kit you will receive a release, payment schedule, and other information concerning this project. Please read it carefully and return the signed release during the festival.

Also, the National Council for the Traditional Arts will be recording all daytime activities for archival purposes and possible use on future records issued by the NCTA. No commercial use will be made of these recordings without prior permission of the artists. If you have any questions about this, speak with a festival staff member at the festival.

If you have any recordings you would like to sell at the festival, bring them along. There will be a booth for record sales on the festival grounds. When you arrive, take your records to the check-in table where you pick up your participant kit. Be sure to have records marked with the sale price. You will be given a receipt showing the number of records and the price. When you're ready to leave, bring your receipt to the record booth. You'll be given cash for the records sold, and the unsold records there.

Your performance schedule is attached.

I hope that this will cover everything you need to know. If you have any problems or questions, feel free to contact the NCTA office (202) 296-5322. After July 28, the staff can be reached at the Wolf Trap Office. Call (703) 938-3810, and ask for the National Folk Festival (or NCTA). For nighttime emergency calls call information (703) 555-1212 and ask for the number for the National Folk Festival in Greenway, Virginia.

We look forward to seeing you at the festival.

Sincerely,

Joseph T. Wilson
Executive Director

SAMPLES OF FESTIVAL COMMUNICATIONS

George M. Holt
Director

Dear Friends,

We are delighted that you will be participating in the 1978 North Carolina Folklife Festival. We look forward to a great event and everyone from the Governor on down is excited about your involvement. Your participation means a lot to us and we hope to make your stay in Durham as comfortable and fun as possible.

Special arrangements for your lodging have been made at Duke University. The University has reserved an entire dormitory quadrangle for our use. You will be assigned a room which best suits your needs, one that is comfortable and well ventilated. However, you may want to bring a small fan along in case of extremely hot weather. Sheets, blankets, pillows, pillowcases, and towels will be provided for you. Bathrooms are conveniently located on each hall.

Breakfast will be served each morning at the dorms. At the festival, you will receive meal tickets for lunches and dinners. There will also be snacks available at the dorms in the evenings.

All of these arrangements have been made at no cost to you.

Because we will be on a tight schedule, it will be important to keep careful track of time. If you are demonstrating a craft, it will be necessary for you to allow sufficient time to set up your materials at the park. Musicians will be provided with a performance schedule so that it will be clear where and when you will be needed. We ask that all musicians arrive at the appropriate stage at least fifteen minutes prior to your performance.

Unless it is simply impossible, please plan to arrive at Duke's West Campus on the afternoon or evening before you are due at the festival. This will eliminate a good bit of confusion and will give you an opportunity to get to know everybody before the festival is in full swing. Our staff will be there to greet you, to help you unload, get settled, and to take care of all needs and problems.

Don't worry about having to find your own way to the festival grounds after you have arrived in Durham. We have chartered special buses for this purpose.

You will hear from us again in late June. We will send a map with directions to the dormitories at Duke, performance schedules, and other important information. If you must come on the day of your performance, come to the dorms first anyway, rather than going directly to the park. We will give you a ride.

There are two things you can do that will really make it easier for us to plan. First, please fill out the enclosed information sheet as soon as possible so that we can make important arrangements with the University. Second, please sign and date one copy of the "letter of agreement" that we have also included. Please return it with the other information. We have included a return envelope for this purpose.

A name for you to know is Julia Morris. She is our hospitality coordinator. Julia will be assisting you at the dorms.

If you have any questions, do not hesitate to call (collect) or write. We have left a space on the return form for this purpose.

We look forward to being with you in July!

Yours,

George Holt, Director

George M. Holt
Director

LETTER OF AGREEMENT

The Undersigned Agrees:

1. to participate in the North Carolina Folklife Festival to be held at Eno River Park in Durham, North Carolina on July 1, 2, 3, and 4, 1978.

2. to grant to the North Carolina Office of Folklife Programs and to the North Carolina Folklife Institute the rights to:

    use the participant's name, photograph, or likeness in any reasonable and appropriate manner and

    record, amplify, reproduce or photograph the participant's vocal and instrumental music or other performances or product and

    publish, distribute, transmit or exhibit the same by any electrical or mechanical means so long as such use is limited to educational and non-profit purposes, and commercial uses for profit requiring the further express approval of the participant.

The Office of Folklife Programs Agrees:

3. to provide suitable lodging at Duke University dormitories or elsewhere;

4. to provide meals;

5. to make every reasonable effort to insure that participants are treated cordially, and that conditions for performances and demonstrations meet with the participant's approval;

6. to pay the undersigned participant an honorarium of _____ which includes travel expenses for his/her participation on _____ of July, 1978, such payment constituting the total financial obligation;

7. this agreement is expressly subject to the additional provision set forth on the back hereof which is hereby made a part of this agreement.

Date _____   FESTIVAL DIRECTOR _____

                                 PARTICIPANT _____

National Council for the Traditional Arts

1346 Conn. Ave., N.W. - 1118
Washington, D.C. 20036
Telephone 202/296-0068

Dear Festival Participant:

We're looking forward to seeing you at the 41st NATIONAL FOLK FESTIVAL at Wolf Trap Farm Park in Vienna, Virginia, July 28 and 29, 1979. This letter should tell you all you need to know until you get to the festival.

Arrival: If you are arriving by plane or train, a festival staff member will meet you and take you to Madeira School. Look for a friendly staffer holding a NATIONAL FOLK FESTIVAL sign. If you are arriving by auto Friday, July 27, come directly to the Madeira School in Greenway, Virginia (map enclosed). If you are arriving by auto Saturday, July 28, or Sunday, July 29, come directly to Wolf Trap (map enclosed). Security personnel at the gate to backstage parking will have your name on a list if you are driving directly to the park from home.

Housing & Food: When you arrive at Madeira, follow the signs to Check In. Bill Kornrich, Jay Udall, or Joe Guice will be in the festival office to take care of you.

Festival participants and staff are invited to attend a buffet supper Friday evening at 7:30 in the Madeira School cafeteria.

From our current information we are arranging housing and food at Madeira School for the following people in your group:

_____ _____ _____
_____ _____ _____
_____ _____ _____

For those of you who have made ADVANCE arrangements with our office for non-performers traveling with you to stay at Madeira, the approximate daily charge for food and housing will be $24. If you have not made advance arrangements, please don't bring additional guests--we have no more space!

Festival Participant Kits: When you arrive at Madeira, pick up your participants' kit in the festival office when you check in. If you are not arriving Friday night or if for some reason you don't get your kit, it will be held for you in the Green Room at Wolf Trap, where you can get it Saturday morning. Your kits contain lunch and dinner meal tickets and tickets for evening concerts. Guard them carefully.

SAMPLES OF FESTIVAL COMMUNICATIONS

Recording and Photographing: See enclosed form.

Telephone Numbers: If you want to leave telephone numbers where you can be reached by your family, they are: Madeira School - (703) 893-2155; Wolf Trap - (703) 938-3810.

Transportation between Madeira and Wolf Trap: Buses will depart Madeira School for Wolf Trap at 9:00 a.m. and 9:45 a.m. Buses will leave Wolf Trap for Madeira after the evening concert. If you must return to Madeira during the day for any reason, please inform Lee Udall or Anne Labovitz in the Green Room and they will arrange transportation. If you do not plan to stay for the evening concert, let Lee or Annie know as early as possible. Vehicles cannot leave the backstage parking area during the performance, so transportation must be planned in advance. Finally, buses will depart Wolf Trap for Madeira after the evening performance. Buses arrive at and depart from the Green Room at Wolf Trap.

Performers' Lounge: There is a comfortable, air-conditioned performers lounge adjoining the Green Room in the Filene Center at Wolf Trap. There will be soft drinks and plenty of chairs for resting. This is also the area where musical instruments and craft work and tools can be locked up when they are not in use.

Saturday Morning Schedule: You'll have to be up bright and early Saturday morning as workshops begin at 11:00 a.m. Breakfast will be served from 7:00-8:00 in the cafeteria and buses will depart for Wolf Trap at 9:00 a.m. and 9:45 a.m.

We hope this takes care of what you need to know. If you have questions, call us at (202) 296-5322. After July 27, we'll be at the Wolf Trap offices. Call (703) 938-3810 and ask for National Folk Festival.

Again, we look foward to seeing you.

JOE WILSON   LEE UDALL   ANNE LABOVITZ

FRANK PROSCHAN   BILL KORNRICH

National Council for the Traditional Arts

1346 Conn. Ave., N.W. - 1118
Washington, D.C. 20036
Telephone 202/296-0068

Dear Festival Participant,

Enclosed please find a few copies of the leaflet we've been sending out to tell people about the National Folk Festival. We'll also have a very nice program book when you get here.

You'll also find enclosed a schedule of the workshops and concerts we have planned for you during the Festival. This is to give you an idea of the kind of things we are going to be presenting. Some of the workshops are 30 minute or 45 minute mini-concerts in which you or your group will be performing for the entire time. Others are workshops which will include musicians from several groups. These will either be planned so that you perform for 15 or 20 minutes sometime during the workshop or you may be on stage for the whole thing, trading songs with the other performers. You may notice some times when you are scheduled for one performance right after another. We will work things out so that you will have the time to get from one to the other.

There may be some changes in this schedule before you arrive. When you get here, we will give you a final schedule. If you have any questions before then, please give us a call. We're all looking forward to your arrival.

Sincerely,

Joe Wilson,
Executive Director

RELEASE

The National Council for the Traditional Arts will be recording all of your performances for archival purposes and for possible future use on records which may be issued by the NCTA. No commercial use of these recordings will be permitted without further permission from you. We will also be taking photographs at the festival which will be used for publicity and program books for future festivals. Following is a release which gives us your permission to make these recordings and photographs. (Don't send back this copy. We will have one for you at the festival.) If you have any questions about this release, or if recording or photographing violates your religious beliefs, please contact Frank Proschan before the festival so that we can be sure there will be no problems.

I, _____ hereby agree that the National Council for the Traditional Arts may photograph and record my performances at the 41st National Folk Festival. These photographs and recordings may be used for educational, non-profit purposes, including festival planning, program books, and publicity. These photographs and recordings may not be used for any commercial, profit-making purposes without my specific permission.

_____
Signature

_____
Date

National Council for the Traditional Arts

1346 Conn. Ave., N.W. - 1118
Washington, D.C. 20036
Telephone 202/296-0068

I _____ hereby agree that the National Council for the Traditional Arts may photograph and record my performances at the 41st National Folk Festival. These photographs and recordings may be used for educational, non-profit purposes, including festival planning, program books, and publicity. These photographs and recordings may not be used for any commercial, profit-making purposes without my specific permission.

_____
Signature

_____
Date

National Council for the Traditional Arts

1346 Conn. Ave., N.W. - 1118
Washington, D.C. 20036
Telephone 202/296-0068

Dear Friends,

After weeks of telephone calls, travel arrangements, letters back and forth, and, we hope, a pleasant journey to Washington, it is good to finally welcome you to the 41st National Folk Festival. The next few days will be busy for all of us, so we want to take a moment right now to tell you how grateful we are that you are here to join with us in celebrating America's rich cultural heritage. We hope that you don't run into any problems while you're here; but if you do, please let one of our staff members know so that we can do whatever is possible to solve it. Listed below are a few things we want to let you know about the festival.

Buses between Madeira and Wolf Trap

We have very limited parking at Wolf Trap, so we must ask everyone to leave their cars at Madeira and take the bus.

Buses will leave Madeira School each morning at 9:00 a.m. and 9:45 a.m. to go to Wolf Trap. They will return to Madeira after the evening concert, so plan to spend the full day at the festival. If you need to return to Madeira any time during the day, or you would rather not stay for the evening concert, please tell Lee Udall or Anne Labovitz in the Green Room at the Filene Center so that they can arrange transportation. (Wolf Trap will not allow cars to leave during the evening concert; if you don't plan to stay until the performance is over, you must leave before it begins.)

Buses will leave Madeira School from the circle. They will leave Wolf Trap from the parking lot immediately behind the Green Room at the Filene Center.

Meals

Breakfast is served at Madeira from 7:30 to 8:30 a.m. in the cafeteria. Lunch is served at Wolf Trap from 11:30 to 1:00 in the dinner tent at the top of the hill. Supper is served at the dinner tent from 5:30 to 7:30. There are tickets for both meals in your participant kit. You must have these tickets to be served lunch and dinner. There will also be sodas at each of the stages and in the crafts tent, and snacks available in the Participants' Lounge under the Filene Center. We will also have snacks available at Madeira after the evening concerts.

Participants' Lounge

On the ground floor level of the Filene Center, next to the Green Room, there is a Participants' Lounge. This is a comfortable, air-conditioned room which will be provided with soft drinks, snacks, and plenty of chairs. This is also where you will be able to leave your instruments or tools while you are not using them. (Please don't leave your valuable instruments out on the grounds unattended. Instrument theft is a common problem at large festivals. The festival staff at the stages can watch your instruments for a short while, but don't leave them unattended or in the hands of people you do not know.)

Badges and Tickets

Your name badge is enclosed. This serves as your pass onto the grounds and identifies you to everyone. Please wear it whenever you are at Wolf Trap. There are also tickets for the evening concerts in your kit. If you do not plan to use these tickets, please turn them in to the Green Room as early as possible so that we can give them to someone else. It looks like we may sell out the concerts, so please return any tickets you won't be using so that someone can see the concert who would otherwise be turned away.

Program Books and Tee-Shirts

If you would like to have more program books as souvenirs of the festival, please go to the Sales/Concessions tent at Wolf Trap. You will be able to purchase extra copies for 50¢ apiece. There are also very nice festival tee-shirts available at the sales tent. There is a special price for staff and participants of $3.00. You must show your name badge when you buy the shirts to receive the special discount.

Washington Friends and Relatives

In order to be sure that you and others are not bothered by hangerson, drunks, and others who have no business there, we have guards at the Madeira gates. If you have relatives or friends in Washington who want to visit you at Madeira, please leave their names in the festival office so they will be admitted.

Schedule

You should have received a schedule in the mail of the workshops and concerts we have planned for you. Another copy is enclosed, which may have a few changes from what you received before. This schedule is the latest information on what is planned. If for any reason you think you will not be able to make it to a workshop we have planned for you, please let Joe Wilson or Mike Holmes in the Green Room know. They will make arrangements with the Stage Managers. Don't just pass on a message to someone - make sure you talk to Joe or Mike so there won't be any confusion. If you

Schedule - Continued

are scheduled for an evening concert, it is very important that you get to the sound check at the time scheduled. We are running the sound checks on a very tight schedule and we won't have time to go back and do someone we miss.

Uninvited Performers

One of the problems we have at the National is keeping non-scheduled performers off the stages. Many musicians who are not booked on the festival come to it as members of the audience or work as members of festival staff. We are pleased that so many musicians like this festival and come to it even though they are not booked on it as performers. They are most welcome and they help make it happen. However, if even ten percent of these musicians get on stage as "guests," we would not have time for you, the people we have carefully selected for our program.

The only way we can deal with this is to put on stage ONLY those people we have hired to play. No exceptions. We spend several months planning the festival, and we know who we want to perform. If someone tells you that they want to join in one of your workshops or performances, tell them that you're sorry, but that it can't be done. If that's not enough, tell them that the only person who can give that permission is the festival director, Joe Wilson, and send them to Joe. It will help a lot if you will remember this rule and hold strictly to it.

          Sincerely,

          Joe Wilson
          Festival Director

(alternate for craftspersons)

Crafts

  Jack Loeffler will set up and break down the crafts tent on Saturday and Sunday. He will store your craft work and tools in a secure, locked space in the participants' lounge area. Please speak to Jack or Kathy if you have questions about overnight storage.

  Kathy Loeffler and Ekbal Kornrich will be in the craft tent most of the time during exhibition hours. When you want to go to the participants' lounge to rest or have to leave the craft tent for any reason, please tell Kathy, Ekbal, or one of the staff persons assigned to the craft tent. They will assign someone to watch your things while you are away.

  If you want to take orders from people at the festival, ask Kathy, Ekbal, or one of their assistants for an order form and they will fill it out.

  Again, we're glad you're here and the festival staff is ready to assist you and make your visit a pleasant one.

          Sincerely,

          Joe Wilson
          Festival Director

SAMPLES OF FESTIVAL COMMUNICATIONS

National Council for the Traditional Arts

1346 Conn. Ave., N.W. - 1118
Washington, D.C. 20036
Telephone 202/296-0068

NATIONAL FOLK FESTIVAL INFORMATION

Here is some information which may be helpful to you in planning for the festival. In mid-June you will receive your daily schedule and final details.

1. Evening concerts will begin at 8:00 p.m. Please report backstage at the Filene Center one-half hour before concert time. There will be a "mike" rehearsal at 4 p.m. each concert day. All performers will be expected to attend on the day of their evening performance.

2. Plan approximately 20 minutes for your part of the evening concert. This is very important to its success.

3. There will be four daytime concert areas equipped with stages, sound systems, and three or four microphones, with a sound technician and staff member at each area. Plan to appear in several workshops during the festival, including a forty-five minute concert by your group. Workshops will be from 1 p.m. to 5 p.m. each day. Please report to your workshop area 15 minutes before you are scheduled to perform.

4. You will be housed and fed at Madeira School, a small private school located about 10 minutes away from the Festival in the Virginia countryside. If you wish to stay elsewhere, you may do so, but the festival will pay for food and housing only at Madeira and if you wish to stay elsewhere, it must be at your expense.

5. We ask that you bring only the regular members of your group to Washington. The space at Madeira is very limited and housing and food is expensive here, so we cannot accommodate guests and friends at this location.

6. Because Wolf Trap is a National Park, we must abide by National Park Service regulations concerning all activities there. The records of groups performing at the festival may be sold, for example, but they must be sold only at the one record sales tent which will be operated by the NCTA. If you wish to have your records sold on the

festival grounds, they will be sold at the price you set, and all cash proceeds will be given to you. All other sales are strictly regulated and most are forbidden.

7. Most performers drive to the festival and we pay a roundtrip fee based on Rand McNally mileage and government per diem reimbursement and we pay for meals. If you are so far away that flying is necessary, we'll provide roundtrip tickets which we buy and send to you. If you have any special travel problems, please let us know. We will meet you at the airport, train or bus station if you let us know your arrival time in advance.

8. You'll be paid for your performance and travel expenses at the festival by check. Because it is difficult to cash checks on weekends, please bring enough money with you to pay your expenses back home. If you're worried about checks or have money problems this year, let us know <u>two weeks before the festival</u> and we'll make arrangements <u>to have your check cashed before</u> the festival is over. It is easy for us to do this, <u>but only if we know in advance</u> that you'll need cash.

9. In late June you'll receive a performer's packet which will give you more information and directions.

10. Do you have photographs of you or your group? <u>Send them to us</u>! Do you have any newspaper clippings or <u>press releases about</u> your group? <u>Send them too</u>! These things will help us make you better known and the festival more attractive.

11. Confused by any of this? Have any problems? Let us know and we'll work it out.

SAMPLES OF FESTIVAL COMMUNICATIONS

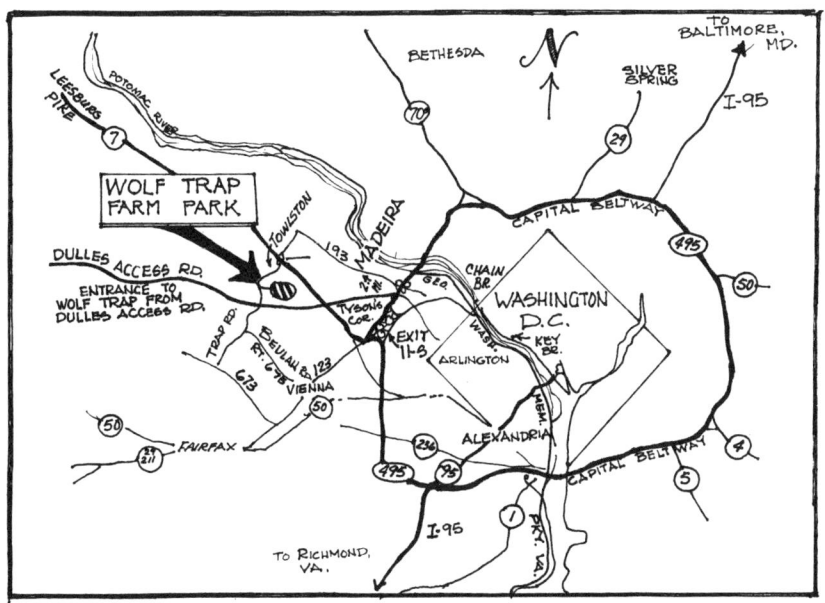

DIRECTIONS TO MADEIRA SCHOOL

TAKE INTERSTATE #495 (CAPITAL BELTWAY) to ROUTE #193 TOWARD GREAT FALLS, VA. (AT EXIT #13) - GO APPROXIMATELY 2.4 MILES - TURN RIGHT AT THE WHITE GUARD HOUSE. NOTE: MADEIRA'S MAIN GATE IS LOCKED AT MIDNIGHT! FOR THOSE UNABLE TO ARRIVE BEFORE THAT TIME, A TELEPHONE IS LOCATED ON A POLE NEAR THE GATE TO BE USED IN CALLING THE SECURITY GUARD (DIAL 60) FOR THE GATE TO BE OPENED. (THIS ONLY WHEN INITIAL ARRIVAL CANNOT BE MADE BEFORE MIDNIGHT -- NOT FOR USE DURING THE FESTIVAL!)

DIRECTIONS TO WOLF TRAP (FILENE CENTER) WILL BE AT MADEIRA SCHOOL OR IF NECESSARY TO GO THERE FIRST, USE THE MAP ABOVE.

National Council for the Traditional Arts

1346 Conn. Ave., N.W. - 1118
Washington, D.C. 20036
Telephone 202/296-0068

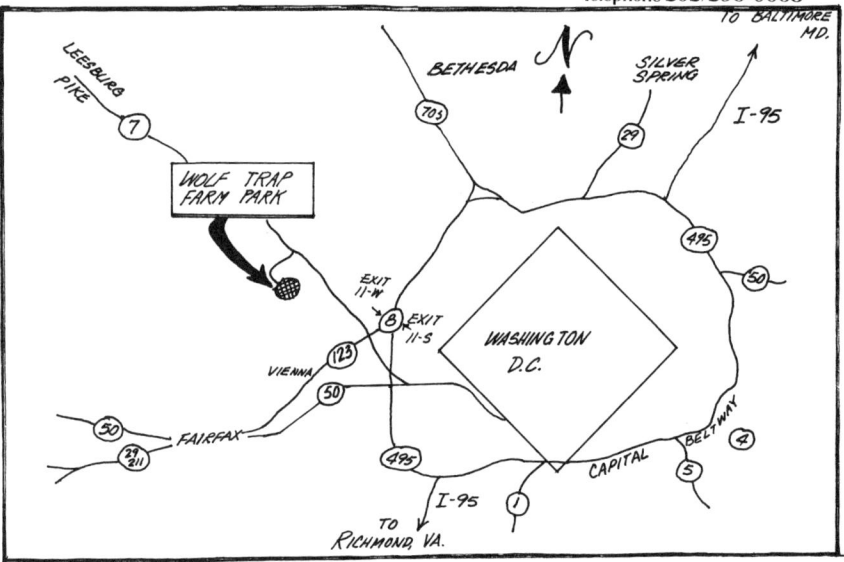

There is NO CAMPING on the festival grounds. The nearest public camping facility can be contacted through the following address:

> Fairfax County Park Authority
> Box 236
> Annandale, VA 22003
> (703) 941-5000

Motels in the Vienna, Virginia area are:

Falls Church Motor Hotel
421 West Broad Street
Falls Church, VA 22046
(703) 533-1100

Vienna Wolf Trap Motel
420 Maple Avenue
Vienna, VA 22180
(703) 281-2330

> Stratford Motor Lodge
> 300 West Broad Street
> Falls Church, VA 22046
> (703) 534-4660

SAMPLES OF FESTIVAL COMMUNICATIONS

National Council for the Traditional Arts

1346 Conn. Ave., N.W. - 1118
Washington, D.C. 20036
Telephone 202/296-0068

42nd NATIONAL FOLK FESTIVAL, July 11-13, 1980
PARTICIPANT INFORMATION SHEET

Name_____

Address_____

City, State, Zip_____

Phone_____(Groups, please attach list with name, address,
　(Area code)　　　　 and telephone number of each member.)

TRAVEL

1. What date do you plan to arrive?_____Depart?_____
2. How do you plan to travel? CAR____BUS____TRAIN____PLANE____
   (Plane reservations will be made by this office.)
3. How many people will be in your group, including yourself?_____
   (Advance arrangements must be made for non-participants and you must pay expenses.)

TECHNICAL

1. Do you require chairs or stools? If so, which and how many?_____
2. How many microphones do you need?_____
3. Do you need amplifiers of any sort?____What kind?_____
4. Do you need a piano?_____
5. Any special requirements or equipment?_____

OTHER

1. Are you a member of the American Federation of Musicians Union?
   _____. Which local?_____(Groups, please attach
   list of all members.)

2. Will you need a dressing room?____For how many people?____
3. Can you suggest any workshops you could lead or take part in?
   _____
4. Anything else you'd like to know?_____
   _____

PLEASE RETURN THIS FORM TO NCTA, Room 1118, 1346 Connecticut Ave., NW, Washington D.C. 20036

SAMPLES OF FESTIVAL COMMUNICATIONS

National Council for the Traditional Arts

1346 Conn. Ave., N.W. - 1118
Washington, D.C. 20036
Telephone 202/296-0068

39TH NATIONAL FOLK FESTIVAL CRAFT AREA
PARTICIPANT INFORMATION SHEET

Name _____

Address _____

City, State, Zip _____

Phone _____
     (Area Code)

TRAVEL

1. What date do you plan to arrive: _____

                           Depart? _____

   Housing provided at Madeira School for out of town participants, July 29 & 30.

   Do you plan to stay at Madeira? _____

2. How do you plan to travel? BUS _____   TRAIN _____
                                 PLANE _____   CAR _____

3. Do you want this office to make travel reservations? ____

4. How many people will be in your group, including yourself?

   _____ (Advance arrangements must be made for non-participants and you must pay expenses.)

TECHNICAL

1. How many tables (2' x 8') will you need? _____

2. How many chairs will you need? _____

3. Are there any materials we will have to supply? _____

4. Will you need electricity? _____

Please list your name, where you are from and what you will be doing at the festival, so that we may make a sign for your exhibit: _____
_____
_____
_____

Any other questions or comments?

SAMPLES OF FESTIVAL COMMUNICATIONS

National Council for the Traditional Arts

1346 Conn. Ave., N.W. - 1118
Washington, D.C. 20036
Telephone 202/296-0068

For those of you who have friends and relatives coming to see you at the festival, here is a list of motels in the vicinity of the festival site. Please be advised that there is no public transportation in the area.

Please make reservations yourself, or write us specifics and we will call and make them for you. You or your friends are responsible for paying all bills.

MOTELS IN THE VIENNA, VIRGINIA AREA

Falls Church Motor Hotel
421 West Broad Street
Falls Church, VA 22046
(703) 533-1100

Vienna Wolf Trap Motel
420 Maple Avenue
Vienna, VA   22180
(703) 281-2330

Stratford Motor Lodge
300 W. Broad
Falls Church, VA 22046
(703) 534-4660

THERE IS NO CAMPING ON THE FESTIVAL GROUNDS - The nearest public camping facility can be contacted through the following address:

Fairfax County Park Authority
Box 236
Annandale, VA 22003
(703) 941-5000

National Council for the Traditional Arts

1346 Conn. Ave., N.W. - 1118
Washington, D.C. 20036
Telephone 202/296-0068

Greetings:

Glad you will here with us this year at Wolf Trap Farm Park.

We are all working hard to ensure that the 39th National Folk Festival is a stimulating event.

Listed below are the activities for which you are currently scheduled. If you have any questions or problems with this schedule, please feel free to write or call our office. You will be notified if there are any last minute changes.

There will be a complete workshop and performance schedule in the performers' area, so you can attend any of the events that interest you. There will also be an open mike stage on the grounds where you can stop by and perform as the spirit moves you.

See you soon.

Sincerely,

Joseph T. Wilson
Executive Director

ACTIVITY   TIME & DAY   PLACE

SAMPLES OF FESTIVAL COMMUNICATIONS

National Council for the Traditional Arts

1346 Conn. Ave., N.W. - 1118
Washington, D.C. 20036
Telephone 202/296-0068

Dear Friend:

Welcome to the 39th National Folk Festival. Following are some basic points of information.

We encourage and ask everyone to leave their cars here and take the bus over to Wolf Trap and back.

Buses leave Madeira at 11:00 and 11:30 in the morning. They will return at 11:00 and 11:45 at night.

If you miss the bus for any reason or wish to be transported back to Madeira School from Wolf Trap, contact the person working in the NCTA office in the Green Room of the Filene Center or the NCTA office at Madeira.

Breakfast is served at Madeira from 8:30 - 10:00 on Friday and Saturday and from 9:30 - 11:30 on Sunday morning.

Lunch is served from 11:30 - 1:00 on the Wolf Trap grounds in the dinner tent on the top of the hill. Dinner is also served in the dinner tent from 5:45 - 7:15.

Enclosed is your participant badge. This serves as your pass onto the grounds, into dinner, etc., as well as identifying you to everyone. Please wear it at all times.

If you have any problems or questions at any time during the festival, please go to the Green Room at the Filene Center or the office at Madeira. Someone there will help you or put you in touch with someone who can help you.

ENJOY!

PERFORMANCE SCHEDULE

PLEASE ARRIVE 15 MINUTES BEFORE EACH WORKSHOP. IF TRANSPORTATION IS NEEDED, PLEASE CONTACT STAGE MANAGERS OR GREEN ROOM STAFF.

DAY	TIMES	AREA	TITLE OF PERFORMANCE	CONTACT PERSON

National Council for the Traditional Arts

1346 Conn. Ave., N.W. - 1118
Washington, D.C. 20036
Telephone 202/296-0068

    Now that we've had a chance to rest up a little, we can look back and remember how successful and enjoyable the 41st National Folk Festival was for all of us. Our ticket sales and attendance were higher than ever, our coverage in the newspapers was good, and the reaction of our audience was excellent. But, most importantly, we had a good time working on it, and we hope you shared that experience. This was truly one of the easiest and most enjoyable festivals we've ever worked on - and much of the credit for that must go to our participants. You were always cooperative and good-spirited, willing to do whatever we asked. We can hardly think of a complaint or a problem that we couldn't solve for you, and none of us can think of a cross word that was spoken. We hope that you also remember the festival as an enjoyable event.

    Enclosed you will find a certificate expressing our appreciation for your taking part in the National Folk Festival. It is only a small token of our gratitude and thanks for your participation, but one that we know you will cherish. Again, thank you very much. We all hope that we will have another chance to see you.

                          Cordially,

Joe Wilson	Lee Udall	Anne Labovitz
	Frank Proschan	Bill Kornrich

*The Board of Directors of
The National Council for the Traditional Arts, Inc.
expresses its deep appreciation to*

---

*for contributing through outstanding performance
to the success of the
42nd National Folk Festival
held July 11 – 13, 1980
at Wolf Trap Farm Park
Vienna, Virginia*

Chairman of the Board   *Director of the Festival*

SAMPLES OF FESTIVAL COMMUNICATIONS

FOR STAFF

National Council for the Traditional Arts

1346 Conn. Ave., N.W. - 1118
Washington, D.C. 20036
Telephone 202/296-0068

Dear

It is time to line up our staff for the 41st National Folk Festival and we are pleased you plan to work with us. I feel it is important that we know what to expect from each other and the nature of the work to be done.

I'll start by saying I'm sure you won't be assigned to a job which will make use of your academic training or intellectual abilities. There is more lugging, tugging, and carrying to be done than thinking, contemplating, and learning. And although everyone (including me) would prefer to work with the performers all the time, there is food to be served, fences to be watched, programs and records to be sold, recording logs to keep, and the like. There is time for fun and our after-festival parties are great.

Some of you will be asked to work from 10:00 a.m. until 7:00 p.m. Others may be asked to work evening shifts. You may be able to trade jobs, but in general we prefer that people stay with the tasks assigned them.

Housing and food is expensive and we pay for every festival pass, so we cannot afford unexpected guests. We hope your friends will come to the festival, but please don't ask us to assume the cost of feeding, housing, or obtaining tickets for them.

Whatever the job assigned to you, I hope you will assume a measure of responsibility which goes beyond it. The people who will be performing for us are carriers of folk traditions and many are older people who have preserved the arts and customs of an earlier age. They deserve our assistance and loving respect.

I would like to call your attention to the following:

1. All staff members should check into Madeira School by 8:30 a.m. Saturday, July 28.

2. You will be assigned to _____

3. Housing arrangements:

    _____ We have NOT planned housing for you.

    _____ You are to be housed at Madeira School. Expect to share your room with another person we will assign.

4. Food arrangements:

   _____ We have made no arrangements to feed you.

   _____ Breakfast provided at Madeira.

   _____ Lunch on your own (there are concessions at the site).

   _____ Lunch provided at performers tent.

   _____ Dinner on your own.

   _____ Dinner provided at performers tent (only for those working late night snack provided at Madeira.)

5. Parking

   Please note that backstage parking is very limited and will be controlled by the National Park Service. Also, there is no movement of automobiles in or out of the backstage area after the evening performance begins. We will provide bus service between Madeira and Wolf Trap at convenient intervals.

6. Some of you must be prepared to come to a staff planning meeting in Washington approximately one month before the festival begins. Are you in this category? _____

If you have any questions, please call us at (202) 296-0068 or (202) 296-5322. The phones are busy this time of year, so please be patient.

With my appreciation and best regards.

                                        Sincerely,

                                        Joe Wilson
                                        Executive Director

SAMPLES OF FESTIVAL COMMUNICATIONS

National Council for the Traditional Arts

1346 Conn. Ave., N.W. - 1118
Washington, D.C. 20036
Telephone 202/296-0068

39TH NATIONAL FOLK FESTIVAL VOLUNTEERS
HERE IS WHAT NEEDS TO BE DONE . . .

Please circle the jobs you'd like (or would be willing) to do at the festival or before. Be sure to indicate days and time available under each item. We especially need folks who can work the same job all three days. This year I would like some help coordinating the volunteers, which will require dependability and time commitment. If you are interested, please indicate this when listing experience on the back.

HOSPITALITY:

1. Participant assistance and check in. (Thurs. at Madeira; 2 1/2 hour shifts from 10 a.m. to 8 p.m. at Wolf Trap, Friday, Saturday, Sunday; Monday at Madeira)

2. Lunch aides (daily, 11 a.m. to 1:30 p.m.)

3. Supper check in (Fri. & Sat., 1 hour)

TRANSPORTATION: (18 years of age minimum)

1. Driving to and from airports, bus and train stations. Station wagons and vans are helpful but not a requirement. Circle days and times available: Thurs., Fri., Sat., Sun., & Mon.; morning, afternoon, evening; car size_____

WORKSHOP AND CRAFT AREAS:

1. Early set-up crews. (Thurs. July 15)
   Post festival take-down crew. (Mon. July 19)

2. Morning set up crew for stages, sound equipment, crafts area, etc. daily 11:00 to 1:00.

3. Afternoon take down crew. (Daily 5:00 to 7:00; after dance party 7:00 to 8:00, Fri. & Sat.)

4. Assistant to music stage manager. (Daily 12:45 to 3:15; 3:00 to 5:30)

5. Cataloging -- listing contents of workshops to go with tape recordings. (Daily 12:45 to 3:15; 3:00 to 5:30).

6. Craft area aides: Doll Making and Instrument Building. We would like to assign volunteers to work with a particular craftsman throughout the festival (2 to 3 hours per day, times to be arranged.)

SUPPORT TO FESTIVAL PUBLIC:

1. Program and record sales and/or service in the information booth. (Daily 12:30 to 3:00, 3:00 to 5:30; 7:00 to 8:30 and intermission.)

2. Fence watchers: To gently discourage fence jumpers between daily events and the evening concert. (6:30 to 8:30, Fri. and Sat.) You won't miss any festival workshops.

SUPPORT TO FESTIVAL STAFF:

1. Distribute posters and brochures before the festival. Needed badly! Area _____. Do you have any special contacts that we could use to publicize the festival?

2. Festival office help before _____, during _____, and after _____ the festival. We would like to have 2-3 special helpers to train in the office before the festival to relieve the office staff.

3. Runners, drivers and intercom operators to be on call in the festival office at Wolf Trap.

NAME _____ AGE _____

PHONE _____

ADDRESS _____
        STREET   CITY   STATE   ZIP

PLEASE INDICATE AS WELL, ANY AREAS OF SPECIAL INTEREST AND EXPERTISE.

SAMPLES OF FESTIVAL COMMUNICATIONS

National Council for the Traditional Arts

1346 Conn. Ave., N.W. - 1118
Washington, D.C. 20036
Telephone 202/296-0068

Dear Friend,

We're glad that you will be joining us for the 40th National Folk Festival to be held at Wolf Trap Park for the Performing Arts in Vienna, Virginia, July 28-30.

This letter is to confirm all arrangements concerning your assistance to us at the festival.

JOB ASSIGNMENTS

_____

_____

The above is your job assignment. Unless you make arrangements with us in advance, we cannot change your job. You are responsible to be on that assignment at the time specified. If there is any question about this, please let us know.

HOUSING AND FOOD

We will provide lunch and dinner on the festival grounds for our staff. However, in some cases you will be asked to wait until later in the dinner hour until most of the performers have eaten. We are expecting to use meal tickets this year which you will receive when you check in. We cannot provide food or housing for any unexpected guests or friends of staff members.

The participants are housed at Madeira School in Greenway, Virginia, near the festival grounds. We have limited space for staff members to stay at Madeira. Local staff are asked to stay at home. Those of you who are travelling from out of town, we may house for Friday and Saturday nights. If you are coming from a distance and it is necessary for you to stay on either Thursday or Sunday night, please let us know in advance. We have limited housing on those nights. Those staying at Madeira will receive breakfast there.

Late night snacks are served at Madeira School for the performers. All staff members who wish a late night snack will be requested to buy a ticket for $2.75. Tickets will be available at Madeira and in the festival office in the Green Room at Wolf Trap. You will not be served without a ticket.

The following is the arrangement we have for you concerning food and housing:

_____

_____

COMPLIMENTARY TICKETS

We receive a limited number of complimentary tickets to the evening concerts. The rest of the tickets we pay for. The complimentary tickets will be given out to performers first. It is possible that we may ask staff members to purchase their ticket for the evening concert at a cost of approximately 60¢. You will be notified of the policy concerning this when you arrive at the festival.

PARKING

Please note that backstage parking is very limited. When you arrive at Wolf Trap, you will have to receive a parking pass to be admitted to the backstage parking lot. Staff members will be on a list at the gate. Give your name to the park guard if you are stopped. Also, there is no movement of automobiles in or out of the backstage area after the evening performance begins. We will provide bus service between Madeira and Wolf Trap at convenient intervals.

I hope this provides any information you may need to know for now. You will receive any other pertinent information when you arrive at the festival.

If you have any questions, please call us at (202) 296-5322 or (202) 296-0068.

We are glad you will be joining us for the 40th National Folk Festival.

                              Sincerely,

                              Joseph T. Wilson
                              Executive Director

SAMPLES OF FESTIVAL COMMUNICATIONS

National Council for the Traditional Arts

1346 Conn. Ave., N.W. - 1118
Washington, D.C. 20036
Telephone 202/296-0068

INSTRUCTIONS FOR RECORDING TECHNICIANS

1. Record tapes in one direction only. Leave them wound tails out. Record at 7.5 i.p.s. Use a wax pencil to mark each reel with the date, area, and reel. Mark each box, along the spine, with the following information in this order:

   DAY/DATE   AREA   REEL   OF

2. Please be sure that the logger is properly filling out the logging forms. If there is no logger, or the logger is not doing the job, let the stage manager know immediately. Work out an interim arrangement with the assistant stage manager while we are sending a replacement.

3. You should be at the sound/recording headquarters by 8:30 Saturday morning to pick up your recorder, tapes, and to go with your stage crew to help set up the sound system.

4. The equipment that you are using is portable professional equipment on loan to the NCTA and is delicate and expensive. Treat it gently and be certain that it is not abused by others. Regular cleaning of the heads is important, so when there is a lengthy break between workshops, grab your swabs and alcohol.

5. Keep an eye on the recording level meters. Very important!! Don't be afraid of occasional peaks into the red portion of the meter scale. Professional recorders are more tolerant of overload than are home recorders, and it's better to have an occasional overload than to have everything recorded at such a low level that it is masked by hiss and noise. Of course, if the meter is running into the red all the time, you've got it set too high. If it never gets above -6, it's set too low. Try to keep your adjustments smooth, and try to make them between selections rather than during a song. During a song, you can touch up the setting, but please keep the fiddling to a minimum. Don't get knob happy and ride the controls all the time.

6. If there's a break between workshops, and your heads are recently cleaned, take a minute to play back a few seconds of the last song you recorded. It is often very difficult to hear distortion while you are recording, but very easy when there is no other noise.

7. If you hear nothing but foot-stomping, let the sound technician know so that the mikes can be repositioned or somehow isolated from the foot-stomping. In listening to tapes from past festivals, the major problems have been distortion and foot-stomping.

8. Richard Derbyshire is in charge of recording. Mike Rivers is assisting with technical trouble-shooting. Contact the Green Room immediately if you have problems and one of them will respond. Don't wait until you run out of tape before calling the Green Room and asking for more.

SAMPLES OF FESTIVAL COMMUNICATIONS

National Council for the Traditional Arts

1346 Conn. Ave., N.W. - 1118
Washington, D.C. 20036
Telephone 202/296-0068

41st NATIONAL FOLK FESTIVAL

JULY 28 and 29, 1979

TAPE LOGGING INSTRUCTIONS

Your equipment consists of a supply of logging forms (sample attached), a spiral notebook, carbon paper, ball-point pens, and ears. Everything except the ears you will pick up from the sound/recording headquarters in the performer's lounge under the Filene Center, and they should be returned there at the end of the day.

Your responsibility is to keep track of what is going onto the tape recordings, who's doing what, who's playing which instruments, etc. If you do your job well, and the tapes are logged while they are being recorded, the tapes can be used easily and conveniently for the various purposes for which they are being made. If the tapes aren't logged, an immense amount of additional work is involved before they can be used for anything.

Each tape should be logged on a new form. Attach a carbon to the form and attach both to the spiral notebook, so that you will have two copies of the log. As each log is completed, the original should be TAPED to the inside of the tape box. The notebook will be returned Saturday night to the sound/recording headquarters and you will receive the same notebook Sunday morning. The top part of the form is self-evident. Fill in ALL of the information requested, as shown on the completed sample attached.

The bottom half of the forms is where the logs will be written. The format for the logs is shown on the attached sample. The information needed is:

Name of program, workshop, concert
Name of performer(s); who plays what; who sings;
    Song titles; changes in personnel or instrumentation

The songs should be numbered in one sequence for each tape, regardless of how many times performers change. If there is a long period of talking or introduction, note that but do not number it. If a song is incomplete, at the beginning or end of a reel, it still gets a number, but note that it is incomplete. If there are a number of vocalists in a group, but the lead vocal rotates, note which person is singing for a particular song. Note whether a song is an instrumental or a vocal song. If there are a number of solo performers on a song-swap, list them all and then note, beside each song, who is the performer. The attached sample should include almost every possible situation you will encounter.

It is important that you try to get every song title. With many performers, this will not be easy, either because they don't introduce the songs or the titles are not in English. Immediately after each workshop, find the performer, introduce yourself and ask for the titles that you missed. It is much easier for you to get the title when it is fresh in the performer's mind than it is for us to try to figure things out months later. Get help from the stage manager or assistant stage manager if you need to get song titles and you also are busy logging the next performance.

NEATNESS COUNTS

SAMPLES OF FESTIVAL COMMUNICATIONS

National Council for the Traditional Arts

1346 Conn. Ave., N.W. - 1118
Washington, D.C. 20036
Telephone 202/296-0068

41st NATIONAL FOLK FESTIVAL - 1979

TAPE LOG

DAY/DATE   AREA   REEL   OF

SOUND TECHNICIAN: STARTING TIME:

RECORDING TECHNICIAN: ENDING TIME:

LOGGER:

PROGRAMS:

NEATNESS COUNTS!!

National Council for the Traditional Arts

1346 Conn. Ave., N.W. - 1118
Washington, D.C. 20036
Telephone 202/296-0068

41st NATIONAL FOLK FESTIVAL - 1979

TAPE LOG

DAY/DATE: SATURDAY, JULY 29, 1972   AREA: 2   REEL: 4 OF 7

SOUND TECHNICIAN: OLIVER CROMWELL   STARTING TIME: 2:15
RECORDING TECHNICIAN: NAPOLEON BONAPARTE   ENDING TIME: 3:00
LOGGER: ROSE MARY WOODS
PROGRAMS: BLUES CONCERT; BALLAD SWAP

BLUES CONCERT
SAM CHATMON, VCL, GTR; SANDY HERFORTH, FIDDLE
 1. CORRINNE, CORRINNA - INCOMPLETE
 2. SITTING ON TOP OF THE WORLD - VCL.
 3. ST. LOUIS BLUES - INSTRUMENTAL

HARMONICA FRANK FLOYD, VCL, GTR, HCA.
 4. ROCKIN' CHAIR DADDY - VCL, GTR, HCA
 5. POOR GIRL BLUES - VCL, GTR.
 6. SNORTIN' THE BLUES - VCL, HCA.
 7. BLUE YODEL - INST., HCA, GTR.

BANAD SWAP
NORMAN KENNEDY, VCL; ALMEDA RIDDLE, VCL; LOU KILLEN, VCL.
 8. THE GYPSIES - NORMAN KENNEDY, VCL.
 9. BLACK JACK DAVY - ALMEDA RIDDLE, VCL.
 10. THE BOLD PRINCESS ROYAL - LOU KILLEN, VCL.
 11. MERRY GOLDEN TREE - ALMEDA RIDDLE, VCL. - INCOMPLETE

SAMPLES OF FESTIVAL COMMUNICATIONS

National Council for the Traditional Arts

1346 Conn. Ave., N.W. - 1118
Washington, D.C. 20036
Telephone 202/296-0068

MEMORANDUM TO: Claire St. Jacques, Tom Rother, Ralph Hoffman

FROM: Joe Wilson

SUBJECT: Timetable - 40th National Folk Festival

Thursday, July 27

10:00 AM -- Site preparation begins. Tent locations staked out. NFF crew sets up tents, signs, stage coverings, NPS crew sets up stages, one blue & white concession tent. Sound crew tests equipment. (Sound equipment will be locked in boxes in Theatre in Woods & Meadow tent.)

4:00 PM -- Move office equipment, program books, records, to locked storage unit in Filene Center.

Friday, July 28

9:00 AM -- Move into Green Room. Sound crews set up staging areas, NPS crew distributes tables, chairs, water coolers, rope off areas.

10:00 AM -- NPS security person at front gate and Filene Center entrance
-- Site security staff reports to posts
-- Press room open

11:30 AM -- Box office open
Security staff at work (NPS & NFF)
-- Lunch served in Dinner Tent

12:00 -- Kiosk set up for information and program book sale
-- Concession booth set up

1:00 PM -- Program begins -- all areas open

4:00 PM -- Begin first sound checks

5:00 PM -- End first sound checks
          -- Break down kiosk (store program books in Green Room)

5:30 PM -- Dance party, Area 3

6:00-7:30-- Dinner in Tent

6:30-7:00-- Late sound checks

8:00-11:00- Evening concert in Filene Center

12:00 PM -- All NFF staff and performers clear of Filene Center

Saturday, July 29

Same as Friday

11:30 PM -- Sound crew breaks down equipment on main stage

Sunday, July 30

Same as Friday

11:00 AM -- Box Office opens

12:30 PM -- Programs begin, all areas open

5:00 PM -- All areas close, clear Green Room

5:00 PM -- Dance Party

National Council for the Traditional Arts

1346 Conn. Ave., N.W. - 1118
Washington, D.C. 20036
Telephone 202/296-0068

41st NATIONAL FOLK FESTIVAL
July 28 & 29, 1979

GENERAL INSTRUCTIONS TO STAGE MANAGERS

AND ASSISTANT MANAGERS

You have been assigned to a stage area. The crew at your area is as follows:

    STAGE AREA #_____   STAGE MANAGER:
                                          ASSISTANT MANAGER:
                                            SOUND:
                                            RECORDING:
                                            LOGGING:
                                            SALES
                                            REPRESENTATIVE:

1. Keep your stage on schedule. A concert or workshop which runs overtime is likely to interfere with programming on other stages as your performers are likely to be scheduled elsewhere. Starting on time is one way to assure that you have time enough to complete a workshop. THIS IS IMPORTANT!

2. Read the festival program book. It contains information about each performer. The amount of information varies because we know some better than others, but there is sufficient information to provide an introduction to any performer.

3. Try to establish some rapport with each performer you'll introduce before the workshop or concert featuring this person. Even a brief conversation and a few questions about their art shortly before going onstage is preferable to a "cold" introduction and will help put performers at ease.

4. Keep unscheduled non-festival performers off stage. Every audience includes some would-be performers and a few are aggressive enough to attempt to interject themselves into the performance and this should be firmly discouraged. Occasionally such a person will approach a performer and request inclusion in his or her part of a workshop or concert. Such requests place the performer in an awkward position and are difficult to refuse. If a non-festival performer tells you that he has secured the approval of a performer, respond by telling him or her that such programming decisions are made by the programming staff and are generally refused. If the person is insistent, refer them to festival headquarters.

Keep your own staff professional in this regard. Most of
the people working on this festival are performers of one
kind or another, but only festival participants are booked
as performers. Yes, this rule applies even if a performer
asks a stage worker to join a performance. They may not
know the philosophy of this festival. We do. Also, we'll
have opportunities to jam at Madeira.

The purpose of these rules is to keep hangers-on and non-
festival performers off stage. It should not restrict the
normal give and take of a festival and occasionally a festival performer who is not part of a particular workshop may
join a fellow festival performer. Use your judgment in
such cases.

5. Be sensitive to on-stage performer needs. We'll try to
provide you with an assessment of each performer which indicates the amount of on-stage guidance we feel the performer
may need from you and this will range from zero to your
introducing each song, dance or story and eliciting personal information from the performer. However, our knowledge of these performers varies, and in some cases you
will need to use your own judgment If a performer seems,
worried or not at ease, don't hesitate to move in and
help him or her. Conversely, if you feel yourself becoming
an encumbrance, turn it over to the performer.

6. Do some planning on your own for each workshop. We're hoping
to provide you with a rough plan for each performance, but
if you find that you'll be handling a subject about which
you know little, try to learn a bit more about it before the
festival.

7. Keep introductions and comments to the point. It is good to
place performers and workshop subjects into context and you
should assume that the audience knows little about what
they are seeing and hearing. A comment which explains that
a particular performer or group has never before performed
for such an audience may help bridge the gap to an audience
expecting slick professionalism from persons onstage. Also,
to point out the unique features of a performer's style,
repertoire, or background will lead to heightened appreciation by the audience--which is the purpose of all introduction. At the same time, there is a thin line between
instructing an audience and boring it. Keep it to the point.

8. With a few exceptions, **performers** will be staying at Madeira
on Friday night. If you feel it would be helpful to talk
with a particular performer or group before you present them
on stage, this might be a good time to do it. If you want to

talk to a particular performer on that evening, check with the office to see when they will be arriving. There will be a social gathering at Madeira School Friday evening beginning at 7:30. If you could arrange to stop by some time during the evening, you could meet and visit with performers scheduled to appear on your stage.

9. Plug performers' records, NCTA records, program books, evening concerts, and T-shirts. A sales representative will be assigned to each stage area and he/she will be selling the NCTA record and program books. Performers' records will be available at the concession stand. The stage representative will have an idea of which performers are available.

10. Performers are requested to report to each stage area at least 15 minutes before they are scheduled to perform whenever this is possible. Be prepared to switch the order of things if someone does not show up on time.

11. We hope to provide each stage area with communication to festival headquarters. If you need help, call and ask for it. However, try to use this system only for real problems. Don't call half an hour before your workshop and complain that your performers have not shown up yet. Keep the line free for real problems and emergencies as much as possible. Also, keep in mind that others may wish to get in touch with you even though your stage is in fine shape. So have someone monitoring your radio at all times.

12. In most cases, the stage manager will do the announcing at his area, unless a guest host has been assigned. The assistant manager should help out whenever he/she is needed and fill in for the stage manager whenever necessary. One of the two of you should be at the stage area throughout the day.

13. Keep in mind that we will be going through all the tape made on your stage looking for items that can be issued on LPs as part of a forthcoming series. Paying attention to levels is important. Logs are important. Records must not be left unattended. If a logger does not obtain the name of a song, the manager should introduce him/her to the performer so that every song or story can be listed.

14. Sound "bleed" from one stage to another can be a serious problem when electric bands are on stage and /or someone becomes power-happy with the volume. Be considerate of others who wish to hear people on other stages. There is a tendency to push the sound up toward the end of the day. Guard against it.

15. The stage manager is the manager and should not hesitate to assert himself/herself when others need direction.

National Council for the Traditional Arts

1346 Conn. Ave., N.W. - 1118
Washington, D.C. 20036
Telephone 202/296-0068

41ST NATIONAL FOLK FESTIVAL: INSTRUCTIONS
FOR RAIN (PERISH THE THOUGHT)

We will run all stages as long as possible. The stage manager and sound technician should close down the stage when they feel it is no longer safe to operate. The stage manager should interrupt the program and announce that it will be temporarily suspended. He or she should tell the audience that when activities resume, they will resume according to the schedule, at the times shown, and that we will not attempt to squeeze in things that were rained out. The sound technician and stage crews should then secure the sound equipment - it should be turned off, unplugged, and the mikes and cables should be broken down. The recorders and consoles should be covered quickly with plastic, which will be provided to each stage, and then the speakers should be covered.

Performers should wait at or near the stages if shelter is available; if not, they should go to the Green Room (we will try to provide pargos for performers - call the Green Room). Stage staffs should remain at the stages. Under no circumstances should equipment be left unattended.

We will wait out all rain storms short of the Biblical Deluge. For shorter showers, the stage manager and sound technician should decide when it is safe to resume operation, and programming will begin according to the schedule. Final decisions on closing down for the day must be made jointly by the stage manager and the Green Room staff.

SAMPLES OF FESTIVAL COMMUNICATIONS

40TH NATIONAL FOLK FESTIVAL STAGE STAFF

AREA 1

Stage Manager	Jane Bergey
Assistant S.M.	Roddy Moore
Sound Technician	George Reynolds
Recording Technician	Kenneth Law
Logging	Chuck and Nan Perdue

AREA 2

Stage Manager	Charlie Camp
Assistant S.M.	John Holum
Sound Technician	Peter Reiniger
Recording Technician	Steve Hamp
Logging	Julia Olin

AREA 3

Stage Manager	Hal Bruno
Assistant S.M.	Barry Bergey
Sound Technician	Pat Goodman
Recording Technician	Blanton Owen
Logging	Ann Scheinberg

AREA 4

Stage Manager	Jim Griffith
Assistant S.M.	Tom McHenry
Sound Technician	Mike Herter
Recording Technician	Cotton Queen
Logging	Pete Hartman

AREA 5

Stage Manager	Dave Whisnant
Assistant S.M.	George Holt
Sound Technician	Nick Hawes
Recording Technician	Sherrod Reynolds
Logging	Saul Broudy
RECORDING SUPERVISOR	Richard Derbyshire
RECORDING TROUBLESHOOTER	Mike Rivers
COMMUNICATIONS SET-UP, TROUBLESHOOTER	Al Taylor, Stan Fowler
FILENE CENTER STAGE MANAGER, SOUND CHECKS	Frank Proschan

National Council for the Traditional Arts

1346 Conn. Ave., N.W. - 1118
Washington, D.C. 20036
Telephone 202/296-0068

Dear Friends,

Welcome!!! We're glad you made it here safely and we promise we'll keep you busy in the next few days. There are a few last-minute things we wanted to let you know, a few things that might have confused you that we want to explain, and a few things we've told you before that we just want to remind you of.

You should already know that you've been assigned to work on:

You may not know who your supervisor is, where to report at Wolf Trap, and when:

When you get to Wolf Trap each morning, check in at the Green Room (we'll have a staff list for you to initial) so we'll know you have arrived on the site, then go to the location listed above. In the Green Room you can also pick up chits for the Evening Concerts. Because there is a possibility that we will sell out both concerts, staff and performers are not guaranteed seats in the Filene Center. Your name badge and a festival chit will qualify you to stand in the wings or sit on the lawn. (We will brief all of the ushers, but it is possible that some will not get the word, so please cooperate if they ask you to move.) If there will be enough seats, the Green Room folks will give you a real ticket.

Lunch at Wolf Trap will be served from 11:30 to 1:00 and supper from 5:30 to 7:30 in the meal tent. Meal tickets are attached. If you are assigned to a job that you absolutely cannot leave, give your meal ticket to a trustworthy person who can pick up your meal and bring it to you. For most jobs you should be able to alternate with someone assigned to a related task. (If you are staying at Madeira, breakfast is served from 7:30 to 8:30, no meal tickets needed.)

After the evening concert, you are welcome to join us at Madeira School. We ask that you not bring an entourage of friends and acquaintances along with you to the party. (A spouse, friend, or date is welcome). There will be evening snacks at Madeira which are intended for participants and staff who worked on the evening concert. If there is extra food, you will be welcome to have some. We have to make sure, however, that the food does not get eaten up before the performers' bus arrives, so we'll ask that you be patient and cooperative. (We'll have beer to keep you from starvation's door.)

SAMPLES OF FESTIVAL COMMUNICATIONS

We must carefully control access to Madeira. If people ask you whether they can drop in where the performers are housed, tell them that the site is private property and that the only people welcome there are the participants and workers and a few people invited there by the festival director. In the past we have had cases of theft, vandalism, and drunken, aggressive party-crashers who had to be forcibly evicted. There are dangers in such situations and we feel a responsibility to insure that participants and workers are safe and can rest. Also, we cannot afford to run a huge party open to everyone. We appreciate your understanding and assistance in this matter.

We have very limited parking at Wolf Trap, so we must ask everyone to leave their cars at Madeira and take the bus. Buses leave Madeira each morning at 9:00 a.m. and 9:45 a.m. to go to Wolf Trap. They will return to Madeira after the evening concert, so please plan to spend the full day at the festival. Buses leave Madeira School from the circle. They will leave Wolf Trap from the parking lot immediately behind the Green Room at the Filene Center.

Lest you think that we have nothing but orders and instructions for you, we also have an immense gratitude. This festival depends just as surely on its volunteer staff as it does on its performers and its audience. We couldn't get by without all of you. We know than many of you have given up more lucrative pursuits for the weekend, that some of you have gone to great personal expense to get here, and that none are being paid. You'll be working hard for at least two days (our promise) and won't get many rewards, other than the gratitude of performers and audience members. There may be frayed tempers, hot workers, or hasty conversations. And, because everyone leaves at different times on Sunday and Monday, you may not even get a personal thank you from our staff.

So, we want to thank you ahead of time. Your time, your energy, and your devotion to the performers and craftspeople we present at the festival are all important -- important in ways that are apparent but also in ways that are sometimes invisible. Since the performers won't all get a chance to thank you, and since the audience members won't tell you how much they've enjoyed the festival, and since we may not even get to say goodbye, let alone thanks, we want to say it right now. **THANKS.**

Joe Wilson   Lee Udall   Anne Labovitz

Frank Proschan   Bill Kornrich

P.S. If you would like to have more program books as souvenirs of the festival, please go to the Sales/Concessions tent at Wolf Trap. You will be able to purchase extra copies for 50¢ apiece. There is also a special price for the festival tee-shirts of $3.00, available at the Sales tent. You must show your badge to receive the discount price.

TUCSON, MEET YOURSELF

FESTIVAL TECHNICAL CALENDAR

By April

    Pick dates for the festival
    Write City Parks and Recreation reserving stage, booths and parks
    Have fund raising program under way

April

    Get new ethnic clubs list from Chamber of Commerce
    Set date for May introductory meeting, reserve room
    Call ethnic groups and get new officers' names; advise about meeting
    Send letter to clubs telling about festival and giving festival and meeting dates
    Make follow-up calls a week before meeting

May

    Introductory meeting: Show slides from last year
    Invite interested groups to sign up
    Announce dates and health requirements
    Ask for leads on musicians and dancers
    Offer pictures from last year for sale

June – July

    Arrange for and hold competition for poster at University of Arizona School of Fine Arts, Graphic Arts division

August

    Set date for September booth rep meeting
    Arrange for representative from Pima County Health Department to come to meeting
    Send letter explaining meeting and booth deposit to ethnic group representatives
    Make follow-up calls
    Invite Cultural Arts rep. from City Parks to meeting

September

    First week – booth meeting in evening

        Accept deposits and fees
        Give health permits
        Draw booth members
        Sign up musicians
        Explain progress and developments
        Answer questions

SAMPLES OF FESTIVAL COMMUNICATIONS

Early in month - send money and specific requirements list re: stage and booths to City Parks. Don't forget dumpster bin, garbage cans, chairs, benches
Send letters to Mayor, City Manager, Police and Fire Departments, notifying them of festival
Send letters to other County offices requesting needed facilities
Request off-duty police for 6:00 PM Friday through noon Sunday
Line up sound system, technicians, photographer
Distribute posters, give interviews, distribute P.S.A.s
Check concerning need for piano, risers for stage, umbrellas for information booth
Get a tentative schedule together and make it available to publicity folks and poster distributors. Check out schedule with each performing group
Get volunteers for poster distribution, provide them with maps and list of places to go

October

See that booths and wiring are done correctly
Request from City Operations a key for breaker box in the park (this is vital, as there is an average of 10 blown fuses daily)
Volunteer meeting one or two Saturdays before festival

This does not include the publicity schedule in its full detail, nor does it include the timing for the programmer. This latter will be chaotic and slow, but it must be solidly done with the program checked by all participants by the Monday before the festival. If reservations are made with the printer, this usually gives enough lead time. This must be checked each year, however.

Every plan change must be double checked with participants, and all details with participants must be by letter, followed up by a phone call.

FESTIVAL CALENDAR
(new Festival)

Note: Application for tax-exempt status, fieldwork, and organizational planning should begin more than a year in advance. This assumes a first-time festival.

A Year to Go --

    First meeting of planners
    Administrative structure decided
    Initial programming concepts decided
    Program committee appointed
    Director appointed
    Date selected
    Budget planned
    Meet with state folklorist
    Apply for state, federal and local funds
    Begin active fieldwork

Ten Months to Go --

    Site selected
    Legality determined
    Begin recruiting top volunteers
    Housing reserved
    All funding applications completed

Eight Months to Go --

    Apply for permits
    Determine bonding, insurance needs
    Plan site arrangements
    Re-consider concepts in light of fieldwork findings
    Assess funding, vigorous follow-up
    Site contracts signed
    Meet potential club and church concessionaires

Six Months to Go --

    Final budget determination
    Send out first participant contracts
    Ask TV stations for PSA time reservation
    Prepare poster for wide-area distribution
    Housing contracts signed
    Obtain bids for feeding participants, staff
    Key staff and volunteer positions filled
    Decide number of volunteers needed

SAMPLES OF FESTIVAL COMMUNICATIONS   229

Four Months to Go --

    Full-time staff at work
    Fieldwork completed
    Send out all contracts, letters of agreement
      and questionnaires to participants
    Gather publicity materials
    Establish press release schedules
    Outline program book, assign articles
    Set up administrative and filing system
      to deal with participant information as it
      comes in, making sure that all pertinent staff
      persons get what they need to do their job
    Make cash request of funding agencies
    Get bids from sound companies, based upon written
      specifications

Three Months to Go --

    Send out general press release announcing dates, location,
      overall theme
    Complete volunteer recruitment
    Follow-up on participant information, contracts
    Sign contract for sound
    Complete documentation planning
    Begin preparing instructions for stage managers, others
    Meeting of key staff, volunteers
    Sign contract for food without listing exact number to
      be fed
    Prepare festival schedule listing concerts, workshops,
      crafts, other

Two Months to Go --

    Make sure all participant contracts and information sheets
      are in hand
    Make travel arrangements; compile lists of needs for each
      area, i.e. production, scheduling, housing, transporta-
      tion, etc., based on participant information sheet
    Record and distribute radio PSAs
    Press releases begin to go out, one a week, beginning with
      third week
    Sound, staging, tent, booth, and other production require-
      ment contracted, ordered, and scheduled
    Participants kits prepared and duplicated, ready for
      mailing
    Buy any radio and/or TV spots
    Complete festival staffing, both paid and volunteer. Set up
      festival organization and assign all jobs. Notify everyone
      in writing as to where to be, when to be there, and what
      they'll be responsible for
    Make sure all program book material is in hand; allow at
      least four weeks for program book designer to do art work.

Four Weeks to Go --

    Send out final information kits to participants
    Meet with production crew to set final plans
    Send out press release
    Program book blueline proofread and sent to printer
    Arrange for pre-festival coverage with media through interviews, try to set up advance features in newspapers
    Performers on local TV, radio

Three Weeks to Go --

    Send out press release
    Newspaper ads bought and prepared
    Housing and food lists completed
    All local transportation arranged for participants, i.e. to and from airports, bus stations, housing facilities, and site
    Signs for festival site completed
    Press kits prepared

Two Weeks to Go --

    Yet another press release
    Housing and food lists submitted to contractor or party providing service
    Press kits distributed to media
    Finalize all production arrangements
    Adjust schedule for last minute changes and notify concerned parties of changes that affect them
    Meet with critical staff who are to carry out the festival to establish a clear chain of communication during the event
    Hold meeting for all volunteers

One Week to Go --

    Send out final press release, which should be general summation of event
    All advertising in effect
    Site preparations under way -- stages erected, covered; tents set up, booths built, signs distributed, areas roped off, sound systems tested in place, phones installed
    Festival operation moves to site
    Check and double check everything

SAMPLES OF FESTIVAL COMMUNICATIONS

National Council for the Traditional Arts

1346 Conn. Ave., N.W. - 1118
Washington, D.C. 20036
Telephone 202/296-0068

Before we all scatter to the four corners of the world (Joe to Tennessee and Louisiana, Lee to Arizona, Bill to Tennessee, Frank to Texas, and Anne back home to her family) we want to thank you for all of the help you gave us with the 41st National Folk Festival. None of us can remember a Festival that happened so successfully, with so few emergencies, no cross words, and such an excellent, congenial, and cooperative staff. We've gotten compliments and thanks from participants and visitors, and want to pass those thanks on to you.

We've been able to collect such a good staff by calling upon many of you year after year, and we hope we can continue to do so. This doesn't mean that we're taking your help for granted-- we do appreciate it. More important, we want you to let us know where you think we can improve our planning, programming, and organization so that we can continue to call on you for assistance. If you have thoughts -- favorable, unfavorable, complimentary, or condemning - please take a moment to jot them down so that we can take them into account in our future plans.

Again, we thank you for your valuable contributions to the success of the 41st National Folk Festival. We'll see you soon.

Cordially,

Joe Wilson

Lee Udall

Anne Labovitz

Frank Proschan

Bill Kornrich

FOR THE MEDIA

National Council for the Traditional Arts

1346 Conn. Ave., N.W. - 1118
Washington, D.C. 20036
Telephone 202/296-0068

39TH NATIONAL FOLK FESTIVAL

NEWS RELEASE

FOR IMMEDIATE RELEASE

CONTACT: 202/296-5322

NATIONAL FOLK FESTIVAL TO BE HELD JULY 29-31 AT WOLF TRAP FARM PARK
FOR THE PERFORMING ARTS IN VIENNA, VIRGINIA

Once again this year Wolf Trap Farm Park for the Performing Arts will be given over to the finest traditional music, dance and crafts as the National Council for the Traditional Arts pays tribute to the cultural heritage of the United States at its 39th NATIONAL FOLK FESTIVAL.

Since the First National Folk Festival was held in St. Louis in 1934, performers and artisans from all over the country have gathered each year to participate in this annual celebration of the diversity of American folk music and dance. It is the oldest and largest ongoing folk festival in the U.S.

In the upcoming National Folk Festival to be held July 29-31 at Wolf Trap, presentations ranging from Ukrainian music and dance, Chinese Opera, and Arab dance to Cajun music, traditional bluegrass, Afro-American blues, old time, gospel, and country music will dramatize the variety of ethnic cultures which make up the richness of the traditional American folk arts.

SAMPLES OF FESTIVAL COMMUNICATIONS

PROGRAM. Evening concerts at 8 p.m. in the Filene Center
will feature such couriers of traditional music as The Pine
River Boys and Maybelle, an old time band from Southern
Virginia; John Jackson, blues guitarist and singer, storyteller,
and banjo player; Cheremoch, Ukrainian-American musicians,
dancers and singers; the Balfa Brothers, a Cajun band from
Louisiana; Rose Maddox, the country's first country music queen;
Jerry McCain, Alabama rhythm and blues harmonica player and
singer; and Ted Lundy, Bob Paisley and the Southern Mountain
Boys, a traditional family bluegrass band.

Workshops, small concerts, and special activities for
children also will be held from 1:00 to 5:00 p.m. on July 29,
30, and 31. These daytime events will take place in informal
stage areas in the meadows and woods surrounding the Filene
Center.

CRAFTS. In addition to the usual exhibits of musical
instruments, instrument making, recordings and books related
to the performing folk arts, the National Folk Festival features one particular craft each year. This year's focus will
be on woodcarving. An Alaskan totem carver, a Seminole Indian
dugout carver, and woodcarvers representing other regions and
cultures will be on hand to demonstrate their crafts.

DANCE PARTIES. Dancing is always a popular feature of
the National Folk Festival. There will be demonstration and
participation sessions during daytime workshops and each
day's activities will culminate in a 5:30 dance party where

Festival-goers and performers gather in the meadows to the music of Chief Ellis and the Barrelhouse Rockers and other bands participating in the Festival.

PRICES. Advance tickets for evening concerts at 8:00 p.m. in the Filene Center are available from East Coast Ticketron outlets or from the Wolf Trap Farm Park Box Office (938-3810). Prices are $6.00 for reserved seats in the Filene Center and $4.00 for lawn seating. Both include free daytime admission. Daytime only admission is $3.00. Admission for six to twelve is $1.00; the programs are free to children under six.

SAMPLES OF FESTIVAL COMMUNICATIONS

National Council for the Traditional Arts

1346 Conn. Ave., N.W. - 1118
Washington, D.C. 20036
Telephone 202/296-0068

39TH NATIONAL FOLK FESTIVAL

NEWS RELEASE

FOR IMMEDIATE RELEASE

CONTACT: 212/296-5322

NATIONAL FOLK FESTIVAL TO BE HELD JULY 29-31 AT WOLF TRAP FARM PARK FOR THE PERFORMING ARTS IN VIENNA, VIRGINIA.

The 39th NATIONAL FOLK FESTIVAL will feature a variety of daytime activities which should attract the interest of any lover of traditional music, dance, art, or folklore. On July 29, 30, and 31 from 1:00-5:30 p.m., four outdoor stages in the woods and meadows of Wolf Trap Farm Park for the Performing Arts will provide the setting for a series of small concerts, workshops, storytelling, sing-alongs, and special activities for children.

On Friday, July 29, Andean musicians (Rumisongos), hammered dulcimer players (The Sinclair Brothers), and an old time string band, The Pine River Boys and Maybelle, will be performing on one stage while a host of noted vocalists gather to sing Jimmie Rodgers songs on another. Later the same day, the Balfa Brothers will share the traditions of the French Cajuns of Louisiana, while on another stage the Foddrell Brothers belt forth blues and country music. Dance-oriented festival goers have yet another choice: the clog-dance workshop conducted by old-time fiddler Thorton Spencer. And on the same day there will be blues guitar, old-time band and harmonica workshops, storytelling, brother style songs, and an unusual instruments workshop hosted by Jonathan Eberhart.

Saturday, July 30, brings another day of activities on four stages simultaneously. Ukrainian musicians and dancers will share their traditions on one stage while Canada's favorite fiddler, Graham Townsend, holds forth on another. In yet another area, a sing-along barroom workshop will feature John Jackson, Rose Maddox, the Paisley Brothers, Henry Townsend--and their audience. There will be time for festival-goers to visit the craft area and resume a tour of concerts involving Ireland's prize-winning uillean piper Joe McKenna, traditional bluegrass band Lundy, Paisley, and the Southern Mountain Boys, and a capella vocalists Cas Wallin and Evelyn Ramsey. Other choices range from Arab dancers to folk piano, Virginia banjo styles, and a bones workshop conducted by the Sinclair Brothers.

The three-day celebration of American folk tradition will be culminated Sunday, July 31, in performances which include gospel singers E.C. and Orna Ball, the Chinese Opera, and Speedy Tolliver, noted Southern Appalachian banjo and fiddle player. Other stages will feature Hazel Dickens, who appeared in the award-winning film, <u>Harlan County USA</u>, blues harmonica player Jerry McCain with Chief Ellis and the Barrelhouse Rockers, and Albert Hash and his old-time Whitetop Mountain Band. Festival-goers might want to settle in with the blues piano workshop, participate in a Ukrainian dance demonstration or join some of the country's finest vocalists to sing along Songs My Mother Taught Me.

PROGRAM. Evening concerts at 8:00 p.m. in the Filene Center will feature traditional bluegrass, Cajun, old-time western, blues and gospel music, and ethnic music and dance.

CRAFTS. In addition to the usual exhibits of musical instruments, instrument making, recordings and books related to the performing folk arts, the National Folk Festival features one particular craft each year. This year's focus will be on woodcarving. A Hopi kachina doll carver, an Alaskan totem carver, and woodcarvers representing other regions and cultures will be on hand to demonstrate their crafts.

DANCE PARTIES. Dancing is always a popular feature of the National Folk Festival. There will be demonstration and participation sessions during daytime workshops and each day's activities will culminate in a 5:30 dance party where Festival-goers and performers gather in the meadows to dance to the music of one of the bands participating in the Festival.

PRICES. Advance tickets for evening concerts at 8:00 p.m. in the Filene Center are available from East Coast Ticketron outlets or from the Wolf Trap Farm Park Box Office (938-3810). Prices are $6.00 for reserved seats in the Filene Center and $4.00 for lawn seating. Both include free daytime admission. Daytime only admission is $3.00. Admission for children six to twelve is $1.00; the programs are free to children under six.

The 39th National Folk Festival is co-sponsored by the National Council for the Traditional Arts and the National Park Service as an annual celebration of the diversity of American folk music and dance. It is the oldest and largest ongoing folk festival in the U.S.

National Council for the Traditional Arts

1346 Conn. Ave., N.W. - 1118
Washington, D.C. 20036
Telephone 202/296-0068

39TH NATIONAL FOLK FESTIVAL

NEWS RELEASE

FOR IMMEDIATE RELEASE

CONTACT: 212/296-5322

NATIONAL FOLK FESTIVAL TO BE HELD JULY 29-31 AT WOLF TRAP FARM PARK FOR THE PERFORMING ARTS IN VIENNA, VIRGINIA

Among performers making their first appearance at the NATIONAL FOLK FESTIVAL are Rumisongos, a group of Andean musicians; Rose Maddox, country and bluegrass singer; and the Sinclair Brothers, hammered dulcimer, bones, and piano players. Sponsored by the National Council for the Traditional Arts, the 39th annual festival will be held at Wolf Trap Farm Park for the Performing Arts in Vienna, Virginia, July 29-31.

Rumisongos bring to the festival a music rich in the tradition of the Andean peoples of Southern America. Now Washingtonians, Carlos Arrien, Alfredo Escobar, and Alvaro Montenegro are from Bolivia. Rento Salazar, the fourth member of the group, is Chilean. Their instruments include guitar, guena (flute), tarka (wind instrument carved in wood), zampona (reed pan pipe), the stringed charango, and the bombo, a percussion instrument. Their instrumental work is fired with excitement and their vocal trios and quartets contain breathtaking harmony and lyrics which evoke an imagery of the ancient civilizations of the Andean Mountains.

SAMPLES OF FESTIVAL COMMUNICATIONS

Rose Maddox, formerly of the Maddox Brothers and Rose, is claimed to be the country's first nationally recognized country music queen. Maddox is a versatile artist whose repertoire includes bluegrass, country, and western swing. Her uninhibited showmanship and rambunctious repertoire have won her a devoted following.

Cloise and Harley Sinclair are quick to explain that their hammered dulcimer is an instrument with roots in Biblical times and should not be confused with the Appalachian dulcimer, a creation of relatively recent vintage. The hammered dulcimer is a box-like, primitive-looking instrument rendering an airy music which defies its appearance and which, among other things, is the precedent of the piano.

The Sinclair Brothers hail from Sheridan, Michigan. Both play the hammered dulcimer. Cloise also plays bones and Harley plays country piano.

PROGRAM. Evening concerts at 8 p.m. in the Filene Center will feature such couriers of traditional music as the Pine River Boys and Maybelle, an old time band from Southern Virginia; Graham Townsend, Canada's best known fiddler; and Jerry McCain, Alabama rhythm and blues harmonica player and singer. Workshop artists will include Joe McKenna, a fantastic player of the Irish pipes, direct from Ireland; Joe Politte, a delightful Missouri French fiddler with an unusual repertoire; the Chinese Opera

Company, who perform traditional works 2,000 years old; Big Chief Ellis and his Barrelhouse Rockers, presenting the best of boogie and blues; and many other folks.

Workshops, small concerts, and special activities for children will be held from 1:00 to 5:00 p.m. on July 29, 30 and 31. These daytime events will take place in informal stage areas in the meadows and woods surrounding the Filene Center.

CRAFTS. In addition to the usual exhibits of musical instruments, instrument making, recordings and books related to the performing folk arts, the National Folk Festival features one particular craft each year. This year's focus will be on woodcarving. An Alaskan totem carver, Seminole and Cherokee wood sculptors, a Hopi kachina doll carver and woodcarvers representing other regions and cultures will be on hand to demonstrate their crafts.

DANCE PARTIES. Dancing is always a popular feature of the National Folk Festival. There will be demonstration and participation sessions during daytime workshops and each day's activities will culminate in a 5:30 dance party where festival-goers and performers gather in the meadows to dance to the music of the Balfa Brothers and other bands participating in the Festival.

PRICES. Advance tickets for evening concerts at 8:00 p.m. in the Filene Center are available from East Coast Ticketron outlets or from the Wolf Trap Farm Park Box Office (938-3810). Prices are $6.00 for reserved seats in the Filene Center and

SAMPLES OF FESTIVAL COMMUNICATIONS 241

$4.00 for lawn seating. Both include free daytime admission. Daytime only admission is $3.00. Admission for children six to twelve is $1.00; the programs are free to children under six.

The 39th National Folk Festival is co-sponsored by the National Council for the Traditional Arts and the National Park Service as an annual celebration of the diversity of American folk music and dance. It is the oldest and largest ongoing folk festival in the U.S.

National Folk Festival
L:NFF-48-60

SLIDE #14	(Fiddle music begins as low background simultaneously with narrative)
SLIDE #15	(first audio)
SLIDE #16	THERE ARE MANY CULTURES IN AMERICA, MANY SONGS, MANY DANCES, MANY STORIES...AND EACH
SLIDE #17	YEAR THE NATIONAL FOLK FESTIVAL BRINGS A RICH SAMPLING OF AMERICA'S CULTURES TO
SLIDE #18	WOLF TRAP FARM PARK... SO MANY THAT FOUR
SLIDE #19	STAGES ARE NEEDED . . . AND YOU'LL NEED THREE DAYS TO SEE IT ALL . . .
SLIDE #20	YOU CAN WADE IN A STREAM (volume of fiddle music increasing) OR MARVEL AT THE SKILLS
(SHOTS OF FIDDLER AND DANCER, FULL, CLOSE-UP, ETC.)	OF A FIDDLER (end of first audio cut: 21 sec.)
(SUPER FIDDLER) (SUPER DANCER)	(second cut) (13 sec.) (:45 in) THE 40th NATIONAL
(SUPER VOICE OF)	FOLK FESTIVAL AT WOLF TRAP,
SUPER: (FULL SCREEN CHIRON)	JULY 28, 29 and 30. TICKETS ON SALE AT TICKETRON OUTLETS AND THE WOLF TRAP BOX OFFICE.

SAMPLES OF FESTIVAL COMMUNICATIONS   243

PSA FOR TELEVISION

The preceding shows script, audio voice, audio music and visuals for a 37 second television PSA. Color slides of scenes from a previous festival and live videotape footage of a fiddler and flat foot dancer are combined. The production sequence was as follows: The script was written and timed by festival staff and slides chosen which illustrated the script. The audio voice was recorded at a separate session at the TV studio by a festival staff member. These elements were brought together with the fiddler and dancer when the PSA was filmed. At the same session 8, 14 and 19 second PSAs were filmed. Because of AFTRA union contracts with the station, the performers (fiddler, back-up guitarist, dancer, voice) had to be either non-professionals identified at some point by a superimposed name on the screen or be paid union scale. In this case they were non-professionals. An hour of production time was required and was donated by the TV station which also made copies of the PSAs for use by 6 other Washington area TV stations. The station was WRC-TV, the Washington NBC affiliate. The fiddler was John Ashby of Marshall, Virginia, who made his first National Folk Festival appearance in 1938, the dancer was Laurie Wilson, a fourth generation flat foot dancer from East Tennessee.

National Council for the Traditional Arts

1346 Conn. Ave., N.W. - 1118
Washington, D.C. 20036
Telephone 202/296-0068

Start: 7-9-77

Discontinue: 7-30-77

Contact: Lee Udall (296-0068)

PSA 10 seconds

Celebrate the summertime at the National Folk Festival at Wolf Trap. Daily programs from 1 to 5 July 29 thru 31, Friday and Saturday concerts at 8:00. For information call the Wolf Trap Box Office, 938-3800.

SAMPLES OF FESTIVAL COMMUNICATIONS

National Council for the Traditional Arts

1346 Conn. Ave., N.W. - 1118
Washington, D.C. 20036
Telephone 202/296-0068

Start: 7-9-77

Discontinue: 7-30-77

Contact: Lee Udall (296-0068)

PSA 10 seconds

That's the haunting sound of Cajun music, and it will be a part of the many musical offerings at the 39th National Folk Festival at Wolf Trap, July 28, 29 and 30. For tickets call the Wolf Trap Box Office 938-3800.

National Council for the Traditional Arts

1346 Conn. Ave., N.W. - 1118
Washington, D.C. 20036
Telephone 202/296-0068

Start: 7-9-77

Discontinue: 7-30-77

Contact: Lee Udall (296-0068)

PSA 20 Seconds

There'll be only one major folk festival in the Washington area this summer -- the 39th National Folk Festival at Wolf Trap. You'll see 200 folk artists representing the many cultures of America -- on Friday, Saturday and Sunday, July 29, 30 and 31 at Wolf Trap, beginning at 1 p.m. For information call 938-3800, that's 938-3800.

SAMPLES OF FESTIVAL COMMUNICATIONS

National Council for the Traditional Arts

1346 Conn. Ave., N.W. - 1118
Washington, D.C. 20036
Telephone 202/296-0068

Start: 7-9-77

Discontinue: 7-30-77

Contact: Lee Udall (296-0068)

PSA 30 Seconds

Get out your instruments and put on your dancing shoes. The National Folk Festival is coming to Wolf Trap, July 29, 30 and 31. Three days of the best blues, bluegrass, old-time, gospel, Cajun and ethnic music and dance. Small concerts and workshops from 1 until 5:30 each day, evening concerts on Friday and Saturday evening at 8 o'clock. See the Balfa Brothers, Ted Lundy, John Jackson, Rose Maddox and hundreds of other great folk artists. That's the National Folk Festival, July 29 thru 31. Tickets available from Ticketron or the Wolf Trap Box Office. Call 938-3800, that's 938-3800.

National Council for the Traditional Arts

1346 Conn. Ave., N.W. - 1118
Washington, D.C. 20036
Telephone 202/296-0068

Start: 7-9-77

Discontinue: 7-30-77

Contact: Lee Udall (296-0068)

PSA 30 Seconds

The faces and sounds of America's grassroots -- that's the 39th Annual National Folk Festival at Wolf Trap -- people from throughout America who have preserved their traditional culture -- Ukrainians, Irish, Appalachian Mountain people, blacks, Louisiana French, Arabs -- the rich cultural roots and sounds of America. At Wolf Trap, Friday, Saturday, Sunday, July 29 thru 31, programs begin at 1 p. m. For more information call 938-3800, that's 938-3800.

FOR THE AUDIENCE

Algia Mae Hinton

Algia Mae Hinton was born August 29, 1929, in the O'Neal Township of Johnston County, North Carolina. She was raised in a musical environment, with most of her family members playing reels, spirituals, and blues. Her mother, Ollie O'Neal, played guitar, autoharp, accordion, harmonica, and jaw harp; and she was so proficient a musician that legends concerning her selling her soul to the devil still persist in that area. Ollie's brother played guitar, and her sister picked guitar and banjo. Of her fourteen children all nine sons and four of the five daughters learned to play guitars. Algia Mae was the baby girl, and by the time she began to play, many of her brothers, sisters, cousins, and brothers-in-law (at least two of whom played fiddle and banjo) had made quite a reputation for the family playing at frolic dances and house parties. Before too long, Algia Mae was playing with the best of them, and through the years she has continued to do so, singing now primarily for family and friends. Among her show-stopping skills is her ability to buckdance to her own guitar accompaniment.

—Glenn Hinson

Algia Mae Hinton.

photo: courtesy Glenn Hinson

Stanley Hicks

Do you know the story of Jack and the Beanstalk? It is only one of the many traditional stories about Jack, most of which had never been recorded until collectors found their way to the Hicks family of Beech Mountain in Watauga County, North Carolina.

The story came to the Hicks' from a grandparent, Council Harmon, and in these stories Jack is a witty lad who serves the King and himself by catching unicorns, lions, wild hogs, robbers, and other dangerous creatures.

The Hicks family has been self-sufficient in far more than its literature. Members of the family have made their own tools, medicine, food, implements, houses, and musical instruments for generations.

Stanley Hicks grew up absorbing these old ways from his father. He helped his father distill oils from birch, mountain tea, and sassafras. He gathered and sold roots and herbs. He knows the home-made games children played to pass the long winter nights in the mountains.

Stanley will tell you that he is "from out of the Beech", one of the highest and most remote of the Southern Appalachian peaks. He had to go elsewhere, to the North Carolina Piedmont and even to upstate New York, to earn enough money to buy his little farm, but he returned to his mountains when enough money had been saved.

Stanley makes fine traditional banjoes and dulcimers and sells them, grows good burley tobacco, keeps some cattle, and has a big garden. He still tells the tales he learned from his father and grandparents, plays the banjo and dulcimer, and sings songs he learned around firesides as a child. A good fiddle or banjo tune is likely to persuade him to show his skills as a buckdancer.

Stanley Hicks

Van Holyoak

Van Holyoak was born in 1928 in Clay Springs, Arizona, and has been singing all his life. He learned many songs from his father, Joe Holyoak, who, like Van, was a cowboy. Van owns and operates a ranch in the White Mountains of Arizona, where he also works for the State Highway Department. A fine story teller as well, Van has performed at the 1976 Bicentennial Festival of American Folklife and at numerous local and regional events. He says: "I think everyone should sing all the time. If the good Lord gave you a beautiful singing voice, it's a fine way to say 'thank you'. If he never, it's a good way to get even."

SAMPLES OF FESTIVAL COMMUNICATIONS

Van Holyoak

John Jackson

John Jackson

John Jackson was born in Rappahannock County, Virginia, the son of a tenant farmer. Music was an integral part of this rural black community in which John grew up. Dances, house parties, field hollers, and church singing were community activities in which most people took an active part. John's father played guitar and banjo and sang blues songs. His mother sang hymns and played the accordion and harmonica. John began to play around with the guitar when he was four years old and by the time he was eight, he was a competent musician.

Today John Jackson is considered one of the finest blues performers in the country. A resident of Fairfax Station, Virginia, John plays frequently in the Washington area, and has toured the U.S., Europe, and South America.

Haywood Blevins

Haywood "Woodie" Blevins has played the piano for over fifty years and is noted for his keyboard talent around his native home of Galax, Virginia. The Blevins family has deep roots in the Baywood section of Grayson County and Haywood still has the original deed to the family farm that his ancestors signed in the late 18th century. His earliest memories are of his grandfather, who was a veteran of the Civil War. His grandfather entertained him as a youngster with stories of the War and tales about his time spent in a Union prison camp just before the end of the conflict. He often played marches and tunes that he learned in the service and could tell stories of incidents that related to each march. In addition to his musical talent, Haywood's grandfather had much artistic ability and gave Woodie a series of sketches of the Yankee prison camp where he spent time.

Haywood also learned music from his father, who was a banjo player. His interest in the piano extended beyond playing. By the time he was 18, he had learned to tune and rebuild pianos. Haywood's reputation as a tuner and repairman spread far and wide and his clientel stretched from North Carolina to Maryland. He divided his time between tuning the piano and farming and even did occasional factory work in the mills around Galax. A disagreement with a plant foreman caused him to leave home in the early '30s. He and his wife moved to Maryland for several years, only to move back to Galax to take over the family farm full-time. They lived there until the Appalachian Power Company bought the place for the New River Dam Project. He now lives in Sparta with his daughter and her family.

—Pete Hartman

Reprinted by permission of Pete Hartman

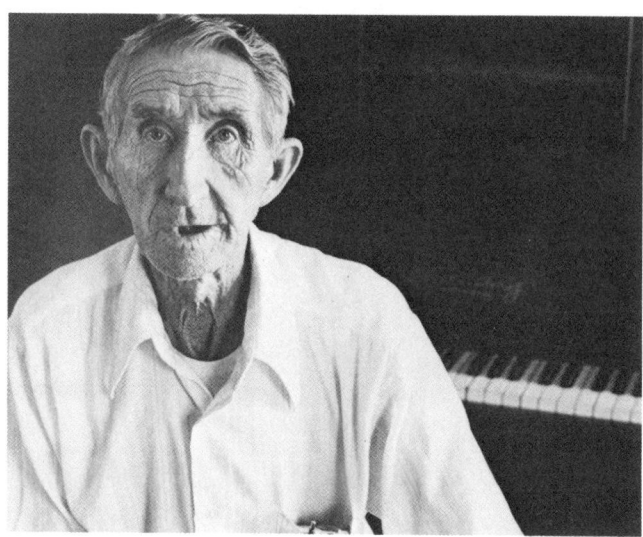

Photo: Pete Hartman; copyright © 1981 by the Blue Ridge Institute; reprinted by permission.

Haywood Blevins.

Joe Cormier Band

Joe Cormier.

Joe Cormier was born in the tiny fishing village of Cheticamp on the north shore of Cape Breton Island in eastern Canada. Even today Cheticamp is a French-speaking place, although most of Cape Breton is English-speaking (albeit with a bit of a Scottish burr and the rolling cadences of eastern Canada).

Cheticamp was settled in the 1780's by fourteen Acadian French families, victims of the expulsion of the French from what is now Nova Scotia by the British. The same expulsion sent thousands of Acadian French families to what is now the United States—to Philadelphia, to Charleston, and especially to southwest Louisiana where in time the word Acadian became Cajun.

Joe grew up in a musical and dancing family. His father played fiddle, as did his older brother Paul. Stepdancing and jigging came from his grandmother. His first important non-family model was Placide Odo, an older French fiddler who included in his repertoire the tunes played by Quebec fiddlers as well as the special Cape Breton repertoire.

Few places on the North American continent were as isolated as Cheticamp in those days, or as intensely musical. Good fiddlers were respected community figures there, weekly house dances were held, and any man who married off a daughter without hiring Placide Odo and sponsoring a dance would be known as a cheapskate for years thereafter. Commercial entertainment was totally absent, so Cheticampers made their own: parties in the summer, wedding parties in November and January, and especially *mi-careme*, the mid-Lent week when Cheticampers disguised themselves in old clothes and masks and went from house to house. Community comedians could be as coarse as they wished, and self-made entertainment flourished during this wonderful week which has a striking resemblance to Mardi Gras in Louisiana villages and the *Guignolee* of the upper Mississippi Valley French villages.

Although Cheticamp is a strikingly beautiful place, its resources have long been unequal to the population it has produced. For over 80 years its people have migrated to Quebec, Ontario, western Canada, and the New England states. The Boston area has long been a center for Cape Breton migrants, and some of its best fiddlers have lived there. They include Angus Chisolm, a fiddler of extraordinary ability and feeling who left a strong influence upon Cape Breton's intricate styles. Even today three of Cape Breton's finest make their homes there. Joe Cormier is the best known, but fellow Islanders John Campbell and Bill Lamey share with Joe the respect of those who know their complex art.

Most Cape Breton fiddlers—Joe included—will tell you that their music is largely Scottish in origin, and some say that it is the "pure" form of Scottish fiddling. That a major part of the repertoire consists of Scottish tunes is easily proven. But the source of the style is more elusive. One doubts that any music held in the hearts and minds of people can remain "pure" (at least in the sense of being unchanged) across the many decades since Highlanders became the dominant people of Cape Breton during the early 1800's. What seems more likely is that Cape Bretoners took a Scots-based music and made it suit their needs for both dance and concert. The result is an important contribution to musical art.

Cape Breton people listen to music, but they also dance to it. Stepdancing is found everywhere on the Island, and every family has at least one. In Joe's family it is his niece Arleen. Now age 18, Arleen began dancing at 5 and won a Canadian Junior Stepdance Championship at age 14. At one point she apprenticed to Don Gilchrist, a highly respected Canadian stepdancer. Arleen is the daughter of Joe's brother Sam, and their home is in Ottawa.

Also along this weekend are two of Joe's long-time musical associates. Edmond Boudreau shares the Cheticamp origins of the Cormiers and is a respected back-up musician on guitar, bass, or mandolin. Joe Patenaude is a Massachusetts-born pianist of French ancestry who has played background piano for many fiddlers at the French-American Victory Club in Waltham, Massachusetts. The latter place is one of several where you can hear more of this music should you be around Boston on a weekend.

James "Son" Thomas

James "Son" Thomas was born in 1926 and reared on a farm near Eden in the Mississippi Delta county of Yazoo. As a youth, he frequented the jukes, joints, and barrelhouses in the Greenville area, obtaining a blues education in the appropriate traditional way. While there were many musical influences upon "Son", those of Arthur "Big Boy" Crudup and Elmore James were strongest. Like many other excellent traditional folk artists from the southern United States, "Son" has found an appreciative audience overseas. His first recordings were released on the Transatlantic and Matchbox labels in England, and he is currently planning a tour of the Scandinavian countries. Yet there has been some recognition at home, particularly in Mississippi. He has appeared in various films and on numerous television shows. "Son's" music emerges from the Delta musical tradition and is particularly significant because it shows the blues in its most basic form, without the urban filtering and blending that has affected so much of the blues. "Son" and his family now live in Leland, Mississippi.

James "Son" Thomas.

Photo: Robert Jones

The Olympian Brotherhood

Olympian Brotherhood "glendi" in Baltimore.

Olympus is said to be the oldest settlement on the Greek island of Karpathos. One of 12 villages on the island, it is perched in the mountains and until very recently has been accessible only by rocky mountain paths.

Perhaps because of its isolation, Olympus has maintained its rich traditions—and the large numbers of Olympians who have emigrated to other areas of Greece and to the United States have kept many of those traditions alive in their new communities. Pressed to leave by the lack of work, Olympians living outside the village now greatly outnumbered those remaining on the island. The largest numbers live in Athens, Rhodes, New York and Baltimore.

The Olympian Brotherhood of America this year celebrates its 20th anniversary. It was established to encourage Olympians in America to preserve their traditions and their close ties to the village.

Traditional music, song and dance are well-loved in the Olympian community of Baltimore. They are integral parts of every *glendi*. In most of Greece today, the word *glendi* means "party". However, in the Olympian community, the word *glendi* carries its traditional meaning. To the Olympians *glendi* is a ritual celebration which occurs on many occasions, but does not directly mean "party". The inter-relationship of music, song and dance at a *glendi* is complex, based on rules maintained for generations and adhered to closely by the Olympians in Baltimore.

Singing is the central part of every *glendi*. But it is more than singing. To the Olympians, it is highly ritualized conversation, conducted by singing improvised couplets called *mantinathes*. At a *glendi* singers of *mantinathes* are men. Women may be present and will participate in dancing, but will sit apart from the men and will not be included in the singing.

The most important participants of the *glendi* are the *meraklithes*—the men who are acknowledged as "glendi specialists". They hold this status for many reasons—not only for their good singing and expert composition of *mantinathes*, but also for the knowledge of the complex rules of *glendia*. It is the *meraklithes* who guide the course of the *glendi*, who begin the singing, who indicate when it is appropriate to dance, and when it is appropriate to shift from one group of *mantinathes* to another.

Possible themes of the *mantinathes* are many. They are the singer's expression of his feelings—about the occasion of the *glendi*, about someone else in the community, and very often about the experience of being an immigrant far away from the island of Karpathos.

The *lyra, laouto*, and *tsambouna* (bagpipe) are the three traditional instruments of Karpathos. There are very few *tsambouna* players in the United States, but *lyra* and *laouto* are essential to every *glendi*, as an accompaniment to both the *mantinathes* and the dancing. The Olympians have four traditional dances: *Kato, Horos, Gonatistos, Pano Horas,* and *Zervos*. They also do dances from Crete and other areas of Greece, but there is a clear distinction maintained between the traditional dances and the others. The non-Karpathian dances—*Kalamatiano, Kefalonitika, Pentazali,* and *Kritiko*—are done only at the end of an evening of dance. Together these four dances are done for only a short time after many hours of Karpathian dances.

—Judy Tiger & Anna Caraveli

Village music and dance, Olympus, Island of Karpathos.

photo: Liliane de Toledo

SAMPLES OF FESTIVAL COMMUNICATIONS

FOLK FESTIVALS

SATURDAY WORKSHOP SCHEDULE

	AREA 1	AREA 2	AREA 3	AREA 4
1:00	CHEREMOSH Ukrainian	Graham Townsend	Foddrell Brothers	BAR Room Songs -Hostess- Bess Hawes Rose Maddox, John Jackson Bob + Dan Paisley Henry Townsend
1:30	"Song-Music-Dance" ROSE MADDOX & THB	JERRY MCCAIN	Pine River Boys + Marybelle	REED MARTIN
2:00			Unaccompanied Ballads Hostess- Bess Hawes with - Evelyn Ramsey Cas Wallin, Dewey Balfa Hazel Dickens	Fiddle Workshop - comparisons/contrasts Ukrainian - Oldtime Cajun - Black with: Joe Pancho, Dewey + Will Balfa, Cheremosh, Irvin Cook Leonard Bowles Walton Morris Graham Townsend
2:30	SOUTHERN QUARTET	Henry & Vernon Townsend		
3:00		FOLK PIANO Nicole Lacaille Hartley Sinclair	CARTER FAMILY WORKSHOP HOST: GARY HENDERSON with E.C. + Oona Ball Bob + Dan Paisley Rose Maddox Emily Spencer	VIRGINIA BANJO STYLES
3:30	Sady Courville Dennis Magee & Marc Savoy			
4:00		BONES WORKSHOP SINCLAR BROTHERS	JOHN JACKSON	Ted Lundy + Bob Paisley
4:30	ARAB DANCERS			
5:00	Joe McKenna IRISH PIPER	SCOTTISH FOLK DANCING	Cas Wallin & Evelyn Ramsey	THE SOUTHERN MOUNTAIN BOYS
5:30				

DANCE PARTY: Chief Ellis + The Barrelhouse Rockers

"I AM ZUNI"
by Clydia Nahwooksy

NATIVE AMERICANS

Native Americans each year bring to the Mall the richness and beauty of their traditional cultures. Participants are carefully selected through a continuing fieldwork program. Important criteria in their selection are a knowledge of their tribe and their skills in a particular artistic area.

Southwestern tribes from the states of New Mexico and Arizona are guests at this year's Festival. Pueblos, Papagos, and Pimas, along with Navajos and Apaches share the enduring ways of life of their communities with the public. The constant yet often imperceptible change of color and harmony in the lives of the people is all a part of the pottery, weaving, dances, and stories of these desert dwellers.
Cydia Nahwooksy

During a recent Arts Festival in a southeastern state, an extremely inquisitive group of spectators were talking to one of the participants.

Their curiosity transgressed the boundaries of good manners as they quizzed the straight, slight young man who stood in back of the table. They asked about the turquoise and silver jewelry on the table, commented on its value and quality. They commented on his white, flared trousers and red velvet shirt and said that he was surely not Indian because he did not wear feathers.

The spectators drifted away, except for one who had traveled in the Southwest and who tarried to say that he knew the young man was Navajo. The young man had courteously and carefully answered each question, with warmth and often with a generous though half-shy smile. To that last spectator, he simply said, "I am Zuni."

Randolph Lalio is Zuni. He is gentle, kind, loving, a listener. He is the young product of an ages-old heritage of dignity and discipline.

Zuni Pueblo, located in New Mexico, is one of numerous Pueblo Indian communities still in existence in the southwestern United States. The Spanish explorer Coronado came among the Zuni people in 1540, looking for the Seven Cities of Gold. Instead, he found multilevel villages and people who were outstanding agriculturists. Some years later, Catholic priests founded missions in the Zuni communities.

Randolph lives across the courtyard from the Zuni Mission. His house is one of the oldest in the old part of his village. Tall, steep steps carved from solid pieces of stone lead up to the door. The steps, worn from centuries of use, are swept clean, as is the inside of the neat, unadorned interior.

The same half-shy, yet completely confident smile greets you when you visit Randolph in his home. There is a sparkle of pride in his eyes as he introduces his grandmother and younger brothers and sister. His grandfather is away tending the family's flock of sheep and his mother and father are elsewhere on business.

On other days after school, when his mother is at home, Randolph would be helping her with the silver jewelry that she makes. He has been learning jewelry techniques and crafting from her for some time; he doesn't feel that he has to, but that he wants to do this. "Seldom do our

Randolph Lalio at the Smithsonian's Montreal Expo Program, 1971.

Photo:
National Anthropological Archives, Smithsonian Institution.

parents and grandparents tell us what to do, we only learn from watching them and listening to stories."

I asked him why he had gone with three other Zuni young people to the Arts Festival, and in a few sentences I learned much about Zuni today. "We went there at the request of our leaders to share some of our dances and arts. However, they aren't exactly the same as we would do them at Zuni. Many of our dances have religious significance and have to be treated differently when they are done away from home. We went there to learn. Today's youth will someday be the leaders at Zuni and we will need to know as much as possible about everyone and everything. We went there to talk about Zuni so that people would understand better about all Indians."

The Zuni Tribal Council is seeking a more adequate income and better health and education facilities for the people, so that they may compete equitably in the twentieth century. At the same time, the council and the religious leaders of Zuni are tenaciously holding on to the old religion and ceremonies, knowing that the strength and cohesiveness of the tribe rest on those qualities. They are striving successfully for a continuance of the valuable and significant lifestyle that makes the people Zuni.

Randolph will go away to college this fall. He will take with him a well-grounded awareness of Zuni history and religion; he will also take with him an ability to function well in a broader society. His skills as a craftsman, and the patience learned by practicing his craft, will serve him in many ways. His knowledge of Zuni songs and ceremonies will fill gaps as he adjusts to a new situation. Most importantly, he will come back and be a part of the sinew of continuance that is Zuni Pueblo.

A Zuni youth standing by an eagle cage in 1879. Eagles were and are prized by the Zunis for their feathers, and were captured when young and kept alive in the Pueblo. (BAE photo)

Zuni Pueblo of the 1880s, looking southwest, toward Corn Mountain. Corn and chilis are drying on the roof-tops in the foreground. (BAE photo)

A Zuni silversmith in his home/workshop. Taken in 1891, this photo shows the interior of a typical Zuni house. (BAE photo)

Photos: National Anthropological Archives, Smithsonian Institution.

Bibliography of Folklore in America
CHARLES L. PERDUE, JR.

Collecting and Field Work

Brunvand, Jan H. *A Guide for Collectors of Folklore in Utah.* Salt Lake City: Univ. of Utah Press, 1971.

Goldstein, Kenneth S. *A Guide for Field Workers in Folklore.* Hatboro, Pa.: Folklore Associates, 1964.

Ives, Edward D. *A Manual for Field Workers* (issued as Vol. XV, 1974, *Northeast Folklore*). Rev. ed. Orono, Me.: Northeast Archives of Folklore and Oral History, Univ. of Maine, 1974. *The Tape-Recorded Interview: A Manual for Field Workers in Folklore and Oral History,* Knoxville: Univ. of Tennessee Press, 1980. A revision of *A Manual for Field Workers.*

Leach, MacEdward, and Henry Glassie, *A Guide for Collectors of Oral Traditions and Folk Cultural Material in Pennsylvania.* Harrisburg: Pennsylvania Historical and Museum Commission, 1968.

Information Sources

BIBLIOGRAPHICAL AIDS

"Annual Bibliography of Folklore." *Journal of American Folklore Supplement,* 1955-1963.

Abstracts of Folklore Studies. Philadelphia: American Folklore Society, 1964. (Successor to "Annual Bibliography.")

Coffin, Tristram P. *An Analytical Index to the Journal of American Folklore.* Austin: American Folklore Society, Bibliographical and Special Series, Vol. 7, 1958.

Dundes, Alan. *Folklore Theses and Dissertations in the United*

States. Austin: American Folklore Society, Bibliographical and Special Series, Vol. 27, 1976.

Flanagan, Cathleen C., and John T. Flanagan. *American Folklore: A Bibliography, 1950-1974.* Metuchen, N.J.: Scarecrow Press, 1977.

Funkhouser, Myrtle. "Folklore of the American Negro." *Bulletin of Bibliography* 16 (1937-1939):28-29, 49-51, 72-73, 108-10, 136-37, 159-60.

Gillis, Frank, and Alan P. Merriam, comp. and annot. *Ethnomusicology and Folk Music: An International Bibliography of Dissertations and Theses.* Special Studies in Ethnomusicology, No. 1, 1966.

Haywood, Charles. *A Bibliography of North American Folklore and Folksong.* 2nd ed. New York: Dover Books, 1961.

Index Medicus. Usually in the medical library; check under "Folklore" or other specific topics.

Leach, Maria, and Jerome Fried, eds. *Standard Dictionary of Folklore, Mythology, and Legend.* 2 vols. New York: Funk, 1949, 1950.

Publications of the Modern Language Association. April supplement (annual), folklore section.

Randolph, Vance. *Ozark Folklore: A Bibliography.* Bloomington: Indiana Univ. Publications, Folklore Institute Monograph Series, Vol. 24, 1972.

Southern Folklore Quarterly. Annual spring issue is bibliography.

Wildhaber, Robert. *A Bibliographical Introduction to American Folklife.* Reprint from *New York Folklore Quarterly,* Dec. 1965.

PERIODICALS

Bluegrass Unlimited
JEMF Newsletter (John Edwards Memorial Foundation)
Journal of American Folklore
Journal of the Folklore Institute
Living Blues
Old-Time Music
Publications of the Texas Folklore Society
Southern Folklore Quarterly
The Devil's Box

Virginia Folklore Society Newsletter and *Journal Western Folklore* (formerly *California Folklore Quarterly*)

Anglo-American Folklore

GENERAL WORKS

Brunvand, Jan H. *The Study of American Folklore: An Introduction.* Rev. ed. New York: Norton, 1978.
Dorson, Richard M. "Current Folklore Theories." *Current Anthropology* 4(1968):93-112.
_____. *Folklore and Folklife: An Introduction.* Chicago: Univ. of Chicago Press, 1977.
Dundes, Alan. *The Study of Folklore.* Englewood Cliffs, N.J.: Prentice-Hall, 1965.
Toelken, Barre, *The Dynamics of Folklore.* Boston: Houghton Mifflin, 1979.

OBSCENITY

Goldstein, Kenneth S. "Bowdlerization and Expurgation: Academic and Folk." *Journal of American Folklore* 80 (1967):374-86.
Maledicta: The International Journal of Verbal Aggression.

URBAN FOLKLORE

"The Urban Experience and Folk Tradition." *Journal of American Folklore* 83(1970):113-270. A symposium consisting of several articles dealing with folklore in the city, mostly considering what happens when rural "folk" move to urban areas.

FOLKLORE OF OCCUPATIONAL GROUPS

Miners
Korson, George. *Black Rock: Mining Folklore of the Pennsylvania Dutch.* Baltimore: Johns Hopkins Univ. Press, 1960.

Sailors
Beck, Horace. *Folklore of the Sea.* Middletown, Conn.: Wesleyan Univ. Press, 1973.

NARRATIVES

General

Bascom, William. "The Forms of Folklore Prose Narratives." *Journal of American Folklore* 77 (1965):3-20.

Hand, Wayland D., ed. *American Folk Legend: A Symposium.* Berkeley: Univ. of California Press, 1971.

Oral History

Gould, Richard A. "Indian and White Versions of 'The Burnt Ranch Massacre': A Study in Comparative Ethnohistory." *Journal of the Folklore Institute* 3(1966):30-42.

Jokes

Legman, Gershon. *Rational of the Dirty Joke: An Analysis of Sexual Humor.* New York: Grove Press, 1968.

――――. *No Laughing Matter: Rational of the Dirty Joke, 2nd Series.* New York: Breaking Point, 1975.

Randolph, Vance. *Pissing in the Snow & Other Ozark Folktales.* Urbana: Univ. of Illinois Press, 1976.

Tales

Roberts, Leonard. *South from Hell-for-Sartin: Kentucky Mountain Folk Tales.* Berea, Ky.: Council of Southern Mountains, 1964.

――――. *Old Greasybeard: Tales from the Cumberland Gap.* Detroit: Folklore Associates, 1969.

Heroes

Abrahams, Roger D. "Some Varieties of Heroes in America." *Journal of the Folklore Institute* 3(1966):341-62.

Turner, Frederick William, III. "Badmen, Black and White: The Continuity of American Folk Traditions." Ph.D. diss., Univ. of Pennsylvania, 1965.

MUSIC — SECULAR

Ballads

Bronson, Bertrand H. *The Traditional Tunes of the Child Ballads.*

4 vols. Princeton: Princeton Univ. Press, 1959, 1962, 1966, 1971.
Child, Francis James. *The English and Scottish Popular Ballads.* New York: Dover Publications, 1966.
Coffin, Tristram P. *The British Traditional Ballad in North America.* Rev. ed. Austin: Univ. of Texas Press, 1977.
Davis, Authur Kyle, Jr. *Traditional Ballads of Virgina, Collected Under the Auspices of the Virginia Folklore Society.* Charlottesville: Univ. Press of Virginia, 1957.
Hodgart, M.J.C. *The Ballads.* New York: Norton, 1962.
Laws, G. Malcolm, Jr. *American Balladry from British Broadsides: A Guide for Students and Collectors of Traditional Song.* Philadelphia: American Folklore Society, 1957.
―――. *Native American Balladry: A Descriptive Study and a Bibliographical Syllabus.* Rev. ed. Philadelphia: American Folklore Society, 1964.
Toelken, J. Barre. "An Oral Canon for the Child Ballads: Construction Application." *Journal of the Folklore Institute* 4:75–101.

Folksongs

Cray, Edward. *The Erotic Muse.* New York: Pyramid Communications, 1969.
Glassie, Henry: Edward D. Ives: and John F. Szwed, *Folksongs and Their Makers.* Bowling Green, Ohio: Bowling Green Univ. Popular Press.
Lomax, Alan. "The Good and the Beautiful in Folksong." *Journal of American Folklore.* 80(1967):213–35.
Nettl, Bruno. *An Introduction to Folk Music in the United States.* Detroit: Wayne State Univ. Press, 1962.
Sharp, Cecil M. *English Folk Songs from the Southern Appalachians.* Rpt. (2 vols. in 1). London: Oxford Univ. Press, 1960.

Minstrels

Toll, Robert C. *Blacking Up: The Minstrel Show in Nineteenth-Century America.* New York: Oxford Univ. Press, 1974.
Hugill, Stan. *Shanties from the Seven Seas: Shipboard Work-Songs and Used as Work-Songs from the Great Days of Sail.* New York: Dutton, 1961.

Folksongs of Protest
Greenway, John. *American Folksongs of Protest.* New York: Barnes, 1960.

Occupational Folksongs
Green, Archie. *Only a Miner: Studies in Recorded Coal-Mining Songs.* Urbana: Univ. of Illinois Press, 1972.

Hillbilly and Country and Western
"Hillbilly Issue." *Journal of American Folklore* 78(1965):195-287.
Malone, Bill C. *Country Music U.S.A.: A Fifty-Year History.* Austin: American Folklore Society, 1968.
Wolfe, Charles K. *The Grand Ole Opry: The Early Years, 1925-35.* London: Old-Time Music, 1975.

Bluegrass
Artis, Bob. *Bluegrass.* New York: Hawthorne Books, 1975.
Rosenberg, Neil V. "From Sound to Style: The Emergence of Bluegrass." *Journal of American Folklore* 80(1967):143-59.

Musical Instruments
Mugwumps. A periodical devoted to musical instruments; occasionally contains information on traditional folk instruments.

The Urban Folksong Revival
Denisoff, R. Serge. *Great Day Coming.* Urbana: Univ. of Illinois Press, 1971.

Black-White Cross-Cultural Influences
Russell, Tony. *Blacks Whites and Blues.* New York: Stein and Day, 1970.

Music — Sacred
Cobb, Buell E., Jr. *The Sacred Harp: A Tradition and Its Music.* Athens: Univ. of Georgia Press, 1978.
Jackson, George Pullen. *White and Negro Spirituals.* New York: Augustin, 1943.

RELIGION — OFFICIAL AND UNOFFICIAL (BELIEFS, SUPERSTITIONS, MAGIC, WITCHCRAFT, CURING, ETC.)

Hand, Wayland D., ed. *American Folk Medicine.* Berkeley: Univ. of California Press, 1976.
Hufford, David J. "Folklore Studies and Health: An Approach to Applied Folklore." Ph.D. diss., Univ. of Pennsylvania, 1974.
Montell, William Lynwood. *Ghosts Along the Cumberland: Deathlore in the Kentucky Foothills.* Knoxville: Univ. of Tennessee Press, 1975.
Mullen, Patrick B. *I Heard the Old Fisherman Say: Folklore of the Texas Gulf Coast.* Austin: Univ. of Texas Press, 1978.
Vogt, Evon, and Ray Hyman. *Water Witching USA.* Chicago: 1959.
Wallace, Anthony F.C. *Religion: An Anthropological View.* New York: Random House, 1966.
Yoder, Don. "Official Religion versus Folk Religion." *Pennsylvania Folklife* 15, No. 2 (Winter 1965–66):36–42.

LINGUISTICS

Speech
Dillard, J.L. *American Talk: Where Our Words Came From.* New York: Vintage Books, 1977.

Proverbs and Proverbial Expressions
Burke, Kenneth. *The Philosophy of Literary Form.* New York: Vintage Books, 1957.
Taylor, Archer. *The Proverb and An Index to the Proverb.* Hatboro, Pa.: Folklore Associates, 1962.

Riddles
Taylor, Archer. *English Riddles from Oral Tradition.* Berkeley: Univ. of California Press, 1951.

Rhymes
The Frank C. Brown Collection North Carolina Folklore, Vol. 1, Durham: Duke Univ. Press, 1952, pp. 31–219.

GAMES

Abrahams, Roger D., ed. *Jump-Rope Rhymes: A Dictionary.* Austin: American Folklore Society, 1969.
Botkin, B.A. *The American Play-Party Song.* New York: Frederick Ungar, 1963.
Knapp, Mary, and Herbert Knapp. *One Potato, Two Potato . . . The Secret Education of American Children.* New York: Norton, 1976.
Roberts, John M.; M.J. Arth, and R.R. Bush, "Games in Culture." *American Anthropologist* 61(1959):597-605.
Sutton-Smith, Brian. *The Folkgames of Children.* Austin: American Folklore Society, 1972.

DANCE

Lomax, Alan. *Folk Song Style and Culture.* Washington, D.C.: American Assoc. for the Advancement of Science, Publ. No. 88, 1968, pp. 222-73.
Stearns, Marshall, and Jean Stearns. *Jazz Dance: The Story of American Vernacular Dance.* New York: Macmillan, 1968.

MATERIAL CULTURE

Glassie, Henry. *Pattern in the Material Folk Culture of the Eastern States.* Philadelphia: Univ. of Pennsylvania Press, 1968.
———. *Folk Housing in Middle Virginia.* Knoxville: Univ. of Tennessee Press, 1975.
Pillsburg, Richard, and Andrew Kardos. *A Field Guide to the Folk Architecture of the Northeastern United States.* Geography Publications at Dartmouth, No. 8, n.d.
Swain, Doug, ed. *Carolina Dwelling.* Raleigh: Vol. 26, Student Publication of the School of Design, 1978.
Yoder, Don, ed. *American Folklife.* Austin: Univ. of Texas Press, 1976.

Art

Andrews, Ruth, ed. *How to Know American Folk Art.* New York: Dutton, 1977.

Crafts

Eaton, Allen H. *Handicrafts of the Southern Highlands.* New York: Russell Sage Foundation, 1937.

FOLKLIFE

Roberts, Leonard. *Sang Branch Settlers: Folksongs and Tales of a Kentucky Mountain Family.* Austin: American Folklore Society, 1974.
Watkins, Floyd C., and Charles Hubert Watkins. *Yesterday in the Hills.* Chicago: Quadrangle Books, 1963.

Folklore of American Indians

Kluckhohn, Clyde. *Navaho Witchcraft.* Boston: Beacon Press, 1967.
Radin, Paul. *The Trickster: A Study in American Indian Mythology.* New York: Philosophical Library, 1956.
Tantaquidgeon, Gladys. *Folk Medicine of the Delaware and Related Algonkian Indians.* Harrisburg: Pennsylvania Historical and Museum Commission, 1972.

Afro-American Folklore

GENERAL

Abrahams, Roger D. *Deep Down in the Jungle: Negro Narrative Folklore from the Streets of Philadelphia.* Rev. ed. Chicago: Aldine, 1970.
Dundes, Alan. *Mother Wit from the Laughing Barrel: Readings in the Interpretation of Afro-American Folklore.* Englewood Cliffs, N.J.: Prentice-Hall, 1973.
Jackson, Bruce, ed. *The Negro and His Folklore in Nineteenth-Century Periodicals.* Austin: Vol. 18, 1967. American Folklore Society, Bibliographical and Special Series, 1967.
Kochman, Thomas, ed. *Rappin' and Stylin' Out: Communication in Urban Black America.* Urbana: Univ. of Illinois Press, 1972.
Levine, Lawrence W. *Black Culture and Black Consciousness:*

Afro-American Folk Thought from Slavery to Freedom. New York: Oxford Univ. Press, 1977.

Savannah Unit of the Georgia Writers' Project W.P.A. *Drums and Shadows: Survival Studies Among the Georgia Coastal Negroes.* Athens: Univ. of Georgia Press, 1940.

Whitten, Norman C., Jr., and John F. Szwed. *Afro-American Anthropology: Contemporary Perspectives.* New York: Free Press, 1970.

MUSIC

Secular

Odum, Howard W., and Guy B. Johnson. *Negro Workaday Songs.* Chapel Hill: Univ. of North Carolina Press, 1926.

———. *The Negro and His Songs* Hatboro, Pa.: Folklore Associates, 1964.

Southern, Eileen. *The Music of Black Americans: A History.* New York: Norton, 1971.

African Roots

Waterman, Richard Alan. "African Influence on the Music of the Americans." In *Acculturation in the Americas,* ed. Sol Tax. Chicago: Univ. of Chicago Press, 1952.

Early Afro-American

Allen, William F., C.P. Ward, and L.M. Garrison. *Slave Songs of the United States.* New York: Peter Smith, 1951.

Epstein, Dena J. *Sinful Tunes and Spirituals: Black Folk Music to the Civil War.* Urbana: Univ. of Illinois Press, 1977.

Higginson, Thomas Wentworth. *Army Life in a Black Regiment.* Boston: Beacon Press, 1962.

Work Songs

Jackson, Bruce. *Wake Up Dead Man: Afro-American Worksongs from Texas Prisons.* Cambridge, Mass.: Harvard Univ. Press, 1972.

Protest Songs

Gellert, Lawrence. "Negro Songs of Protest: North and South

BIBLIOGRAPHY

Carolina and Georgia." In *Negro Anthology*, ed. Nancy Cunard. London: Wishart & Co., 1934.

Blues
Bastin, Bruce. *Crying for the Carolines*. London: Studio Vista, 1971.
Titon, Jeff Todd. *Early Downhome Blues: A Musical and Cultural Analysis*. Urbana: Univ. of Illinois Press, 1977.

Jazz
Stearns, Marshal W. *The Story of Jazz, with an Expanded Bibliography and a Syllabus of Fifteen Lectures on the History of Jazz*. New York: New American Library, 1958.

Soul
Garland, Phyl. *The Sound of Soul*. Chicago: Henry Regnery, 1969.

Sacred—Spirituals
Odum, Howard W. "Religious Folk-Songs of Southern Negroes." *American Journal of Religious Psychology and Education* 3 (1908-1909):265-365.
Wilgus, D.K. *Anglo-American Folksong Scholarship Since 1898*. New Brunswick, N.J.: 1959. (Appendix I: "The Negro-White Spirituals.")
Yoder, Don. *Pennsylvania Spirituals*. Lancaster, Pa.: Pennsylvania Folklife Society, 1961.

Sacred—Gospel Songs
Heilbut, Tony. *The Gospel Sound: Good News and Bad Times*. New York: Simon & Schuster, 1971.

Cantometrics
Lomax, Alan. "The Homogeneity of African-Afro-American Musical Style." *In Afro-American Anthropology: Contemporary Perspectives*, ed. Norman E. Whitten, Jr., and John F. Sqwed. New York: Free Press, 1970.

Choreometrics — Dance

Emery, Lynne Pauley. *Black Dance in the United States from 1619–1970.* Palo Alto: National Press Books, 1972.

NARRATIVES

Oral History

Fry, Gladys-Marie. *Night Riders in Black Folk History.* Knoxville: Univ. of Tennessee Press, 1975.

Montell, William Lynwood. *The Saga of Coe Ridge: A Study in Oral History.* Knoxville: Univ. of Tennessee Press, 1970.

Perdue, Charles L., Jr., Thomas E. Barden, and Robert K. Phillips. *Weevils in the Wheat: Interviews with Virginia Ex-Slaves.* Charlottesville: Univ. Press of Virginia, 1976.

General

Crowley, Daniel J., ed. *African Folklore in the New World.* Austin: Univ. of Texas Press, 1977.

Hurston, Zora Neale. *Mules and Men.* New York: Harper & Row, 1970.

Perdue, Chuck. "I Swear to God It's the Truth if I Ever Told It!" *Keystone Folklore Quarterly* 14(1969):1–54.

Jokes

Middleton, Russell, and John Moland. "Humor in Negro and White Subcultures: A Study of Jokes Among University Students." *American Sociological Review* 4(1959):61–69.

Toasts

Jackson, Bruce. *Get your Ass in the Water and Swim Like Me: Narrative Poetry from Black Oral Tradition.* Cambridge, Mass.: Harvard Univ. Press, 1974.

RELIGION — OFFICIAL AND UNOFFICIAL (BELIEFS, SUPERSTITIONS, MAGIC, WITCHCRAFT, CURING, ETC.)

Hyatt, Harry Middleton. *Voodoo — Conjuration — Witchcraft — Rootwork: Beliefs Accepted by Many Negroes and White Per-*

sons, *Those Being Orally Recorded Among Blacks and Whites.* Memoirs of the Alma Eagan Hyatt Foundations, 1978.

Johnson, Clifton H., ed. *God Struck Me Dead: Religious Conversion Experiences and Autobiographies of Ex-Slaves.* Philadelphia: Pilgrim Press, 1969.

Puckett, Newbell Niles. *Folk Beliefs of the Southern Negro.* Montclair, N.J.: Publication No. 22, Paterson Smith Reprint Series in Criminology, Law Enforcement, and Social Problems, 1968.

Raboteau, Albert J. *Slave Religion: The "Invisible Institution" in the Antebellum South.* New York: Oxford Univ. Press, 1978.

Rosenberg, Bruce A. *The Art of the American Folk Preacher.* New York: Oxford Univ. Pres, 1970.

LINGUISTICS

Black English

Brasch, Ila Wales, and Walter Milton Brasch. *A Comprehensive Annotated Bibliography of American Black English.* Baton Rouge: Louisiana State Univ. Press, 1974.

Dillard, J.L. *Black English.* New York: Random House, 1972.

The Dozens

Abrahams, Roger D. "Playing the Dozens." *Journal of American Folklore* 75(1962):209–20.

Rhymes

Talley, T.W. *Negro Folk Rhymes.* New York: Macmillan, 1922.

GAMES

Abrahams, Roger D. "There's a Black Girl in the Ring." In *Two Penny Ballads and Four Dollar Whiskey,* ed. Robert H. Byington and Kenneth S. Goldstein. Hatboro, Pa.: Folklore Associates, 1966.

MATERIAL CULTURE

Vlach, John Michael. *The Afro-American Tradition in Decorative Arts.* Cleveland: Cleveland Museum of Art, 1978.

Folklore of Non-Anglo and Non-Afro Americans

EUROPEANS GENERALLY

Christiansen, Reidar Th. *European Folklore in America.* (Studies Norvegica No. 12) Norway: Scandinavian Univ. Books, 1962.

CAJUNS

Daigle, Pierre V. *Tears, Love and Laughter: The Story of the Acadians.* Church Point, La.: Acadian Publishing Enterprise, 1972.
"The World of Cajun Music: In *The American Folk Music Occasional,* compiled and edited by Chris Strachwitz and Pete Welding. New York: Oak Publications 1970.

GERMANS

Pennsylvania Folklife, various issues
Pennsylvania German Society Proceedings, various issues
Pennsylvania German Folklore Society Publications, various issues

ITALIANS

Williams, Phyllis H. *South Italian Folkways in Europe and America.* New Haven: Yale Univ. Press, 1938.

HISPANO CULTURE

Brown, Lorin W. *Hispano Folklife of New Mexico: The Lorin W. Brown Federal Writers' Project Manuscripts.* With Charles L. Briggs and Marta Weigle. Albuquerque: Univ. of New Mexico Press, 1978.
Madsen, William. *Mexican-Americans of South Texas.* New York: Holt, Rinehart and Winston, 1964.

SLAVIC CULTURE

Pirkova-Jacobson, Svatava. "Harvest Festivals Among Czechs and Slovaks in America." *Journal of American Folklore* 69:266-80.
Sokolov, Y.M. *Russian Folklore.* Hatboro, Pa.: Folklore Associates, 1966.

Index

(The facsimile examples comprising Part Two of this book have not been indexed.)

Academic culture, 13-14
Acculturation, 16-18
Administration, festival: staff, 25-30; structure, 25-26
Admission charges, 44-46
Appalachian: crafts, 7-8; dance, 6, 71; music, 6-7, 21, 50
Archive of Folk Song (Library of Congress), 68
Arlington Three, A.L. Steely's, 7
Arts agencies, state, 67
Arts councils, state, 50-51
Attorney, consulting, 36, 38
Audience, 30-34, 44-46, 83

Badges, festival identification, 99
Behavior, maintaining appropriate, 120-21
Blue Ridge Folklife Festival, 123-24
Bluegrass music, 4-6, 68-69, 93
Board of Directors, festival, 38-39
Bonds, 37
Bookkeeping, 28-29
Booths, 36, 107
Breakdown, postfestival, 126-27
Brochures, 36, 95-96
Broussard family (Cajun bands), 7
Budget, festival, 28-29, 34-36
Business entity, form of, 38-39
Butchering, attitudes toward, 83-84

CB radios, 121-22
Campa, Arthur L., 7
Caterers, 105

Chamber of Commerce, directory of organizations, 67
Check-out, from housing, 103
Churches, involvement in programming, 54, 72
Cockfighting, 84
Collectors, folklore, 59-60
Communications, during festival, 121-22
Community: celebrations, 65; gathering places, 64
Complimentary tickets, 94, 99
Concert sequence, 85-86
Concessions: as part of programming, 29, 123; personnel and operation, 125-26; physical arrangements for, 125; security, 125
Consultants, 28; budget, 34; festival planning, 48, 56-57; legal, 36, 38
Contracts: festival site, 126; landlord, 101; participants, 28, 40, 97
Copyright requirements, 40
Corporations, soliciting funds from, 51-52
Crafts, sale of, 124
Crafts groups, 65
Cross-cultural sensitivities, 83-85
Culture, types of, 14-15

Dance associations, 70-71
Date, selection of festival, 33-34
Dietary restrictions, among participants, 105
Directory of organizations (Chamber of Commerce), 67

Dobie, J. Frank, 7
Documentation, festival, 115-16

Electrical cable and extension lines, 108
Electricity, 107-108
Equipment, lists of, 99
Ethnic groups, 17, 31, 64-65, 67, 86, 93, 123; Afro-American, 4, 60; American Indian, 4, 6, 16, 24n, 73, 95; Cajun, 7, 55. *See also* Immigrants
Evangeline Band, 7

FCC, regulations about transmitters, 122
Federal Writers' Project, 63
Festival director, duties of, 25, 34
Festival of American Folklife, 6, 8-9
Festivals, types of, 4-6
Fiddlers, 4, 6, 61-62, 67-68, 77, 81-82
Fieldwork, 9, 57-72
Files, participant information, 98
Folk art galleries, 66-67
Folk culture: confusion regarding, 18-19; description of, 13-14
Folk performers, types of, 20-22
Folklore: definition, 13, 24n; form, 12; function, 11-12; oral transmission, 13, 15
Folksong societies, 72
Food: for participants, 103-106; sale of, 123-24
Foundations, soliciting funds from, 51-52
Funding, festival: admission charges, 44-46; donations from corporations and foundations, 51-52; grants, 46-51; subscriptions, 52-53
Funds, reserve ("the nut"), 44

Generators, portable, 32
"Gofer," 29, 117
Grants, 28, 38-39, 46-51
Greyhound races, 84

Hackberry Ramblers, The, 7
Hand clapping, discouragement of, 81-82
Handy, W.C., 7
Health emergencies, 119-20

Honoraria, for participants, 28
Hospitality, 26, 97-106
Housing, 99-103
Humanities committees, state, 50-51
Hurston, Zora Neale, 7

Immigrants, 16-17, 24n, 68-70. *See also* Ethnic groups
Incorporation, advantages of, 38-39
Information: kit, 99; sheet, 97
Insurance, 39-40
Internal Revenue Service: Employer's Identification Number, 41-42; Form 501, 42; Form 941, 42; Form 990, 42-43; Form 1099, 28, 43; requirements, 41-43; tax exemption, 38-39
Interviewing, of participants, 73-74
Interviewing and collecting, 62-63

Jackson, George Pullen, 7
Jacobsen, O.S., 7
Journals, folklore and historical, 71-72

Knott, Sarah Gertrude, 6-8

Latrines, 32, 107-108
Legal considerations, 36-41
Letters, to participants, 97-98
Libraries, folklore collections in, 62-64
Library of Congress, Archive of Folk Song, 68
Lundy, Emett, W., 96
Lunsford, Bascom Lamar, 6-7

Map, of festival site, 98, 109
Mariposa Folk Festival (Canada), 6
Meals: for participants, 103-106; schedule and tickets for, 99
Media contacts, 89-90
Meyer, Agnes, 7
Microphone rehearsal, 112-14
Microphones and accessories, 110-15, 117
Milwaukee Journal, 7
Mississippi Valley Folk Festival, 55
Mountain Dance and Folk Festival (Asheville, N.C.), 6
Music stores, 64
Musical instruments, amplified, 112
Musicians, network of, 61-62

INDEX

National Council for the Traditional Arts, 68
National Endowment for the Arts: Expansion Arts Program, 46, 50; Folk Arts Program, 46-50; grants applications, 47-50
National Folk Festival, 6, 68; admission charges, 45; communications, 122; concession policy, 125; food arrangements, 105; late-evening gatherings, 100; program book, 95-96; publicity, 88; sound systems, 111-12; workshops, 74, 79, 99
National Foundations for the Arts and Humanities, 38
National Park Service, 6, 8, 68
Newport Folk Festival, 8
Newspapers: publicity in, 64, 93; as sponsors of folk festivals, 7
New York Post, 7

Occupational groups, 68-70

Participants, identifying, 56-72
Parking, 107-108
Partnership, advantages of, 38
Payroll, 41-42
Performance schedule, 117-18
Permits and restrictions, 36-38, 124
Petty cash, 28
Philadelphia Folk Festival, 6
Philadelphia Inquirer, 7
Photographs, of participants, 92, 97
Photography, 115-16
Pigs, greased, 84-85
Pony pull, 84
Popular culture, 11, 13
Post, Lauren C., 7
Posters, 95-96
Presentation, of performers, 80-87
Presenters: introductions of performers, 81-83, 86, 114, 116; selection of, 22-23
Press: kits, 94; releases, 90; room, 94
Production, 26, 107-27; schedule, 108
Program: book, 36, 94-96, 99; committee, 25-26, 29, 94
Programming, 54-87; concessions as part of, 29, 123; establishing concept of, 54-56

Public Service Announcements, 92
Publications, festival, 94-96
Publicity, 26, 31, 88-96; committee, 88, 94; follow-up details, 94; kinds of, 26; prefestival, 89-93; theme of, 89-90

Radio, publicity, 92-93
Radio communications, 121-22
Rain: insurance, 40; procedures in case of, 118
Recap meeting, 30, 127
Record collectors, 60-61
Recording: log, 29, 117; technician, 29, 117
Recordings, of performers: for publicity, 92-93; prohibitions against, 40; sale of, 124-25
Rest area, for performers, 106, 108, 119
Revival performing arts, 7-8, 16-18
Room assignment, 101-102
Roosevelt, Eleanor, 7

Sacred Harp singing, 6-7, 16
St. Louis Globe-Democrat, 7
San Diego Folk Festival, 6
Sanitary facilities, 32, 107-108
Security: of concessions, 125; of personal property, 119; of supplies, 108; staff for, 120-21
Senior citizens, 64-65
Sheeting, plastic, 109, 118
Signs, 108-109
Site: preparation, 107-109; selection, 30-33
Smithsonian Institution, 6, 8-9, 68
Sound: check, 112-14; reinforcement, 109-15; system operator, 29, 111-12, 117
Staff, festival: 27-30; as hosts or houseparents, 102-103; safety and security, 118-21; schedules for, 108
Stage: anxiety, 86-87; cues, 86-87; manager, 29, 116-18; manager, assistant, 29, 117
Stages: presentation on, 80-83; source of, 107
Storage, 108, 125

Subscriptions, 52–53
Survival performing arts, 7–8, 16–18

Tables and chairs, sources of, 107–108
Tape recorders and tape, 115–16
Tax exemption, 38, 44, 47
Taxes, 43. *See also* Internal Revenue Service
Telephones, 107
Television: publicity, 92–94; videotaping, 116
Tents, 32, 36, 107
Tools and supplies, 109, 125
Transportation, local, for participants, 98, 100, 103
Travel expenses, of participants, 28, 98–99

Unemployment compensation, state, 43
Unions, 40, 114

Videotaping, 40, 90–93, 116
Volunteers, festival, 29–30, 108, 119

Walkie-talkies, 121–22
Washington Post, 7
Water, 32, 107–108
Welcoming, of participants, 102–103
White, Clarence Cameron, 7
Workshops: participatory, 78; planning of, 74–87; press releases about, 90; scheduling of, 79; themes for, 74–78

Folk Festivals has been composed on the Compugraphic Phototypesetter in 10-point Times Roman type with 2-point spacing between the lines. Vivaldi and Times Roman were selected for display. The book was designed by Judy Ruehmann; set into type by Metricomp, Inc., Grundy Center, Iowa; printed offset by Thomson-Shore, Inc., Dexter, Michigan; and bound by John H. Dekker & Sons, Grand Rapids, Michigan. The paper on which the book was printed bears the watermark of S. D. Warren and is designed for an effective life of at least three hundred years.

THE UNIVERSITY OF TENNESSEE PRESS
Knoxville